Nietzsche's Political Skepticism

Nietzsche's Political Skepticism

Tamsin Shaw

PRINCETON UNIVERSITY PRESS

PRINCETON AND OXFORD

Copyright © 2007 by Princeton University Press

Published by Princeton University Press, 41 William Street, Princeton, New Jersey 08540

In the United Kingdom: Princeton University Press, 3 Market Place, Woodstock, Oxfordshire OX20 1SY

All Rights Reserved

Library of Congress Cataloging-in-Publication Data

Shaw, Tamsin, 1970–
   Nietzsche's political skepticism / Tamsin Shaw.
      p.   cm.
   Includes bibliographical references and index.
   ISBN 978-0-691-13322-5 (cloth: alk. paper)
   1. Nietzsche, Friedrich Wilhelm, 1844–1900—Political and social views. 2. Legitimacy of governments. 3. Authority. I. Title.
   JC233.N52S43 2007
   320.01—dc22   2007018560

British Library Cataloging-in-Publication Data is available

This book has been composed in Sabon

Printed on acid-free paper. ∞

press.princeton.edu

Printed in the United States of America

10   9   8   7   6   5   4   3   2   1

To my parents, Robin and Kate Shaw

Contents

Abbreviations

I have used the abbreviations below for Nietzsche's works. I have cited the translations listed with some modifications. I have used the *Werke: kritische Gesamtausgabe*, edited by Giorgio Colli and Mazzino Montinari, (Berlin: de Gruyter, 1967–), which, where cited, I have abbreviated to *KGW* followed by volume and page number.

BT   *The Birth of Tragedy*, in *The Birth of Tragedy and Other Writings*, trans. Ronald Speirs, ed. Raymond Geuss and Ronald Speirs (Cambridge: Cambridge University Press, 1999)

OTL   "On Truth and Lying in a Non-Moral Sense," in *The Birth of Tragedy and Other Writings*, trans. Ronald Speirs, ed. Raymond Geuss (Cambridge, 1999)

UM   *Untimely Meditations*, trans. R. J. Hollingdale (Cambridge: Cambridge University Press, 1983)

      i   "David Strauss, the Confessor and the Writer"
      ii "On the Uses and Disadvantages of History for Life"
      iii "Schopenhauer as Educator"
      iv "Richard Wagner in Bayreuth"

HTH   *Human, All Too Human*, trans. R. J. Hollingdale (Cambridge: Cambridge University Press, 1986, 1993)

      I Volume 1
      II Volume 2: "Assorted Opinions and Maxims"
                       "The Wanderer and his Shadow"

D   *Daybreak*, ed. Maudemarie Clark and Brian Leiter, trans. R. J. Hollingdale (Cambridge: Cambridge University Press, 1997)

GS   *The Gay Science*, ed. Bernard Williams, trans. Adrian Del Caro (Cambridge: Cambridge University Press, 2001)

TSZ   *Thus Spoke Zarathustra*, trans. Walter Kaufmann, in *The Portable Nietzsche*, ed. Walter Kaufmann (New York: Viking, 1954, 1976)

BGE   *Beyond Good and Evil*, ed. Rolf-Peter Horstmann and Judith Norman, trans. Judith Norman (Cambridge: Cambridge University Press, 2002)

GM   *On the Genealogy of Morality*, ed. Keith Ansell-Pearson, trans. Carol Diethe (Cambridge: Cambridge University Press, 1994)

    i   First Essay: "Good and Evil," "Good and Bad"
    ii Second Essay: "Guilt," "Bad Conscience," and Related Matters
    iii Third Essay: What Do Ascetic Ideals Mean?

TI   *Twilight of the Idols*, in Aaron Ridley and Judith Norman, eds. *The Anti-Christ, Ecce Homo, Twilight of the Idols*, trans. Judith Norman (Cambridge: Cambridge University Press, 2005)

AC   *The Anti-Christ*, in Aaron Ridley and Judith Norman, eds. *The Anti-Christ, Ecce Homo, Twilight of the Idols*, trans. Judith Norman (Cambridge: Cambridge University Press, 2005)

EH   *Ecce Homo*, in Aaron Ridley and Judith Norman, eds. *The Anti-Christ, Ecce Homo, Twilight of the Idols*, trans. Judith Norman (Cambridge: Cambridge University Press, 2005)

WP   *The Will to Power*, ed. Walter Kaufmann, trans. Walter Kaufmann and R. J. Hollingdale (New York: Vintage, 1967–68)

In citing Schopenhauer I have used E.F.J. Payne's translation of *The World as Will and Representation*, 2 vols. (New York: Dover, 1958, 1969), which is abbreviated to *WWR*, followed by volume and page number.

Nietzsche's Political Skepticism

Introduction

> Without the assistance of priests, no power can become
> "legitimate" even today.
>
> —*Human, All Too Human*, I, 472

Nietzsche is a frustrating figure for political theorists. Those who take seriously his insights into morality, culture, and religion have often been struck by the fact that he abstains from developing these insights into a coherent theory of politics. There are two ways in which we might nevertheless try to derive a political theory from his work.

One way would be to uncover an implicit theory underlying his avowed political views. This route has not been widely held to hold much promise. He does, of course, indulge in some strident criticisms of naïve or decadent political ideals. But these have often been simply dismissed as being churlish rather than profound.[1] And detailed, scholarly studies of his attitudes to political phenomena have failed to discover a unifying basis in some implicit and coherent normative political theory.[2]

---

[1] Cf. e.g. Bernard Williams, *Shame and Necessity* (Berkeley: University of California Press, 1993), 10. Williams tells us that, although Nietzsche's views developed beyond his early aestheticism, "he did not move to any view that offered a coherent politics. He himself provides no way of relating his ethical and psychological insights to an intelligible account of modern society—a failing only thinly concealed by the impression he gives of having thoughts about modern politics that are determinate but terrible."

Brian Leiter has recently concluded that Nietzsche "has no political philosophy, in the conventional sense of a theory of the state and its legitimacy." He does, Leiter admits, occasionally express views about political matters, "but, read in context, they do not add up to a theoretical account of any of the questions of political philosophy." *Nietzsche on Morality* (London: Routledge, 2002), 296.

And Keith Ansell-Pearson points out that, in his later works, Nietzsche makes normative suggestions about politics, but he never develops a notion of legitimacy to support them. Cf. *An Introduction to Nietzsche as Political Thinker* (Cambridge: Cambridge University Press, 1994), 41.

[2] The two most detailed scholarly reconstructions of Nietzsche's political views and their development in response to contemporary political events may be found in Peter Bergmann, *Nietzsche: "The Last Anti-Political German"* (Bloomington: Indiana University Press, 1987); and Urs Marti, *"Der grosse Pöbel- und Sklavenaufstand": Nietzsches Auseinandersetzung mit Revolution und Demokratie* (Stuttgart: Verlag J. B. Metzler, 1993). Marti writes (296): "Was in der Forschung als Nietzsches politische Philosophie bezeichnet wird, ist eine

The other way would be to spell out the political implications of his broader philosophical views. These might be seen to be compatible with his political opinions.[3] Or they might be seen as implications that he himself failed to discern and which are therefore at odds with his own political remarks.[4] But attempts to extract a political theory from his work in this way have yielded such diverse conclusions that it is hard to resist drawing the inference that his ethical and epistemological views do not themselves have any very determinate political consequences.[5]

In this book, I would like to defend the view that Nietzsche indeed fails to articulate any positive, normative political theory. It is tempting to assume that there are only uninteresting reasons (lack of understanding, lack of interest, unreflective parochialism) for this failing. But I want to make a case for the claim that there is an interesting reason. I shall argue that, in his early and middle works in particular, Nietzsche articulates a deep political skepticism that can best be described as a skepticism about legitimacy.[6]

In using the term *political skepticism*, I am not alluding to the established positions that generally go by that name in the Anglophone tradition, such as those associated with Michael Oakeshott and Isaiah Berlin. The former involves a claim about the limitations of technical expertise in politics;[7] the latter an insistence that we cannot assume there will be

---

Ansammlung von Stimmungen, tiefen Ängsten, vorsichtigen Hoffnunge und realitätsfernen Zukunfstvisionen."

[3] Some commentators have seen the hierarchical and aristocratic tendencies in his later writings as being deeply rooted in his philosophical insights. Cf. esp. Bruce Detwiler, *Nietzsche and the Politics of Aristocratic Radicalism* (Chicago: University of Chicago Press, 1990); and Frederick Appel, *Nietzsche contra Democracy* (Ithaca: Cornell University Press, 1999).

[4] This discrepancy is stressed especially by Mark Warren in *Nietzsche and Political Thought* (Cambridge, Mass.: MIT Press, 1991).

[5] Steven Aschheim has recorded the tremendous diversity of political positions that Nietzsche's work has been employed to defend in Germany. Cf. *The Nietzsche Legacy in Germany: 1890–1990* (University of California Press, 1994). Tomasz Grzegorz Pszczótkowski has provided a detailed typology of interpretations of Nietzsche's politics in his *Zur Methodologie der Interpretation des Politischen bei Friedrich Nietzsche* (Frankfurt am Main: Peter Lang, 1996). Cf. also Tracy Strong's essay, "Nietzsche's Political Misappropriation," in *The Cambridge Companion to Nietzsche*, ed. Bernd Magnus and Kathleen Higgins (Cambridge: Cambridge University Press, 1996), 119–47.

[6] I will use the term *early works* to refer to *The Birth of Tragedy* (1871) and contemporaneous writings. The term *middle works* will refer to the *Untimely Meditations* (1873–76), and all further writings up to and including the first four books of *The Gay Science*. All of the writings including and following the fifth book of *The Gay Science* (1886) will be called the "mature works" or "later works."

[7] Cf. Michael Oakeshott, "Rationalism in Politics," in *Rationalism in Politics* (Indianapolis: Liberty Press, 1991).

any natural harmony between the plurality of political values that we pursue.[8] Nietzsche, I shall argue, is less concerned with the conflicts that arise when we try to realize our values in political life than with our inability to arrive at a form of politics that is genuinely grounded in normative authority.

His guiding political vision, I shall claim, is oriented around the rise of modern state, which requires normative consensus in order to rule, and a simultaneous process of secularization that seems to make uncoerced consensus impossible. The state has the ideological capacity to manufacture this consensus but no necessary concern that it should involve convergence around the right (as opposed to merely politically expedient) norms.

Nietzsche doubts that secular societies can otherwise generate sufficient consensus. They therefore lack any reliable mechanism for placing real normative constraints on state power. But, I shall argue, he does not want to give up either on the possibility of having stable political authority or on his commitment to an independent source of normative authority. So his political skepticism derives from the fact that he holds both to be necessary but cannot see how they can be compatible.

To many of Nietzsche's readers, no doubt, it will sound as though this kind of political skepticism presupposes precisely the kind of normative realism that he has been widely taken to reject. Any interpreter of Nietzsche must face a tricky problem concerning the status of his evaluative claims, particularly in the later works. The anti-objectivist meta-ethics that is suggested there seems to be in conflict with the objectivist-sounding evaluative judgments that he defends.[9] Some interpreters claim that there are readings that can render these aspects of his work compatible, in particular by refusing to take the value judgments at face value. Nietzsche does not mean them, they claim, to express objective normative truths. I shall defend the view that the evidence is mixed, but that the incompatibility thesis provides us with a more plausible and coherent account, as well as one that can help us to make sense of this interesting political dilemma.

If we read Nietzsche, at least in his later period, as a consistent antirealist, we will still encounter a version of the political problem that I have

[8] Cf. "Two Concepts of Liberty," *Four Essays on Liberty* (Oxford: Oxford University Press, 1979), and "The Decline of Utopian Ideas in the West," in *The Crooked Timber of Humanity* (Princeton: Princeton University Press, 1998).

[9] As John Richardson puts it, "The main interpretive puzzle about Nietzsche's metaethics" is "how to reconcile his emphatic 'perspectivizing' of all values, including his own, with his equally vehement 'ranking' of values—a ranking that so clearly purports to some privileged status." *Nietzsche's New Darwinism* (Oxford: Oxford University Press, 2004), 68. Richardson himself defends an interesting compatibility thesis, which will be discussed in chapter 5. Cf. also Richard Schacht, *Nietzsche* (London and New York: Routledge, 1983), 419.

described, concerning an inability to formulate a coherent conception of political legitimacy. On an antirealist view of the status of his own values, Nietzsche must not only lack a normative political theory that can be justified to others, but will also (as we shall see in chapter 4) lack a coherent conception of how his own values might ground political authority.

But even if we take Nietzsche's value-criticism to be objectivist in orientation, that is, if we read him as a moral realist, we will arrive (perhaps more surprisingly) at an antitheoretical view of politics. And on this reading we can make sense of the distinctive form of political skepticism that he discovers.

As I have already indicated, there are many different ways in which we might try to assess Nietzsche's contribution to political thinking. I do not myself believe that the political skepticism that I am attributing to him will provide an interpretive framework that renders coherent every aspect of his thought, or one that is compatible with all the diverse philosophical and political claims that he makes. But I hope to show that it is at least a sufficiently distinctive and interesting strand in his work to merit examination in its own right.

Nietzsche's View of the State

The political skepticism that I attribute to Nietzsche derives from two important descriptive premises. One concerns the nature of modern states and in particular the fact that their ability to rule a society requires convergence, in that society, on some shared normative beliefs. The other concerns the inability of secular societies to generate the required convergence through noncoercive means. I shall take these descriptive premises, which originate in Nietzsche's early and middle-period writings, to be held fairly stably across his career.

Nietzsche sees that modern states cannot rule through direct coercion alone. They must be perceived to be legitimate.[10] This means that they must have a perceived entitlement to rule. Their subjects will accept those political obligations that they believe conform to the correct norms for political legitimacy. For example, if they believe that religion has supplied them with the correct set of norms, they will measure their political obligations against this independent standard for moral appraisal.[11]

States functionally require that the political obligations they seek to impose on their subjects be accepted by them. The aspiration to legitimacy in this sense is a "transactional" feature of states, as John Simmons

[10] *HTH*, I, 472.
[11] Ibid.

has pointed out.[12] It concerns the obligations of particular people to particular states, and not just the justification of the state per se. Although Nietzsche speculates, in passing, about what a world without states would be like, he accepts that political agency in the modern world is concentrated in them.[13] The most interesting questions that he raises about states concern not their basic justification, but rather what we shall refer to as their ideological need. People will only accept the authority of a particular state if that state seems, in its form and its behavior, to conform to independently valid moral norms. The ideological need of the state consists in this need for perceived legitimacy.

Many states are accepted to be legitimate in this sense. Their rule is supported by normative consensus. But as we shall see, Nietzsche claims that insofar as this normative consensus exists in secular societies, it is the product of political coercion. The state, he tells us "lies in all the tongues of good and evil."[14] States are quite capable not only of compelling obedience but also of manufacturing a misguided moral commitment to the obligations that they impose on us.[15]

Although people will not consciously espouse views that they know to be mere prescriptions of state ideology, states, through their control of apparently independent institutions—for instance, educational and religious institutions—have powerful means of implicitly asserting control over belief. States can thereby manufacture the very normative beliefs to which they then appeal in their claims to legitimacy. We will refer to this phenomenon as political self-justification. It is made possible by the ideological capacity of modern states.[16]

---

[12] A. John Simmons, "Justification and Legitimacy," *Ethics* 109, no. 4 (July 1999): 739–71.

[13] In *HTH*, I, 472, he speculates that in the absence of religion the state as a form of political organization might die out. He warns against any rash political experiments that would hasten this process.

[14] *TSZ*, part I, "On the New Idol": "Every people speaks its tongue of good and evil, which the neighbour does not understand. It has invented its own language of customs and rights. But the state tells lies in all the tongues of good and evil; and whatever it says it lies."

[15] States have, for example, co-opted religious authority to this end. "As a rule," Nietzsche tells us, "the state will know how to win the priests over to itself because it needs their concealed and intimate education of souls and knows how to value servants who appear outwardly to represent a quite different interest." *HTH*, I, 472.

[16] Mark Warren has argued that this problem of covert self-justification is the primary political problem that Nietzsche sees as resulting from secularization. He writes: "Because the loss of Christian-moral culture occurs without the formation of a sovereign self, the opportunity exists for the state to provide its own legitimations by manipulating self-identities. In this way, the state assumes a role vacated by the church. Only in the modern period, then, does it become possible for the state to exploit reflexive needs directly by providing a vicarious identity for the self in relation to the community" (*Nietzsche and Political Thought*, 220). I shall explore this same loss of extrapolitical authority, but instead of focusing on the

I shall argue that Nietzsche sees this political self-justification as an inevitable feature of secular polities, for he holds that in the absence of myth or religion we have no other means of generating the required normative agreement. There can be no uncoerced consensus sufficient to support political authority. Nietzsche's reasons for holding this view are complex and will be set out in chapters 3, 4, and 5.

The strength of the claim will depend on how strong an impossibility Nietzsche takes uncoerced normative agreement to be. He might mean that uncoerced agreement is impossible only "for us," that is, for human beings given a particular stage of their intellectual development. Or he might mean that it is in principle impossible for us to achieve. In fact, we shall see, his view is grounded in diverse observations and speculations concerning our intellectual capabilities, as well as philosophical claims about the nature and difficulty of moral criticism. I do not attribute to him any confident view about the extent to which the situation is remediable, should human capacities develop beyond their current state. But I will claim that he seems inclined toward pessimism.

Given Nietzsche's reflections on the state and on the general unreliability of normative belief, he must assume that it is extremely unlikely that any independent source of normative authority will be able to compete with the state's ideological control. This view of the modern political predicament forms the basis of Nietzsche's political skepticism. In itself this is merely a descriptive view, and does not yet amount to a form of skepticism. But I shall argue that insofar as Nietzsche believes that we can neither be satisfied with this state of affairs, nor see a way to overcome it, he must be viewed as a political skeptic.

NIETZSCHE AS A SKEPTIC ABOUT LEGITIMACY

Nietzsche's concern with the state, I shall argue, is normatively driven. He is an opponent of its ideological incursions into the realm of culture. His antipathy is most evident in the middle-period writings, where he has very specific complaints about the German state. But his opposition does not simply derive from a contingent clash between his own values and those promoted by this state. It derives from a principled objection to political ideology. The very fact of having normative convictions entails a rejection of the untrammeled ideological authority of the state.

It would simply be incoherent for anyone to have strong normative commitments and at the same time to concede to the state the power to

---

manipulability of identity as the basis of our vulnerability to state ideology, I shall try to bring out the salience of Nietzsche's claims concerning normative authority.

override all normative authority. If someone acknowledges a distinction between correct and incorrect values, they are acknowledging some determinant of that correctness. The fundamental determinant will be some property such that, in virtue of possessing it, this will be the correct value to have. They might hold that this property consists in its being sanctioned by God, or corresponding to normative facts, or even just being endorsed by their own pro-attitudes. Very few people hold the view that this property consists in being sanctioned by the state. Even political realists, who ultimately value state power above all else, tend do so because it tracks some property such as, in Leopold von Ranke's case, what God wills.[17] To the extent that the state is assigned a role in determining people's values, this authorization will be derivative. It will derive from recognition of some independent source of normative authority.

If we accept some independent source of normative authority, we cannot concede total ideological power to the state. We must preserve the conditions of possibility of valuing. We might call this a "transcendental" argument for limiting the state's ideological capacity. Nietzsche cannot, then, coherently accept or endorse the ideologically predatory state. I shall argue in chapter 1 that he is a vociferous opponent of it. He aims to preserve evaluative independence.

It does not, prima facie, look very difficult to come up with a theory of legitimacy that meets this "transcendental" demand. There are certainly contemporary political theorists who would hold that that is just what is taken care of by the weak, or deflationary, notion of legitimacy that they defend. This weak notion does not require that political institutions conform to objectively *correct* norms. It involves, along with the view that states must justify themselves to their subjects, only what Bernard Williams refers to as the "critical theory principle," or the claim that "the acceptance of a justification does not count if the acceptance itself is produced by the coercive power which is supposedly being justified."[18] So legitimacy in this sense requires that political institutions conform to the

---

[17] There may be a few exceptions among secular reason-of-state theorists. In his *Idee der Staatsräson in der neueren Geschichte* (entitled *Machiavellism*, in the English edition), Friedrich Meinecke tells us that the state "is an organic structure whose full power can only be maintained by allowing it in some way to continue growing; and *raison d'état* indicates the path and goal for such a growth." An understanding of the characteristic way of life of an individual state, Meinecke claims, yields normative insight: "From the realm of what is and what will be, there constantly emerges, through the medium of understanding, a notion of what ought to be and what must be." Friedrich Meinecke, *Machiavellism: The Doctrine of Raison d'État and Its Place in Modern History*, trans. Douglas Scott, (New Brunswick, New Jersey: Transaction, 1998), 1.

[18] Bernard Williams, "Realism and Moralism in Political Theory," in *In the Beginning Was the Deed: Realism and Moralism in Political Argument*, ed. Geoffrey Hawthorn (Princeton, N.J.: Princeton University Press, 2005), 6.

accepted norms of those over whom they rule, and that acceptance of these norms be uncoerced, at least by the political institutions that they purport to legitimate.

But although this weak notion seems helpfully unambitious in demanding conformity to the professed normative beliefs of a population, rather than to the right norms, it presupposes precisely the kind of uncoerced convergence that Nietzsche thinks secularism is making increasingly unlikely. In the absence of any account of how uncoerced convergence might be possible, it must fall short of being a feasible theory of legitimacy.[19]

Nietzsche claims that popular values, in the absence of myth or religion, will not manifest the kind of convergence that is necessary to support a shared form of political authority. As I shall argue in chapter 2, in ancient Greece as well as in the modern world, secularization involves, for Nietzsche, acceptance of the view that reason is the only legitimate guide to belief and value. Reasoning does not, however, appear to lead to normative consensus. And there does not seem to Nietzsche to be any secular institution that can compete with the state in shaping popular belief through some nonrational means. His own initial hopes that art might supply such a galvanizing force turn out, as we shall see in chapter 2, to be flawed.

A moral antirealist would have special grounds for being concerned about this problem. The antirealist holds that moral reasoning cannot generate convergence on the truth, since there are no objective normative truths to converge on. We cannot, then, reliably expect rational consensus to be the outcome of moral reasoning. But at the same time, people in secular cultures will not consciously defer to any nonrational authority, in the way that, for instance, religious people might defer to revelation. So the combination of secularism and antirealism, or the refusal to accept nonrational forms of authority combined with skepticism about moral reason, makes the problem seem especially intractable.

But what about the moral realism or objectivism? It looks as though this might supply a way out of the problem, by offering the hope of rational convergence. A stronger notion of legitimacy, one that aimed for convergence on the correct norms might then appear to offer a more feasible solution. And, as I suggested earlier, there seems to be quite a powerful residual element of moral realism even in Nietzsche's later work (I defend this view in chapter 5). Nietzsche presents his own evaluative

---

[19] I am assuming here that practical impossibility is a knock-down argument for any theory of political legitimacy. If a theory of legitimacy is intended to supply us with standards for the evaluation of political institutions, then an ideal that could never be realized institutionally must fail in a vital respect.

convictions as if they were normative truths that he has discovered. These concern what is good for individuals, for societies and cultures, and for humanity as a whole. So, if there are discoverable moral truths, can we not hope for convergence around them? And would this not constitute a robustly independent form of normative authority that could compete with the state's ideological capacity?

Nietzsche's most distinctive argument for political skepticism, I shall argue, rests on the claim that even if we can assume that there are knowable normative truths, secular societies will still have a tremendous problem in making those truths effective in political life. Even objective normative truth would not be able to provide a basis for genuine political legitimacy because the majority of people would have no means of recognizing it as such. If we read implicitly realist assumptions into Nietzsche's later value-criticism, I shall argue, we will find in his work an even deeper form of political skepticism.

There are two ways in which, we might imagine, we could acquire normative knowledge. First of all, we could try to discover the truth ourselves, through the use of our own reason. I shall argue that Nietzsche thinks most people simply lack the intellectual capabilities to do this. If we take his later evaluation of values to involve a quest for truth, his value-criticism has to be seen to reveal how widespread, deep, and intransigent error inevitably is. Normative truths, we have to infer, are difficult to discover.

The second way in which people might acquire normative knowledge is through deference to experts whose authority they recognize. But even if there were indeed people (such as philosophers) who had the relevant intellectual capabilities and were able to ascertain the truth, most people would still be incapable of recognizing their authority. They would have no reason to defer to any particular individual who claims expertise in this area, for they would not be equipped to assess whose view really should be rationally binding for them.

This problem concerning normative expertise has been explored by Alexander Nehamas, for whom it constitutes the central puzzle of Socrates' ethical teaching. Socrates, he tells us, raises the question of how *aretê* can be taught, given that those who want to learn it face the problem of identifying a teacher with the right expertise. In order to do so, they would already have to be experts themselves "regarding what benefits and harms the soul."[20] Otherwise they risk being harmed by an incompetent teacher.

Socrates' insight, Nehamas tells us, is that "in the case of shoemakers or doctors, we can tell whether the shoe fits or the fever has gone: we

---

[20] Alexander Nehamas, *The Art of Living: Socratic Reflections from Plato to Foucault* (Berkeley: University of California Press, 1998), 80.

have relatively clear ways of recognizing them. But in the case of ethical experts, it is not clear that we can recognize the experts independently of the fact that we find their views and their reasons for them—their reasons for living as they do—convincing. But to find such reasons is already to follow them."[21] We are then presented with a profound problem concerning how knowledge of *aretê* can ever be communicated to others. The Platonic solution, Nehamas tells us, is to claim that people have *aretê* only by divine dispensation.[22]

Nietzsche, I shall argue in this book, is concerned with the distinctively secular problem that arises when theism no longer seems to provide a credible means of resolving the issue. The problem of moral knowledge resurfaces for Nietzsche as a post-Christian problem. And it seems to be a peculiarly destabilizing problem in a world in which social and political ideas and institutions have taken for granted the possibility of popular access to moral truth.

This problem was not apparent so long as people believed that religion was the correct guide to normative truth. Religions have suggested two different solutions. On one model, they have insisted, people might rely on some inner revelation, or their own conscience, as a reliable guide to truth and value. On another, people might defer to the authority of appropriate experts, or a priesthood. But on Nietzsche's view, there are no comparable secular mechanisms for making genuine normative truth popularly authoritative. Our intellectual capacities are generally inadequate. And secular societies conspicuously lack any recognized normative expertise.

So his political skepticism, I shall argue, is motivated by the perception of an important disanalogy between religious and secular worldviews. Organized religions can develop structures through which their normative and nonnormative truth-claims might come to wield authority over popular belief. The exploitation of various nonrational forms of persuasion (involving acceptance of the authority of revelation, scripture, a clerisy) has permitted religions to promote acceptance of the beliefs and values that they take to be correct. Religious authority dictates that our justifications for belief and value must end in some specific place, that is, the faith that comprises that particular religious worldview. A religious priesthood might therefore devise various means of establishing these limits. But secular, rational justifications do not in principle have to end at any particular point. Even if philosophers can identify valid norms, they cannot set themselves up as a secular priesthood and establish similar mechanisms of normative control.

[21] Ibid., 81.
[22] Ibid., 89.

Nietzsche's political skepticism, then, consists in the view that we simply cannot reconcile our need for normative authority with our need for political authority. Given his own historical situation, as we shall see, he was vividly aware of the fragility of any apparent compromise between these demands. He does, in the later writings, occasionally seem inclined to give up on one or the other. But the real challenge that his skepticism presents to modern politics is somehow to find a way of not giving up on either.

CHAPTER 1

The Predatory State

INTRODUCTION

In a speech to the Prussian Chamber of Peers, in 1873, Bismarck defended his *Kulturkampf*, the battle that he had lately been so vehemently waging against the political power of the Catholic Church in Germany. He insisted that it was not "a matter of a struggle between faith and unbelief." Rather "it is a matter," he declared, "of the age-old struggle for power, as old as the human race itself, between kingship and the priestly caste, a struggle for power that goes back far beyond the coming of our Saviour to this world."[1] The conflict between the secular state and religious authority was given the stamp of inevitability and Protestants across the *Reich* hurriedly aligned themselves with the secular cause.

Nietzsche had, by this time, already come to the conclusion that religious belief had been discredited and was destined to die out. But we do not find in his work any celebration of victory on behalf of the secular political powers. Instead we find an increasingly cautious and even hostile attitude to the state and its ideological reach. His wariness arises from an interesting analysis of the nature of political authority in the modern world.

In his early work, he identifies two important features of the modern world. The first is secularization. In *The Birth of Tragedy*, he describes to us the way in which rational reflection eroded the horizons of myth that bounded Greek culture of the Tragic Age.[2] And in the *Untimely Meditations* he describes the "whirlpool of secularization [*Verweltlichung*]" that occurs as Christian faith recedes.[3] The loss of a shared worldview entails a breakdown of previous forms of normative consensus.

---

[1] Otto von Bismarck, *Ausgwählte Reden*, Zweiter Band (Berlin, 1877), pp. 203–4.
[2] Cf. *BT*, 23.
[3] *UM*, iii, 4:

The waters of religion are ebbing away and leaving behind swamps or stagnant pools; the nations are again drawing away from one another in the most hostile fashion and long to tear one another to pieces. The sciences [*Wissenschaften*], pursued without any restraint and in a spirit of the blindest *laissez faire*, are shattering and dissolving all firmly held belief; the educated classes and states are being swept away by a hugely contemptible money economy. The world has never been more worldly, never poorer in love and goodness. The educated classes are no longer lighthouses or refuges in the midst of this turmoil of secularization [*Verweltlichung*].

The second is the rise of the modern state. Political power, in the modern world, must be accepted as legitimate.[4] So the modern state, which cannot rule through force alone, requires allegiance rooted in some degree of normative consensus. It also has the capacity to manufacture this consensus. Nietzsche is struck by the spell-binding charisma of political leaders, but also (as we shall see) by the more insidious means that the state employs, through control of education, to establish its ideological grip.[5]

It is these two phenomena that define, for Nietzsche, the political predicament of the modern world. He paints a vivid picture for us. It is one that will later find echoes in Max Weber's vision of the rise of the modern state and the simultaneous fragmentation of moral life through secularization.[6]

In his *On the Genealogy of Morality*, Nietzsche presents us with a particularly striking image of the state. In its essential, original form, he says, the state was a "pack of blond beasts of prey" that sank its claws into a vulnerable populace.[7] This vision of the predatory state has deep roots in his thought. It dates back to the 1870s, when the founding of the new German *Reich* made him vividly aware of the state as an abstract agent, aggressively pursuing power and doing so, in particular, through ideological control. As we shall see, in that period, his Basel colleague, Jacob Burckhardt, provided him with a view of politics that emphasized the perpetual potential conflict between coercive political power and the realm of culture, governed by the noncoercive authority of norms.

For both Burckhardt and Nietzsche, we will see, the modern state must establish its authority by promoting the acceptance of laws, norms, and obligations. It must aim for "legitimacy" in the merely descriptive sense. But the state's end in promoting such consensus is the maintenance of its own power. In its very essence, the state seeks to control. In its modern historical form it has acquired an especially acute ideological need. Traditional and religious legitimations are being eroded.[8] The maintenance of ideological control becomes the object of an explicit form of calculation, governed by reasons of state.

I shall use the term *ideology* to denote beliefs that are manufactured by the state for the purposes of sustaining its own power. The relevant claim is not that they are all bound to be false. Some of them may adventitiously

---

[4] *HTH*, I, 472.

[5] Cf. *HTH*, I, 43, on the "statesman as the steersman of the passions." Cf. also *D*, 167, on the unconditional devotion inspired by Bismarck.

[6] Cf. esp. "Politik als Beruf," *Gesammelte politischen Schriften* (Tübingen: Mohr, 1980).

[7] *GM*, ii, 17.

[8] Cf. *GS*, 176: "*Pity.*—Those poor reigning princes! All of their rights are now suddenly turning into claims, and all of these claims begin to sound like presumption. Even if they only say 'We' or 'my people' wicked old Europe begins to smile."

coincide with the truth. Rather, it is that they do not aim at the truth. The aim in producing them is to support and legitimate the authority of states.[9]

Nietzsche does not advocate the overthrow of the state.[10] In fact, we will see that stable political authority is a necessary precondition for the kinds of human achievements that he values. But he cannot concede to the state the kind of ideological power that maintenance of its authority seems to require. In this chapter, I will argue that Nietzsche is strongly committed to the view that our values should be determined by an independent form of normative authority, and that this should shape political life rather than vice versa. The problem, as we will see in later chapters, is that he cannot envisage how such an independent source of normative authority might provide a bulwark against the ideological power of the state.

POLITICAL REALISM

The merely descriptive view of the state's ideological need and capacity is perfectly compatible with political realism. But Nietzsche is no political realist, and it is important to distinguish his skeptical view from this position.[11] He, of course, expresses vehement opposition to Bismarckian realpolitik. But he also has deeper, philosophical reasons for rejecting political realism.

Many recent theorists of the state have been political realists of various kinds, who reject the view that questions about normative truths or

---

[9] Raymond Geuss points out:

One must distinguish between the function of supporting, fostering, or stabilizing hegemony and the function of justifying or legitimizing hegemony. Any set of beliefs which legitimizes or justifies a social practice will thereby tend to support it, but the converse is not the case: a belief that a given ruling class is strong and ruthless, so that any resistance to the dominant order is futile, may well be a belief, the acceptance of which by large segments of the population will have the effect of stabilizing the existing relations of dominance, but it is unlikely that such a belief could be used to *justify* these relations.

Guess, *The Idea of a Critical Theory: Habermas and the Frankfurt School* (Cambridge: Cambridge University Press, 1981), 15.

[10] Cf. *HTH*, I, 472.

[11] Nietzsche's aversion to political realism has been stressed by those commentators who emphasize the "antipolitical" character of his work. Cf., e.g., Walter Kaufmann, *Nietzsche: Philosopher, Psychologist, Antichrist* (Princeton, N.J.: Princeton University Press, 1975). Cf. also Peter Bergmann, *Nietzsche: "The Last Anti-Political German"* (Bloomington: Indiana State University Press, 1987).

objective values can play any helpful role in thinking about political legitimacy.[12] According to such a view, the functioning of states requires their legitimacy in the sense of conformity to established positive law. But although we might ask descriptive questions about what kind of ethical context promotes acceptance of these laws, we need not (and cannot practicably) require that this acceptance be justified in any higher normative sense.[13] I shall claim that Nietzsche wants to make at least some normative demands on state power, for he holds that our capacity to recognize independent criteria for beliefs and values must be preserved.

Political realism in relation to legitimacy (we will set aside the better-known connotations that the term has acquired as a theory of international relations) can take several different forms. First of all, what I shall call scientific realism is concerned with descriptive claims about the nature of political life. Insofar as this involves confronting salient facts about political reality it seems uncontroversial to say that Nietzsche, like most political thinkers, was a realist in at least this sense. In its most influential form, now associated with Weber, scientific realism stresses the fact that politics inevitably involves the pursuit of power. Nietzsche certainly shares this concern.[14] But some scientific realists might further wish to suspend normative questions about politics altogether, and in this sense Nietzsche is not a pure scientific realist. As we shall see, his concern with the state is normatively driven.[15]

Second, one might be a skeptical political realist. By this I shall mean a position that (unlike the view that I am calling "political skepticism") is derived from a more general normative skepticism. On such a view, there is no meaningful distinction between normative beliefs and mere ideology; on the most reductive reading, both could only ever be assertions and hence expressions of power. So whereas the scientific realist claims that politics involves the pursuit of power, the skeptical realist makes the

---

[12] Carl Schmitt has perhaps been the most influential adherent of such a view. Cf. "Die Tyrannie der Werte," in *Säkularisation und Utopia—Ebracher Studien: Ernst Forsthoff zum 65. Geburtstag* (Stuttgart: W. Kohlhammer, 1967), 37–62, 45–46. Schmitt sees the attempt to ground politics in objective values as an unnecessary reaction to nineteenth-century nihilism. Cf. also Ernst-Wolfgang Böckenförde, "Zur Kritik der Wertbegründung des Rechts," in *Recht, Staat, Freiheit: Studien zur Rechtsphilosophie, Staatstheorie und Verfassungsgeschichte* (Frankfurt/Main: Suhrkamp 1991), 67–91.

[13] Nietzsche's philosophy of values has been seen as foundational to this realist approach to legitimacy. Cf., e.g., Jürgen Habermas, "On the Logic of Legitimation Problems," *Legitimation Crisis* (Boston: Beacon Press, 1975), 122.

[14] Cf., e.g., *Nachgelassene Fragmente* 1876 bis Winter 1877–1878, *KGW* IV-2.440 (KSA 8.344).

[15] Brian Leiter rightly sees Nietzsche's admiration for Thucydides (cf. *TI*, "What I Owe to the Ancients," 2) as emanating from his attachment to descriptive political realism. Cf. *Nietzsche on Morality*, 48–51.

further claim that politics *cannot* involve anything but the pursuit of power.[16] But I shall argue that Nietzsche's attitude to the state could not be accounted for by such a view. His desire to preserve independence from state ideology rules out this position.

Third, one might be a normative political realist. This would involve making the normative claim that politics *should* not involve anything but the pursuit of power. It is a view that has been widely attributed to Nietzsche, in the form of a politics of "will to power."[17] This would allow us to locate him in the reason-of-state tradition that had come to dominate German political thought. But I shall argue that he is not a normative political realist in this sense. He clearly values things that are threatened by the state's encroaching authority. He does not take state power to be his supreme value.

NORMATIVE POLITICAL REALISM AND REALPOLITIK

In Nietzsche's early and middle writings he clearly aligns himself with the critics of contemporary realpolitik. It is important for us to differentiate his view of the state carefully from that of realpolitik's supporters. The dominant view of the state in the period of the *Reichsgründung* involved a form of normative political realism. The historical school founded by Ranke saw realpolitik as justified by a transcendent norm, one that did not have to be recognized by individual statesmen or subjects but rather provided an external form of justification for political actions.

For Ranke, this justification is essentially theological. States might appear to be forged by very human drives, but these drives themselves are

---

[16] This view of Nietzsche's politics has been elaborated by Henry Kerger, who assimilates Nietzsche's views on state authority to those of the "legal realist" tradition, stressing in particular the congruence of Nietzsche's views with that of the contemporary legal theorist Rudolph von Ihering. Cf. Henry Kerger, *Autorität und Recht im Denken Nietzsches* (Berlin: Duncker and Humboldt, 1987).

[17] This is a view that Nietzsche later writings, in particular, have been seen to support. Mark Warren claims that according to Nietzsche's political construal of the idea of will to power, in works such as *Beyond Good and Evil*, any political exploitation is natural and even desirable. Cf. Mark Warren, *Nietzsche and Political Thought*, 227. It is therefore unsurprising, on Warren's view, that Nietzsche has been frequently interpreted as a defender of realpolitik, in spite of his earlier explicit opposition to this tradition. As examples of this view, he cites Georg Lukács, *The Destruction of Reason*, trans. Peter Palmer (Atlantic Highlands, N.J.: Humanities Press, 1981), 372–78; J. P. Stern, *Nietzsche* (Glasgow: William Collins Sons, 1978), 82–87, and *A Study of Nietzsche* (Cambridge: Cambridge University Press, 1979), 120–22; Alasdair MacIntyre, *After Virtue* (Notre Dame, Ind.: University of Notre Dame Press, 1980), chs. 9, 18.

divinely inspired.[18] States are "Gedanken Gottes";[19] their development is governed by a divine plan. According to this view, in surveying the laws governing the development of states in human history, we are able to occupy a perspective superior to ordinary morality. If we adopt a normative commitment to this political development per se, it will trump any other more parochial moral considerations.[20]

The "realist" tradition founded by Ranke is not, then, normatively disinterested. The position incorporates the view that statesmen must consider reasons of state independently of any moral considerations, that they will often have to transgress customary morality in order to preserve the state's stability and security. But the theoretical position which insists, a priori, that reasons of state have precedence over moral claims, or holds that they must be understood to be justified from some more objective standpoint, is of course itself a significant normative claim.

It would not be incoherent to see the idea of "will to power" as a secular version of this kind of normative realism. It would just be a secular name for the forces that Ranke sees at work in history. According to Ranke even the apparently amoral forces that empower states and generate wars, however destructive they might seem, are in fact "moral energies."[21] History is seen to be infused with a moral significance that is not perceptible to most of the individual actors within it. So, we might imagine, the "will to power" that is equally blind to individual human

---

[18] Cf. *Politisches Gespräch*, in *Die großen Mächte und politisches Gespräch* (Frankfurt/ Main: Suhrkamp, 1995), 110: "Der Geist des Staates ist zwar göttlicher Anhauch, aber zugleich menschlicher Antrieb. Es ist eine Gemeinschaft beschränkterer Natur, über der jene, höherer, von Bedingungen freiere Gemeinschaft schwebt."

[19] Ibid., 95.

[20] In his classic essay contrasting Ranke's and Burckhardt's approaches to history, Hugh Trevor-Roper claims that the German historical school saw the state as "the protective carapace which society created out of its own substance, and which was therefore no less valid, no less autonomous, than the culture which it protected. Thus if different forms of culture were all equally valid and not to be criticized by absolute standards, so were differing states. States too, like cultures, followed their own rules, their 'reason of state,' which was thus legitimized, and not to be criticized from the standpoint of morality or natural law." Hugh Trevor-Roper, "Jacob Burckhardt," *Proceedings of the British Academy* 70 (1984): 359–78 (Master Mind Lecture, 11 December 1984), 361. Cited by Lionel Gossman, *Basel in the Age of Burckhardt: A Study in Unseasonable Ideas* (Chicago: University of Chicago Press, 2000), 439–40.

[21] Cf. *Politisches Gespräch*, 93; and *Die großen Mächte*, 68: Nicht ein solch zufälliges Durcheinanderstürmen, Übereinanderherfallen, Nacheinanderfolgen der Staaten und Völker bietet die Weltgeschichte dar, wie es beim ersten Blicke wohl aussieht. Auch ist die oft so zweifelhafte Förderung der Kultur nicht ihr einziger Inhalt. Es sind Kräfte und zwar geistige, Leben hervorbringende, schöpferische Kräfte, selber Leben, es sind moralische Energien, die wir Entwicklung erblicken." Friedrich Meinecke, commenting on this notion, admits that Ranke must be "interpreting the concept of morality in a much wider sense than in that of the customary unalterable command dictated by conscience" (Cf. *Machiavellism*, 384).

purposes and values constitutes, for Nietzsche, the self-justifying dynamic of human history.[22]

However, this reading would have to obscure not only Nietzsche's powerful epistemic and evaluative commitments, but also the critique of realpolitik that they entail.[23] The normative political realist cannot acknowledge any genuine conflict between normative authority and the ideological power of the state; the whole realm of culture, truth, and value must be subordinated to the superior end of maintaining the state's power. But it is precisely this kind of potential conflict that motivates Nietzsche's political views, and in particular, his "antipolitical" thought.

As Friedrich Meinecke saw, Nietzsche belongs to the opposing political tradition. In his famous 1948 lecture on "Ranke and Burckhardt," Meinecke represents Ranke as the founder of a Berlin tradition that includes Droysen, Treitschke, and Dilthey, and Burckhardt as the founder of a Basel tradition that includes Nietzsche, Overbeck, and Bachofen.[24] The two traditions are grounded in fundamentally different worldviews. It is only the latter that permits us to see the state as a potential threat to our highest values.

THE VIEW FROM BASEL

Nietzsche sees Ranke's "realism," and hence his defense of the Bismarckian *Reich*, as motivated by a discreditable desire to pander to the powerful.

---

[22] For a helpfully concise summary of the positions on will to power, see Brian Leiter, *Nietzsche on Morality*, 138–39. For a detailed analysis of Nietzsche's uses of the concept, refuting the attribution of a metaphysical claim, see Maudemarie Clark, "Nietzsche's Doctrines of the Will to Power," *Nietzsche*, ed. John Richardson and Brian Leiter (Oxford: Oxford University Press, 2001), 139–50.

[23] By contrast, historians of the Rankean school were defenders of Bismarck's realpolitik. Hugh Trevor-Roper remarks: "When Bismarck came to power, the classically and historically trained intellectuals of Germany were ready for him. They could welcome him as the necessary agent of *Weltgeschichte*. Nor would they demur at his methods, his *Realpolitik*. Why should they? The state, they had already decided, was the organ of culture which could not be judged, and had its own morality, which also could not be judged. The state, Hegel had said, was the march of God on earth. The state, Ranke had written, was a living being, a spiritual substance, a thought of God. The state, wrote Droysen, was 'the sum, the total organism of all ethical communities, their common purpose'; it was a law to itself—a moral law; in following its 'real interests, it could not be wrong.' "Jacob Burckhardt," 364.

[24] Friedrich Meinecke, *Werke*, vol. 7, *Zur Geschichte der Geschichtsschreibung* (München: R. Oldenbourg Verlag, 1968), "Ranke und Burckhardt, 93–110. Meinecke says that one day a book will have to be written on Berlin and Basel in the age of the *Reichsgründung*. Two essential contributions to this comparative project are Felix Gilbert's *History: Politics or Culture: Reflections on Ranke and Burckhardt* (Princeton, N.J.: Princeton University Press, 1990); and Lionel Gossman, *Basel in the Age of Burckhardt*.

Contrasting the quality of "strength of soul" with a mere "prudent indulgence towards strength," he says:

> The Germans . . . have finally brought out a very nice classical specimen of the latter, —they have every right to claim him as one of their own, and be proud of him: one Leopold Ranke, this born classical *advocatus* of every *causa fortior*, this most prudent of all prudent "realists."[25]

Burckhardt, on the other hand, is admired for refusing to subordinate intellectual standards to the interests of the *Reich*.[26] Contrary to his popular image, Nietzsche aligns himself with those who are prepared to take a principled stand against political power.

For Burckhardt and for Nietzsche this stance is possible because they reject the theological or quasi-theological attitude to history shared by their German contemporaries. Their more pessimistic view of history derives originally from Schopenhauer.[27] It sees the historical process as devoid of any objective meaning or ultimate goal and therefore does not vindicate any particular set of institutions that have evolved within it.[28]

But it is also Burckhardt's analysis of the state that opens up a distinct set of issues. He was, of course, writing before the modern social scientific definition of the state began to crystallize around Weber's famous formulation. He develops a clear conception of what is distinctive about the modern state and hence a view of what is distinctively dangerous about it. But like all nineteenth-century German historians, he uses the term *Staat* to refer to ancient and modern political entities of all kinds, including the ancient Greek polis. Burckhardt uses the term to identify what he sees as the enduring essence of the state.

The state in its most primitive sense, for Burckhardt, is really any form of social organization that constitutes a distinct entity, to which the ends of individuals are subordinated. Insects can form a state in this sense.[29]

---

[25] *GM*, iii, 19.

[26] *TI*, "What the Germans Lack," 5. cf. also *Nachgelassene Fragmente*, Sommer 1872 bis Ende 1874, *KGW* III-4.394, on Burckhardt as an opponent of the overestimation of the state.

[27] Felix Gilbert tells us that references to Schopenhauer became frequent in Burckhardt's correspondence during the 1860s. *History*, 73.

[28] For Burckhardt, this attitude is clearly expressed in the *Weltgeschichtliche Betrachtungen* (*Reflections on History*), the posthumously published work that derives from lecture notes for a course which Nietzsche attended. But Lionel Gossman points out: "Probably Burckhardt never wholeheartedly embraced the optimistic faith of the Restoration and of some of his Berlin teachers in the providential course of historical development. There seem always to have been reservations or reversals." *Basel in the Age of Burckhardt*, 219.

[29] Cf. Burckhardt, *Weltgeschichtliche Betrachtungen*, in *Gesamtausgabe* (Berlin: Deutsche Verlags Anstalt Stuttgart, 1929–33), 7:32. This posthumously published work was translated and published under the English title, *Force and Freedom: Reflections on History*,

Burckhardt contrasts *Tierstaaten* and *Menschenstaaten*, since the former are in no way free, that is, there is no aspect of individual life in such a "state" that is not subordinated to the demands of the state. The individual ant, for instance, functions only as a part of the "ant-state."

But although human states may be comparatively free, Burckhardt rejects the view that a human state could ever be formed through voluntary association: "Force always comes first," he tells us.[30] The state is formed through the reduction of force to a system. Although Burckhardt explicitly contrasts his view with Rousseau's social contract theory, he does not intend his own view of the origins of the state to be a mere speculative fiction, but rather a realistic account of how states have arisen.[31]

His historical account, however, is intended to bring out a general paradigm and thus to describe an essential feature of states: the compulsory subjection of all individuals to an institutionally realized end.[32] In its most perfectly achieved form, as Lionel Gossman points out, Burckhardt's state "requires the identification of each individual will with that of the whole, and tolerates no deviation, no difference, no independence, within or without." Gossman adds, "It is at least arguable that the ancient polis, as described in *The Cultural History of Greece*, represents, in many respects, for Burckhardt, the very essence of the state."[33] And the most complete polis may be found in the example of the Spartans for whom "the people is an army and the state an armed camp."[34]

Burckhardt does not admire this form of perfection. To him, "power is in itself evil."[35] He resists defining the state in terms of some ethical or metaphysical end, as his German contemporaries had frequently done.[36]

---

ed. and trans. James Hastings Nichols (New York: Pantheon Books, 1943). I shall cite this translation.

[30] Burckhardt, *Force and Freedom*, 109.

[31] Ibid., 109.

[32] Ibid., 117: "As regards the internal policy of the State, it was not engendered by the abdication of the egoisms of its individual members. It *is* that abdication, it *is* their reduction to a common denominator, in order that as many interests and egoisms as possible may find permanent satisfaction in it and, in the end, completely fuse their existence with its own."

[33] Gossman, *Basel in the Age of Burckhardt*, 320. In *Human, All Too Human*, Nietzsche seems to concur with this view of the Greek polis as the paradigmatic form of the ideologically oppressive state. In *HTH*, I, 474, he writes: "*The evolution of the spirit feared by the state.* —Like every organizing political power, the Greek *polis* was mistrustful of the growth of culture and sought almost exclusively to paralyse and inhibit it. It wanted to admit no history, no development in this realm; the education sanctioned by state law was intended to be imposed upon every generation and to rivet it to *one* stage of development. The same thing was later desired by Plato, too, for his ideal state." Cf also *HTH*, "Wanderer," 232, on devotion to the polis.

[34] Gossman, *Basel in the Age of Burckhardt.*, 320: citing Burckhardt's *Gesamtausgabe*, 8:69.

[35] Burckhardt, *Force and Freedom*, 115.

The state, insofar as it necessarily strives above all to sustain its own power, stands outside the realm of normative authority.

Traces of this political vision may be found throughout Nietzsche's work. When he claims, in his *Genealogy*, that the original state was a "pack of blond beasts of prey," he is clearly adopting the Burckhardtian paradigm. He sees the state in its most primitive and essential form as an aggressive band which, "organized on a war footing, and with the power to organize, unscrupulously lays its dreadful paws on a populace which, though it might be vastly greater in number, is still shapeless and shifting." Like Burckhardt, he contrasts this view with the naïve idea that the essence of the state might be understood contractually.[37] It is a nonvoluntary form of association.[38]

This view of the state dates back to the period of his interactions with Burckhardt in Basel. In an unpublished essay on "The Greek State," from around 1871, Nietzsche describes the complete sacrifice of other interests to its own ends, which the state, in its purest form, impels. People are blinded to the "dreadful origin of the state" in violence by an instinctive and uncritical identification with it. But he tells us that this prereflective basis of submission to the state has been eroded; modern states can only sustain their power by duping the majority of people.[39] He is following Burckhardt, too, when he identifies the distinctive set of problems presented to us by the modern state.

Burckhardt on the Modern State

The formation of the modern European *Staatsgeist* took place, Burckhardt contends, in Renaissance Italy.[40] Whilst modern scholars doubt this provenance, Burckhardt's paradigm remains analytically instructive.[41] He claims that the distinctive characteristic of the modern state is its

---

[36] Ibid., 118.

[37] *GM*, ii, 17.

[38] Cf. Dana Villa, "Friedrich Nietzsche: Morality, Individualism, and Politics," *Socratic Citizenship* (Princeton: Princeton University Press, 2001), 125–84, esp. 136–37, on Nietzsche's "primordial state" and its deep antipathy to the form of human freedom that Nietzsche wishes to defend.

[39] "Der griechische Staat"; *KGW* III-2.267.

[40] Burckhardt, *Die Kultur der Renaissance in Italien*, in *Gesamtausgabe*, 5:3. I shall cite translations from Jacob Burckhardt, *The Civilization of Renaissance Italy*, trans. S.G.C. Middlemore (London: Penguin Books, 1990).

[41] Cf. Quentin Skinner, *Visions of Politics*, vol. 2, *Renaissance Virtues* (Cambridge: Cambridge University Press, 2003), ch. 14, 378: "It has often been argued that [in Machiavelli's work] we already encounter an understanding of the state not merely as an apparatus of power but as an agent whose existence remains independent of those who exercise its authority at any given time. There is not much evidence, however, to support this

character as a *Kunstwerk*, that is, a product of conscious reflection and calculation. It is objectified and hence understood as an independent agent, whose ends are distinct from those of particular rulers or subjects. These ends may therefore be the object of a special form of calculation: reason of state.

This new form of understanding gave rise, Burckhardt tells us, to "the great modern fallacy," the idea that a constitution can be consciously created, rather than evolving in an organic relation with the countless other elements in the life of a people that are relevant to political stability.[42] Even Machiavelli, Burckhardt claims, is not entirely free from the illusion of unfettered creative freedom, to which "constitutional artists" are prone.

Burckhardt sees this attitude as misguided because the change in human consciousness that permits such an objective view of the state at the same time engenders the modern, critical individual, who no longer submits unreflectively to political authority. In the most widely quoted passage from his *Civilization of the Renaissance in Italy*, Burckhardt writes:

> In the Middle Ages both sides of human consciousness—that which was turned within as that which was turned without—lay dreaming or half awake beneath a common veil. The veil was woven of faith, illusion, and childish prepossession, through which the world and history were seen to be clad in strange hues. Man was conscious of himself only as a member of a race, people, party, family, or corporation—only through some general category. In Italy this veil first melted into air; an *objective* treatment and consideration of the State and of all things of this world became possible. The *subjective* side at the same time asserted itself with corresponding emphasis; man became a spiritual *individual*, and recognized himself as such.[43]

He therefore sees a necessary tension between the ideological need of the modern state, which must establish its authority or perceived entitlement to command, and the critical awareness, which disallows any unreflective obedience.

For Burckhardt, unlike Ranke, the modern state is not established through any normatively justified process. It is viewed objectively as a structure of power and requires calculations about how to sustain or expand that power, so the distinctive form of political judgment to which it gives rise is reason of state.

---

vision—originally Burckhardt's vision—of the Italian Renaissance as the crucible in which the modern idea of the state was formed." Skinner tells us that when speaking of *lo stato*, Machiavelli is speaking of "*il suo stato*, of the prince's own state or condition of rulership."

[42] Ibid., 54.

[43] Burckhardt, *The Civilization of Renaissance Italy*, 98.

According to Burckhardt's historical analysis, modern states are originally illegitimate. Burckhardt frequently attributes the instability of the
Italian despotic states, which he sees as the first modern states, to their il-
legitimacy; their rulers have seized power without having any perceived
entitlement to rule, either through birth or some religious mandate. The
state's functioning requires the subordination of individual ends to its
own ends, but this cannot take place through recognition that the state's
authority is normatively binding. It must therefore take place through direct or indirect coercion.

In his *Reflections on History*, Burckhardt insists that this opposition
between the state's ideological demands and the critical refusal of its
ideology has been exacerbated by the French Revolution and its consequences. On the one hand, the ubiquitous imitation of "Napoleonic Cae-
sarism" led to an expansion in the idea of the state's power; on the other,
a "spirit of criticism" has been generally awakened in people.[44] Modern
political life is therefore characterized by a stark and irresolvable opposition between the state, which seeks power, and culture, which is the
realm of morality, science, technology, art, and "all that cannot lay claim
to compulsive authority."[45] There is an inevitable opposition, in other
words, between political power and normative authority.

Nietzsche does not explicitly commit himself to the same historical
narrative concerning the rise of modern states (though many of his historical remarks do have a Burckhardtian ring to them). But he clearly
adopts the same conception of the state as an abstract entity oriented by
the primary goal of maintaining its own power. In his "Glance at the
State," in *Human, All Too Human*, he acknowledges that modern states
cannot maintain their power through direct coercion, but rather must
permanently strive to establish and preserve acceptance of norms, laws,
and obligations.[46] For Nietzsche, as for Burckhardt, genuine normative
authority can only be effective if it is able to counter the ideological hegemony of the state. And for both thinkers the new German *Reich* provided
powerful lessons in just how threatening this hegemony might be.

Nietzsche contra the *Reich*

During the first years of the *Reich*, Nietzsche gradually becomes increasingly aware of, and hostile to, the reality of the state's ideological capacity. He comes to fear that the new state's hegemonic aspirations will lead

[44] Burckhardt, *Force and Freedom*, 293–94.
[45] Ibid., 1.
[46] *HTH*, I, 441 and 472. Nietzsche even claims here that the modern state seeks to fill the
gap left by the loss of religious devotion with devotion to the state.

to the appropriation, elimination, or overwhelming of all other forms of authority. In his *Untimely Meditations*, Nietzsche tells us that a mere military victory has been mistaken for a cultural victory, and that this delusion is capable of turning the victory into "*the defeat if not the extirpation of the German spirit for the sake of the 'German Reich.'*"[47] And in his "Lectures on the Future of our Educational Institutions," he perceives that spontaneous popular support is being consolidated by the more insidious subordination of education to political ends.

It was indeed the case that many of the liberal intellectuals in whose hands education lay, owed their academic positions to Falk, the minister responsible for the *Kulturkampf* legislation. They naïvely embraced the imposition of political power as a means of securing the separation of church and state, as well as the state supervision of education that they desired.[48] De jure independence had given way to de facto subservience.[49]

Nietzsche is not simply disgusted by the spectacle of institutions mass producing compliant servants of the *Reich*. He also fears a deeper corruption of intellectual life. When the state appropriates and instrumentalizes a species of authority, he believes, the necessary compromise of its own independent standards will cause it to rot from within. "One only has to recall," he tells us, "what Christianity has gradually become through the greed of the state. . . . Since it has been employed in a hundred ways to propel the mills of state power it has gradually become sick to the very marrow, hypocritical and untruthful, and degenerated into a contradiction of its original goal."[50]

He is here echoing his friend, Franz Overbeck, who in 1873 had complained of the corruption of Christianity by the state, in his "On the Christian Character of Our Present-Day Theology."[51] Gossman sees this form of argument as a natural continuation of the Basel tradition:

An obvious thread connects these ideas with Burckhardt's view of power as inherently evil. Just as Burckhardt dissociated himself from the Prussian nationalist historian's project of combining culture and power in a new national state, which was supposed to provide the

[47] *UM*, i, 1.

[48] Cf. Klaus Christian Köhnke, *The Rise of Neo-Kantianism*, trans. R. J. Hollingdale (Cambridge: Cambridge University Press, 1991), 222.

[49] De jure independence was secured by the principle of freedom of learning and teaching, formulated in paragraph twenty of the Prussian Constitution. Cf. Friedrich Paulsen, *The German Universities and University Study*, trans. Frank Thilly (London, 1906), 75.

[50] *UM*, iii, 6.

[51] *Über die Christlichkeit unserer heutigen Theologie* (1873; Darmstadt: Wissenschaftliche Buchgesellschaft, 1981). Interesting discussions of the relationship between Nietzsche and Overbeck, drawing attention specifically to their "antipolitical" views, may be found in Gossman, *Basel in the Age of Burckhardt.*, ch. 14, and Peter Bergmann, *Nietzsche*, ch. 4.

necessary material and political clout to protect the German *Kulturvolk*, Overbeck denounced the effort to combine religion and power through a Church that was intimately, too intimately, associated with the national state.[52]

Like Burckhardt and Overbeck, Nietzsche sees the encroachment of political power as a very real threat to other forms of authority over belief and value.

Since the state, on Nietzsche's view, cannot tolerate anyone who "applies the scalpel of truth" to politically necessary faith, it has an interest in having broad control over intellectual life, and particularly the disciplines of history and philosophy. As we have seen, the Rankean German historical school was in fact largely subservient to the *Reich*. Nietzsche claims that the dominant school in philosophy, that of the neo-Kantians, has been similarly co-opted.

Even the illegitimate Italian despots in whom Burckhardt first discerned the modern *Staatsgeist* saw the benefit in employing intellectuals.[53] And Bismarck, a notoriously anti-intellectual figure, similarly profited from the willing or unwilling support of the educated classes. Nietzsche indicates two ways in which the state can benefit from such an association.

First of all, states might reinforce their authority through an appeal to philosophical views that seem to provide them with some form of justification. In his 1872 lectures "On the Future of Our Educational Institutions," Nietzsche claims that Hegelianism offers this kind of support. Though by the following year he has come to the conclusion that the present state is sufficiently powerful to dispense with such justifications: "One now possesses power: formerly, in Hegel's time, one wanted to possess it—that is a vast distinction. Philosophy has become superfluous to the state because the state no longer needs its sanction."[54]

Nevertheless, he sees many contemporary neo-Kantian figures as complicit with the same disingenuous defense of the political status quo.[55] Nietzsche sees this vulnerability to political corruption as endemic in the

---

[52] Gossman, *Basel in the Age of Burckhardt*, 422.

[53] Burckhardt, *Gesamtausgabe*, 5:5.

[54] *UM*, iii, 8.

[55] In his *Untimely Meditations*, he singles out three in particular, saying:

Every philosophy which believes that the problem of existence is touched on, not to say solved, by a political event is a joke- and pseudo-philosophy. Many states have been founded since the world began; that is an old story. How should a political innovation suffice to turn men once and for all into contented inhabitants of the earth? But if anyone really believes in this possibility he ought to come forward, for he truly deserves to become a professor of philosophy at a German university, like Harms in Berlin, Jürgen Meyer [sic] in Bonn and Carrière in Munich. (*UM*, iii, 4)

Kantian tradition. He writes: "Even Kant was, as we scholars are accustomed to be, cautious, subservient and, in his attitude to the state, without greatness: so that, if university philosophy should ever be called to account, he at any rate could not justify it."[56]

Even without compelling this kind of philosophical deference, though, there is a second way in which states can benefit from the control of philosophy. A state's ideological grip can be rendered more secure if it effectively restricts philosophical work to issues that do not encroach on its own authority over belief. Nietzsche sees a specific branch of the neo-Kantian tradition as complicit with this politically expedient narrowing.

During the second half of the nineteenth century, Friedrich Trendelenburg's Kantian critique of Hegel's logic inspired many German thinkers to return to Kant and in particular to the first *Critique*. This transition from a *weltanschaulich* mode of philosophy to a more limited *Erkenntnistheorie* struck Nietzsche as an abdication of philosophical responsibility in the areas where it mattered most. He writes in his notebooks: "To turn *philosophy* into a pure science (like Trendelenburg) means to throw in the towel."[57] Philosophers in this tradition are, he complains, "content to assert that they are really no more than the frontier guards and spies of the sciences."[58] It is only outside the university, Nietzsche claims, that philosophy can flourish, free from state power and free from the fear of it.[59] Nietzsche demands that a higher tribunal, independent of state control, should exist to supervise and judge university education. Only philosophy, he says, has the authority to do this.[60] The safeguarding of genuine truth and value requires very deliberate resistance to the predatory state.

Antipolitical Thought

The German historical school saw no such opposition between the coercive authority of the state and the noncoercive authority of norms that was possible in the realm of culture. They saw instead a necessary continuity between the state and culture, maintaining that culture could in fact only survive under the protection of a strong state. So they celebrated the

---

[56] Ibid., 4.
[57] *Nachgelassene Fragmente*, Sommer 1872 bis Ende 1874, *KGW* III-4.318.
[58] *UM*, iii, 8.
[59] Ibid., 8.
[60] "As soon as philosophy departs from the universities, and therewith purifies itself of all unworthy considerations and prejudices, it must constitute precisely such a tribunal: devoid of official authority [*staatliche Macht*], without salaries or honours, it will know how to perform its duty free of the *Zeitgeist* and free from fear of it."

Reich as the transformation of a vulnerable *Kulturvolk* into a powerful *Kulturstaat*.[61]

In both his early and later works, Nietzsche explicitly rejects such a conception. In *Twilight of the Idols*, he writes:

> If you invest all your energy in power, in great politics [*grosse Politik*], in economics, world trade, parliamentarianism, and military interests— if you take the quantum of understanding, seriousness, will, and self-overcoming that you embody and expend it all in this *one* direction, then you will be at a loss for any other direction. Culture and the state—let us be honest with ourselves here—are adversaries: "*Kultur-Staat*" is merely a modern idea. The one lives off the other, the one flourishes at the expense of the other. All great ages of culture are ages of political decline: anything great in the cultural sense has always been unpolitical, even *anti-political*.—[62]

His own antipolitical stance, which earned him the scorn of the Rankean nationalist, Treitschke, is not simply motivated by his desire to defend culture in the sense of artistic and creative life.[63] It is entailed by his normative commitments.

It is easy to see how someone preoccupied with the insights of descriptive political realism, particularly the view that politics consists almost exclusively in more or less complex relations of power, might give in to political pessimism. They might be tempted to give up the hope that politically relevant beliefs might be grounded in any real normative authority. This realism of despair would grant to the state the ideological authority that it naturally seeks. But since this would involve ceding to the state the right potentially to undermine all normative authority, it is not a position that can be coherently advocated. If we have independent normative commitments we cannot coherently endorse a state of affairs that would frustrate them.

It is important, then, that we see Nietzsche's position as antipolitical and not merely unpolitical. The defense of truth in which he begins to engage during the early 1870s involves an explicit opposition to the political threat. In his essay "Schopenhauer as Educator," he describes his ideal of the "Schopenhauerean man," who "*voluntarily takes upon himself*

---

[61] Cf. Trevor-Roper, "Jacob Burckhardt," 361.

[62] *TI*, "What the Germans Lack," 4; cf. also UM, iii, 6. This antagonism between culture and political authority dates back, in Nietzsche's view, to the Greek polis. He tells us in *HTH*, I, 474, that Greek culture "evolved *in spite of* the polis."

[63] Treitschke said of Nietzsche and Overbeck: "The two of you sit there in your corner and see nothing, absolutely nothing of what is now moving the nation." Cited by Gossman, *Basel in the Age of Burckhardt*, 442.

the suffering involved in being truthful.[64] In following this example, he tells us, "we are all *able* to educate ourselves *against* our age."[65] Genuine philosophy can then rediscover an immunity to state power: "For philosophy offers an asylum to a man into which no tyranny can force its way, the inward cave, the labyrinth of the heart: and that annoys the tyrants."[66]

Peter Bergmann, in his *Nietzsche: "The Last Antipolitical German,"* reveals the significance of Schopenhauer to the generation of 1866, as the most important oppositional figure of the new political era.[67] His work was influential outside the academy, providing a compelling alternative to the desiccated neo-Kantianism that reigned within it. The more general disillusionment with politics that had been evident since the 1850s contributed to this popularity. Schopenhauer's philosophy seemed to offer the possibility of remaining aloof from politics and its disappointments. He postulates the existence of an "inner disposition" that cannot be modified from the outside; he thereby draws a boundary which the state cannot cross.[68] He proposes that the power of the state should be restricted to the negative restraint that protects "rights," defined in his own idiosyncratic manner.[69] He thereby seeks to draw a definite line between the state's authority and individual freedom of thought. Nietzsche's account of the power of Schopenhauer's thought in his *Untimely Meditations* suggests that his own confidence in defending the truth against the state's incursions into the realm of belief derives from this early influence.

The defense of intellectual freedom remains a very important theme in Nietzsche's middle and later works.[70] It remains the most important form of freedom to which he is committed, as evidenced by the centrality of the idea of the "free spirit," both to *Human, All Too Human,* and *Beyond Good and Evil.*[71] Even though he raises questions about the value of truth, he remains (as we shall see in chapter 3) powerfully committed to

[64] *UM*, iii, 4.
[65] Ibid., 4.
[66] Ibid., 3.
[67] Bergmann, *Nietzsche*, esp. 50–51.
[68] Schopenhauer, *WWR*, I, 345.
[69] Ibid., 340: "If the will of another denies my will, as this appears in my body and in the use of its powers for its preservation without denying anyone else's will that observes a like limitation, then I can *compel it without wrong* to desist from this denial, in other words, I have to this extent *a right of compulsion.*"
[70] Cf. Dana Villa, "Friedrich Nietzsche," 126, on Nietzsche's desire to defend intellectual integrity in the face of encroaching ideology.
[71] Cf. esp. *HTH*, I, 34, 225, 226, 227, 228, 464; *HTH*, II, 'Assorted Opinions' 211. Cf. also *BGE*, esp. 41, 42, 43, 44, 227, 230. Cf. also *GS* 18: "The Greek philosopher went through life feeling secretly that there were far more slaves than one might think—namely, that everybody who was not a philosopher was a slave. His pride overflowed when he considered that even the mightiest men on earth might be his slaves."

preserving the freedom to seek truth.[72] And he hopes that the truth-seeking free spirits will finally be capable of determining their own values.[73] The philosophers, as free spirits understand him, is "the man with the most comprehensive responsibility, whose conscience bears the weight of the overall development of humanity."[74]

FREEDOM AND SUBORDINATION

What distinguishes the free from the fettered spirits, for Nietzsche, is the ability of the former to determine reflectively their own beliefs and values.[75] His critique of morality, in particular, aims to liberate us from moral prejudices in order to make us capable of a new evaluative freedom. He urges his readers to aspire to "the purification of our opinions and value judgements and to the *creation of tables of what is good that are new and all our own.*"[76] The sustained project of value-criticism in which he engages in the later works is guided by this ambition.

Political life, however, seems to Nietzsche to tend in general to inhibit this kind of critical freedom. He maintains that "all states and orderings within society—classes, marriage, education, law—all these derive their force and endurance solely from the faith the fettered spirits have in them: that is to say, in the absence of reasons, or at least in the warding off of the demand for reasons." Christianity played an important role in repressing the critical spirit that demands reasons. And Nietzsche tells us that "the state in fact does the same thing and every father raises his son in the same fashion: only regard this as true, he says, and you will see how much good it will do you."[77] Only the free spirits, who he acknowledges

---

[72] Cf. *HTH*, II, "Wanderer," 333: "*Dying for "truth."* —We would not let ourselves be burned to death for our opinions: we are not sure enough of them for that. But perhaps for the right to possess our opinions and to change them."

[73] Cf. *HTH*, I, "Preface," 6.

[74] *BGE,* 61.

[75] I will argue in the chapters that follow that an important strand in Nietzsche's work, one that is exemplified by his own critical philosophy, takes this freedom to be rational self-determination, through the discovery of factual and normative truths. Since his epistemological and meta-ethical remarks are at other times inconsistent with this view, there are tricky interpretive problems involved in understanding his conception of freedom. For now, I will assume that it is relatively uncontroversial to claim that he values the freedom to seek truth, in some sense, and the freedom to determine our own values, in some sense.

[76] *GS* 335. This is also an important theme in *Zarathustra*: cf. esp. *TSZ*, Part II, "Of Old and New Law Tables," which Nietzsche then cites in *EH*, "Why I am Destiny," 4; and *TSZ*, Part I, "The Three Metamorphoses." Cf. also *GM*, ii, 2, on the "sovereign individual," "the 'free' man" who "possesses his *measure of value.*"

[77] *HTH*, I, 227.

in his 1886 preface belong to the future and not to the present, ask for reasons rather than contenting themselves with the mere appearance of reasons.[78]

Nietzsche clearly holds, then, that this freedom is extremely difficult to win. Most people are unlikely to attain it. But nevertheless it seems to him to be of supreme importance for the future of humanity that some individuals do. If he wants to sustain the human capacity for such freedom, this will not be consistent with permitting the strongest individuals to introduce new forms of domination that threaten it. His commitment to freedom, then, might appear to be incompatible with his admiration for those "great" political leaders who successfully subordinate entire populations.[79] The apparently "Caesarist" element that crops up in his thought might cause us to suspect that he is only really committed to developing a form of subordination that he prefers.[80]

What we have to bear in mind is that much as Nietzsche admires Caesar, he admires Brutus more. The most beautiful thing about Shakespeare, he tells us, is his admiration for Brutus. And he suggests that it is not an attachment to some superficial freedom that inspired this admiration, but the recognition of "the independence of soul" being realized here.[81] The heroic individuals that Nietzsche admires are seen as the highest exemplars of freedom won through struggle and resistance. They both exploit and foster freedom.

In the age of a Caesar, Nietzsche insists, "the individual is usually ripest and culture is therefore at its highest and most fruitful stage." At these "times of corruption," when established faiths and norms have broken down, the "seed-bearers of the future" are shaken from the tree.[82] Napoleon, we are told, was "one of the great continuators of the Renaissance," since he vehemently opposed received "modern ideas" and modern civilization. He should be credited, Nietzsche claims, with "having enabled *man* in Europe to become the master over the businessman and the philistine."[83]

The businessman and the philistine, like academics and politicians, represent a much more insidious threat than those who wield power in an

[78] Ibid., I, 225.
[79] Cf. e.g. *GM*, i, 16, where he describes Napoleon as "the noble ideal made flesh." Also *TI*, "Skirmishes," 38, on Caesar as "the most magnificent type."
[80] Daniel Conway claims that Nietzsche, inspired by Julius Caesar, has aspirations to create an empire modeled on that of the ancient Romans. He contends that this strand in Nietzsche's thought reveals his affinities with fascism. Cf. Conway, "*Ecce Caesar*: Nietzsche's Imperial Aspirations," in *Nietzsche, Godfather of Fascism?* ed. Jacob Golomb and Robert Wistrich (Princeton: Princeton University Press, 2002), 173–95.
[81] *GS*, 98.
[82] Ibid., 23.
[83] Ibid., 362. Cf. also *TI*, "Skirmishes," 49, on Goethe's admiration for Napoleon.

openly coercive way. For Nietzsche sees a greater threat to truth and value in the routinized practices that support established forms of political organization, at the expense of any critical reflection on their overall rationale or the ultimate values that they serve. In *The Gay Science*, he warns us:

> China . . . is a country where large-scale discontentment and the capacity for *constant transformation* became extinct centuries ago; and in Europe too the socialists and state idolaters, with their measures for making life better and safer, might easily establish Chinese conditions and a Chinese "happiness."[84]

He repeatedly expresses the proto-Weberian fear that the gravest threats to freedom will be those with which we unreflectively cooperate rather than those whose coercive power is obvious to us and provokes our resistance.

Nietzsche claims that modern European states have developed various mechanisms through which people are drawn unwittingly to cooperate in their own subordination. The experience of Bismarck's manipulation of parliaments and democracies clearly colors his view of their potential role in ideological domination. With characteristic cynicism, he writes: "Parliamentarism—that is, the public permission to choose between five basic political opinions, flatters and wins the favour of all those who would like to *appear* independent and individualistic and would like to fight for their opinions."[85] He views political parties, too, as one of the consensus-generating mechanisms that impairs critical thinking.[86]

Those who rule in the modern world, he claims, will inevitably do so by establishing the appearance of legitimacy.[87] They will exploit the perception that their rule is accountable and transparent, while covertly manufacturing the very consensus that they claim legitimates them.

---

[84] *GS*, 24.

[85] Ibid., 174. He adds: "In the end, however, it is irrelevant whether the herd is commanded to have one opinion or permitted to have five. Whoever deviates from the five public opinions and steps aside will always have the whole herd against him."

[86] *HTH*, I, 438: "The demagogic character and the intention to appeal to the masses is at present common to all political parties: on account of this intention they are all compelled to transform their principles into great *al fresco* stupidities and paint them on the wall."

[87] Cf. *BGE*, 199, on "the moral hypocrisy of those commanding": "They do not know how to protect themselves from their bad consciences except by acting like executors of older or higher commands (from their ancestors, constitution, justice system, laws, or God himself) or even by borrowing herd maxims from the herd mentality, such as the 'first servants of the people,' or the 'instruments of the commonweal.'" Of the herd men, Nietzsche says: "In those cases where people think they cannot do without a leader and bellwether, they keep trying to replace the commander with an agglomeration of clever herd men: this is the origin of all representative constitutions, for example."

His vision of political life under modern states is bleak. It suggests a profound disengagement of politics from the sources of belief and value that he himself recognizes.

Normatively Unconstrained Politics

Nietzsche's vision of the predatory state originates in the early works. There, he already seems to see politics in the modern world as something animalistic, as detached from the intellectual, moral, and creative capacities that he admires in human beings. Although we imagine that our institutions are becoming ever more rationalized and ever more participatory, in fact our collective lives seem to him to display a brute imperviousness to reason:

> The tremendous coming and going of men on the great wilderness of the earth, their founding of cities and states, their wars, their restless assembling and scattering again, their confused mingling, mutual imitation, mutual outwitting and down-treading, their wailing in distress, their howls of joy in victory—all this is a continuation of animality.[88]

But in spite of the fact that Nietzsche's ongoing reflections on political life only seem to deepen his pessimism, he does not systematically develop any view of what a potential solution would look like.

This is not because he imagines that we can do without political authority altogether. He displays a Burckhardtian conservatism, even toward the institution of the state.[89] And it is not because he has no view about what a polity shaped by his own independent values would look like. His scattered remarks about politics in the later writings have generally been seen to support an aristocratic view of politics, whether this is construed as radical or conservative.[90] He unambiguously rules out

[88] *UM*, iii, 5.
[89] *HTH*, I, 472:

A later generation will see the state . . . shrink to insignificance in various parts of the earth—a notion many people of the present can hardly contemplate without fear and revulsion. To *work* for the dissemination and realization of this notion is another thing, to be sure: one has to have a very presumptuous idea of one's own intelligence and scarcely half an understanding of history to set one's hand to the plough already—while no one can yet show what seedcorn is afterwards to be scattered on the riven soil. Let us therefore put our trust in "the prudence and self-interest of men" to preserve the interest of the state for some time yet and to repulse the destructive experiments of the precipitate and the over-zealous!

[90] Defenses of this position may be found in Bruce Detwiler, *Nietzsche and the Politics of Aristocratic Radicalism*; Mark Warren, *Nietzsche and Political Thought*; Daniel Conway,

egalitarianism and democracy as the right norms for political life.[91] He pours scorn on the very idea of "the labour question."[92] He repudiates nationalism as a basis for political life.[93]

Although he clearly makes normative claims about politics, none of them are particularly edifying, most of them are undefended, and they are never developed into a coherent political theory. Like Burckhardt, he detests the "stupidity" of politics, the blind striving for power.[94] But like Burckhardt, he has equal contempt for normative political theory.[95]

Burckhardt's reasons are rooted in his pessimistic view of history. He extrapolates from his views on the actual historical development of states to a claim about real human possibilities. States, Burckhardt claims, need to maintain power in the context of the particular historical conditions that they inherit. The acceptance of a state's authority develops in

---

Nietzsche and the Political (London: Routledge, 1997); and Keith Ansell-Pearson, *An Introduction to Nietzsche as Political Thinker.* Cf. esp. *BGE* 257.

Also *BGE* 258: "The essential feature of a good, healthy aristocracy is that it does *not* feel that it is a function (whether of the kingdom or of the community) but instead feels itself to be the *meaning* and highest justification (of the kingdom or the community), —and, consequently, that it accepts in good conscience the sacrifice of countless people who have to be pushed down and shrunk into incomplete human beings, into slaves, into tools, all *for the sake of the aristocracy.*" *BGE* 257.

[91] Cf. *AC* 43:

Let us not underestimate the disaster that Christianity has brought even into politics! Nobody is courageous enough for special privileges these days, for the rights of the masters, for feelings of self-respect and respect among equals—for a *pathos of distance*. . . . Our politics is *sick* from this lack of courage! —The aristocraticism of mind has been undermined at its depths by the lie of the equality of souls; and when the belief in the "privileges of the majority" creates (and it *will create*) revolutions, do not doubt for a minute that it is Christianity, that it is *Christian* value judgements these revolutions are translating into blood and crimes! Christianity is a rebellion of everything that crawls on the ground against everything that has *height*: the evangel of the "lowly" *makes* things lower.

And on democracy, cf. *BT,* "An Attempt at Self-Criticism," 4.
[92] *TI,* "Skirmishes," 40.
[93] *BGE,* 251.
[94] Cf. *TI,* "What the Germans Lack," 1: "It costs a lot to come to power: power makes people *stupid*. The Germans—once they were considered the people of thinkers: do they think at all these days?"
[95] Ibid., 38: "All our political theories and constitutions . . . are consequences, necessary consequences, of decline." And Burckhardt on ancient Athens: *Force and Freedom*, 219: "Speculative thought made its appearance in the guise of a creator of new political forms, but actually as a general solvent, at first in words, which inevitably led to deeds. It appeared on the scene as political theory and took the State to task—a thing that would have been impossible if genuinely creative political power had not been far advanced in decline."

conjunction with faith of various kinds.[96] In order to preserve its power the state has to resist the critical erosion of this ideological basis.

If the development of the state were identical, as Hegel thought, with the progress of rationality in human affairs, it would be possible for rational, reflective individuals to endorse the political arrangements that had thus evolved. But Burckhardt sees no such rational progress in human history.

Human history has, of course, witnessed various attempts to erase all established forms of authority and re-create political life ex nihilo, with the sole authority of rational principles. But these abstractions, Burckhardt claims, have proved incapable of commanding the kind of allegiance that might secure their authority in the face of the more basic competition for power and pursuit of material interests.[97]

In Nietzsche's case, his insight into the disengagement of political authority from any independent normative authority derives from his insight into the nature of normative authority itself. As we shall see, he doubts that the kinds of authority over belief and value that he himself recognizes can ever be popularly effective. They are not themselves capable of securing the kind of consensus that can ground stable political authority. His political skepticism, I shall argue, is rooted in a pessimistic view of individual rational capacities and of the capacity of philosophers to wield any effective intellectual authority.

Keith Ansell-Pearson acknowledges a change in Nietzsche's views about the political effectiveness of philosophical insight, claiming that Nietzsche moves from a "liberal recommendation" model, in the middle period, toward one of aristocratic legislation in the later writings.[98] I hope to show in the following chapters that Nietzsche does indeed experiment with different models of intellectual authority across his career, but he does so because he never arrives at any satisfactory conception of how it can be exercised.

Ansell-Pearson's interprets "aristocratic legislation" to mean the imposition of values through force and violence. He cites section 377 of *The Gay Science* in support of this view. Nietzsche says here,

> We are delighted with all who love, as we do, danger, war, and adventures; who refuse to compromise, to be captured, to reconcile, to be castrated; we consider ourselves conquerors; we think about the necessity for new orders, as well as for a new slavery—for every strengthening

[96] Burckhardt, *Force and Freedom*, "The State Determined by Religion."
[97] Cf. Ibid., "The State Determined by Culture" and "Origin and Nature of the Present Crisis."
[98] Ansell-Pearson, *An Introduction to Nietzsche as Political Thinker*.

and enhancement of the human type also involves a new kind of enslavement.

However, it is important to note that Nietzsche says "we think about" this possibility. Toward the end of this section he adds, "We far prefer to live on mountains, apart, 'untimely,' in past or future centuries, merely in order to avoid the silent rage to which we know we should be condemned as eyewitnesses of politics that are destroying the German spirit."[99] Any political values that he endorses are confined to the realm of wishful thinking; for he still cannot articulate a normative political vision that is coherently related to his own claims about the conditions under which political power is exercised in modern states.

In order to do so he would have to identify some mechanism through which normative authority could determine, directly or indirectly, the kinds of political power that are accepted to be legitimate. He cannot coherently abandon this aim and accept an unconstrained power politics. But neither, we shall see, can he envisage any means through which it might be achieved.

---

[99] Cf. also AC, Preface: "You need to be used to living on mountains—to seeing the miserable, ephemeral little gossip of politics and national self-interest *beneath* you."

CHAPTER 2

The Self-Destruction of Secular Religions

INTRODUCTION

Nietzsche would not have to fear the ideologically predatory state if our capacity to distinguish truth from ideology were sufficiently robust. His fear is that knowledge of truth (and in particular, I shall argue in chapter 5, normative truth) is not only difficult to come by, it is even harder to disseminate. Before setting out his arguments for this view, I would like in this chapter to sketch the way in which he comes to be preoccupied with the problem of intellectual authority that lies at the basis of his concerns.

He comes to this problem, I shall claim, via the nineteenth-century European debate about whether we can or ought to establish a secular religion. I shall argue that in *The Birth of Tragedy*, Nietzsche aims to found something like a secular religion.[1] He hopes, in doing so, to harness the nonrational, persuasive power of art in the service of philosophical insight. It is his recognition that this project will inevitably fail that impels his ongoing concerns about intellectual authority. These concerns seem to me to be deepened by the insights of the later works.

In, *Ecce Homo*, Nietzsche's last published work, he declares, "There is nothing in me of a founder of a religion—religions are affairs of the rabble; I find it necessary to wash my hands after I have come into contact with religious people. —I *want* no 'believers.'"[2] It is a protestation that has been disregarded by many of his followers and rejected by his detractors. Like Marx and Freud, Nietzsche has been widely viewed by posterity as a founder of one of the twentieth century's various secular religions.[3] Unlike Marx and Freud, however, Nietzsche is seen not simply to have created a faith surreptitiously through the insidious employment of

---

[1] The centrality of the work to Nietzsche's oeuvre has always been emphasized by those who see in Nietzsche's thought the ambition to provide some sort of aesthetic substitute for religion. Since the publication of Stefan George's eulogy to Nietzsche in 1900, this tradition has seen in *The Birth of Tragedy* the origins of a redemptive aestheticism that is fundamental to Nietzsche's philosophy. The idea that the Dionysian principle forms the essential core of his thought has provided support for many of the interpretations that have appropriated his name for secular religions. cf. Steven Aschheim, *The Nietzsche Legacy in Germany*, esp. ch. 7, "After the Death of God: Varieties of Nietzschean Religion."

[2] *EH*, "Why I Am Destiny," section 1.

[3] Cf. Steven Aschheim, *The Nietzsche Legacy in Germany*, ch. 7.

"falsification-evading devices" but rather quite deliberately and conspicuously, as a self-styled secular prophet who was occasionally inclined to
identify himself with God.[4]

Recent Anglophone interpreters, in their attempts to take Nietzsche seriously on their own terms, as a philosopher in the modern, professional
sense, have tended to downplay this aspect of his popular image. His
work has been relocated in the tradition of skeptical rationalism, or
philosophical naturalism, which runs from Hume to Quine and Davidson.[5]
But clearly neither Willard Quine nor Donald Davidson ever felt the need
to repudiate the suggestion that they were trying to found a religion. The
fact that Nietzsche is moved explicitly to disavow such a project, even at
this late stage in his career, reveals an important aspect of his intellectual
ambitions.

Nietzsche's naturalistically oriented critical reasoning exists alongside an
apparent religiosity that is never entirely extirpated from his work. In this
his thought is continuous with that of the Left Hegelians and neo-Kantians
who had previously allied a critical project with an attempt to preserve,
if in transfigured form, certain emotional or nonrational aspects of religion. The motivation of much of his writing derives from the concern, so
central to this tradition but largely absent from Anglophone philosophy
and political thought, with the relationship between philosophy and popular belief.[6]

The concern is rooted in the idea that although philosophical criticism can delimit the realm of rationally justified beliefs, this activity is
not available to everyone (as we do not all share the requisite leisure or

---

[4] Ernest Gellner, in his *The Psychoanalytic Movement* (London: Paladin Press, 1988) lists
the kind of techniques and devices which, he believes, psychoanalysis employs in evading
falsification. Cf. ch. 8, "Anatomy of a Faith."

[5] The comparison with Hume has, since Danto and Kaufmann, facilitated Nietzsche's introduction to the world of Anglophone philosophy. Cf. Arthur C. Danto, *Nietzsche as
Philosopher* (New York: Columbia University Press, 1965). Danto sees affinities in areas
such as causality (93–95) and ethics (135–36). Kaufmann states, in his introduction to *The
Portable Nietzsche* (1954; New York, 1976), that "though Hume and Nietzsche are antipodes
in temperament, they are in many ways close to each other in their thinking. . . . Nietzsche
is not only close to the man who was the grandfather of so much in modern English and
American philosophy, David Hume, but also to this modern philosophy itself. Occasionally
he anticipated it by several decades, and it might still profit from his stimulation," 18.
Maudemarie Clark, who pioneered a recent reexamination of Nietzsche's epistemology
views within the Anglophone, analytic literature, suggests affinities between Nietzsche and
Davidson: cf. *Nietzsche on Truth and Philosophy* (Cambridge: Cambridge University Press,
1990), 34–38. Richard Schacht reinterprets perspectivism in Wittgensteinian terms: cf.
Nietzsche (1983; London: Routledge, 1992), 61. Simon May defends a Quinean Nietzsche:
Nietzsche's Ethics and his War on Morality, (Oxford: Oxford University Press, 1999), 141.

[6] On the German tradition, cf. Fritz Ringer, *The Decline of the German Mandarins: The
German Academic Community, 1890–1933* (London: Wesleyan University Press, 1969).

intellectual ability) and most people will not possess the rational expertise necessary to assess the validity of its arguments. So criticism of this type may be necessary to establish reflectively the validity of our beliefs, but it cannot in itself be an effective instrument for influencing popular belief more generally. The kind of authority wielded by intellectuals therefore seems peculiarly problematic.

Intellectual authority seems necessarily to consist in two essential but not self-evidently compatible elements: it requires correctness but also persuasiveness, or effectiveness. Although philosophical expertise might lead philosophers to justified beliefs, it is not obvious that their insights can be made persuasive to those who are not equipped with this expertise and cannot assess the relevant reasons for themselves. We are compelled to ask how critical or rational expertise can be made to inform human understanding more broadly.

The question is one that particularly exercised German philosophers during the second half of the nineteenth century. Whereas Kant and Hegel had sought (for philosophical and political reasons) to establish an essential congruence between their philosophical claims and existing religious belief, their nineteenth century heirs became increasingly skeptical that philosophy could vindicate religious authority or ratify the claims of "common sense." In the absence of an assumed natural congruence between philosophy and popular belief, the question of intellectual authority became increasingly perplexing.

Neo-Kantian thinkers such as F. A. Lange and Kuno Fischer rejected Kant's view that monotheism is a natural ideal of reason and hence that there is a stable, rational core to Christian belief. Left Hegelians such as David Strauss and Ludwig Feuerbach rejected the old Hegelian view that the task of philosophy was to articulate as *Begriff* the *Vorstellung* of biblical revelation.[7] The content of popular belief was therefore seen to diverge radically from the content of philosophy. It no longer seemed that people would inadvertently, that is, without the reflective use of their reason, arrive at rationally justified beliefs. But in the absence of a general capacity for philosophical criticism and evaluation, society at large could not necessarily be relied on to recognize genuine reasons once they were presented to them by philosophers.

It seemed that the philosophers would have to reassess the kind of effective authority that their epistemic advantage allowed. They might aim to facilitate convergence on rationally justified beliefs through some nonrational means. Or they might wish to institute a popular faith that is not constituted by rationally justified beliefs but which accords with some

---

[7] Cf. John Edward Toews, *Hegelianism: The Path toward Dialectical Humanism, 1805–1841* (Cambridge: Cambridge University Press, 1980).

rationally prescribed ends. Reason might then, in a sense, be authoritative, without reflective recognition of its authority being necessary for all.

The aspiration to combine critical philosophy with some such constructive project led, in the second half of the nineteenth century, to the promulgation of diverse kinds of "secular religion." The term will be used here to denote an aspiration to wield intellectual authority, where the validity of this authority resides in rational justification, but its general effectiveness, given an inequality in our rational capacities, is seen to require the employment of some nonrational means.

Any set of beliefs and practices that ostensibly repudiates the authority of revelation yet implicitly demands some form of unreflective allegiance is liable to be called a secular religion. Nationalism and patriotism might be characterized as secular religions in this sense, and some would claim, more controversially, that communism and psychoanalysis should be too. But nineteenth-century Europe saw the advent of secular religions as deliberate human artifacts intended to exercise a genuine form of intellectual authority.

Left Hegelian and neo-Kantian thinkers made both the secularism and religiosity of their enterprise objects of conscious reflection. That is, they attempted consciously to formulate the limits at which reason must make room for faith and to conceive reflectively what sort of faith this should be. The project was lent special urgency by claims that Christianity was culturally or philosophically obsolete and would have to be overcome. These claims were later accompanied by an insistence that if an adequate replacement could not be found, humanity would descend into nihilism. Philosophy, it seemed, must preside over the generation of post-Christian worldviews. Through this aspiration it became allied to epistemic, ethical, and political goals.

None of these ambitious nineteenth-century projects issued in any enduring revolution in popular belief. And few intellectuals have subsequently attempted a similar venture. The conception of intellectual authority on which it was premised seems to have been fundamentally flawed. I shall argue in this chapter that Nietzsche confronts these flaws in the failure of *The Birth of Tragedy*.

POST-CHRISTIAN FAITH: FROM POLITICS TO AESTHETICS

We can identify two distinct tendencies in the nineteenth-century quest for a post-Christian faith, suggesting different ways in which philosophy might inform popular belief. One was political in orientation. It involved viewing the redemption of humanity as an ethical goal, with deep social transformation being a necessary vehicle for the required change in human consciousness that philosophy had identified. In its Kantian and Hegelian forms it aimed to realize in Germany the progressive goals of the French Revolution but without incurring violent social upheaval. The other dominant tendency was aesthetic. It expressed itself in the aspiration to re-create aspects of religious experience through secular, artistic means. In some authors both tendencies were combined (for example, in F. A. Lange, one of Nietzsche's earliest and deepest philosophical influences), but the latter increasingly took precedence for the politically disillusioned post-1848 generation.

Nietzsche, particularly in his early writings, may be seen to represent this aesthetic and antipolitical trend. His encounter with Richard Wagner was undoubtedly decisive here. Wagner, who is perhaps better known to posterity for having too many political opinions rather than too few, came to share with many of his generation a certain political weariness. This was brought about by the gradual recognition by the intellectual classes in Germany of their own political impotence (a situation that was compounded by Bismarck's military founding of the new German *Reich*). A narrowing of the scope of intellectual ambitions was the widespread if not inevitable result.[8]

Wagner and Nietzsche saw in their mutual interaction the possibility of fusing philosophical insight and aesthetic experience, and thereby transforming human consciousness without first requiring a transformation of society. Wagner was at the time the most artistically creative and visible exponent of the idea that we need a secular replacement for a decaying Christianity.[9] His ambitions concerning popular belief may have been somewhat grander than Nietzsche's own. But he had already confronted important questions concerning the extent to which nonphilosophical reality could be relied on to cooperate with any philosophically stated convictions or ideals.

Wagner had once manned the barricades in the Dresden uprising of 1849 and was subsequently exiled to Paris. There he immersed himself in the writings of Ludwig Feuerbach and began to produce his programmatic

---

[8] Friedrich Paulsen remarks on this narrowing in *The German Universities and University Study*.

[9] The most widely quoted statement of this aspiration occurs in Wagner's "Religion and Art" essay of 1880, where he writes, "One might say that where religion becomes artificial [*künstlich*], it is reserved for art to save the essential core of religion by recognizing the figurative [*sinnbildlichen*] value of the mythic symbols which the former would have us believe in their literal sense, and revealing their deep and hidden truth through an ideal representation." Cf. "Religion and Art," in *Religion and Art*, trans. W. Ashton Ellis (Lincoln: University of Nebraska Press, 1994), 213 (translation amended); cf. "Religion und Kunst," *Sämtliche Schriften und Dichtungen* (Leipzig: Breitkopf und Härtel, 1912–14), Sechste Auflage, Zehnter Band, 211.

and notoriously convoluted prose works on the future of art. When he penned the essay "Art and Revolution," he clearly not only expected but desired a social revolution as the means to a new fellowship of man, to which end art must be subordinate.[10] However, by the time Nietzsche came under his charismatic influence, Wagner was revising his early Feuerbachian writings for republication and excoriating their juvenile political posturing.

It is not difficult to see why Wagner initially found in his discovery of Feuerbach a natural affinity between the aims of art and philosophy. The primary human problem outlined in *The Essence of Christianity*, that of hypostasis, cannot be solved through critical analysis alone. The philosophical recognition that theology and metaphysics can be naturalistically reduced to "anthropology" is not sufficient for the abolition of the alienated state that such theistic dogmas have induced in us. The profound emotional significance of these illusions entails that a reorientation of religious feeling is also required.

Feuerbach taught Wagner that this fundamental psychological change could not take the form of some merely superficial, artistic manipulation of people's emotions. It seemed instead to demand a reconfiguration of the whole structure of human needs and hence a process of radical social transformation. It was an inherently political endeavor. The significance of art had to lie in its congruence with greater political objectives. It was therefore reassuring for Wagner to assume that social revolution would be the natural outcome of the immanent logic of history.

The problem with this desired coincidence between the ends of history and the rational goals specified by philosophy lay (as generations of Marx's critics have since pointed out) in a certain opacity concerning history and human agency. The mechanism of revolutionary transformation was not adequately specified. And if in the immediate aftermath of 1849 Wagner retained a cheerful political optimism, the imminence of radical social change came to seem increasingly remote as the 1850s passed with the revolutionary promise unfulfilled. A passive reliance on the logic of history came to seem untenable, but neither was it clear what individual actors could do to promote the kind of radical, unconscious social change that they desired.

Revolutionary agitation and political organization certainly did not seem compatible with the humanistic ends that idealists such as Wagner had embraced as the potential outcome of politics. In the final analysis, the carefully lit atmosphere of the opera house seemed more congruent

---

[10] The theater, he insists here, might play a pioneering role in the reorganization of society because it is most naturally amenable to liberation from the economic imperatives of profit and wages.

with the ideal of human dignity that inspired Wagner than the subterranean world of organizing armed resistance. John Edward Toews has suggested that this sort of problem was endemic to the Hegelianism of the period; that the humanistic ends which inspired radical Hegelians were inherently incompatible with the revolutionary means that would be required for their fullest realization.[11] The highest political ideals that philosophical reflection had generated seemed destined to be eviscerated by the profanity of political life. The apparent antipathy between philosophy and politics, which Nietzsche certainly perceived, was already felt by the post-1848 generation.

Wagner, for his part, wrote a new preface to his Feuerbachian writings in 1872, stating that he had withdrawn from the bewildering stimuli of politics into the realm of a more purely artistic ideal. In 1854 he had read Schopenhauer's *The World as Will and Representation*, and discovered there a new, metaphysically deeper role for music. According to Schopenhauer, music permits a uniquely immediate experience of the inner nature of reality, a reality comprised, on his view, by the relentless and purposeless stirrings of "Will."[12] This quasi-religious construal of musical meaning (which, oddly to us, Schopenhauer retrieved from the works of Mozart and Rossini), made music a perfect nonrational vehicle for the communication of philosophical insight.[13]

In his *Beethoven* essay, of 1870, Wagner explains how one form of secular religion has come to supplant another as the guiding orientation of

---

[11] Toews, *Hegelianism*, 369:

The insistence that the self could discover and appropriate the autonomy and wholeness it had for so long projected onto some alien essence in the concrete reality of its finite activity and consciousness seemed a hollow and impotent claim in the face of the overwhelming "objective" powers of the state and the capitalist economy. Self-liberation and self-affirmation could become "real" only through a revolutionary destruction of the conditions and powers that inhibited and prevented their concrete actualization. The tasks of revolution, however, demanded self-renunciation, devotion to a common goal, commitment to suprapersonal values, belief in an objective meaning in history—that is, a denial of precisely those values of individual autonomy, self-expression, and self-enjoyment that constituted the goal of a revolution which would finally "make an end" to the historical pathology of self-alienation. Self-liberation and the liberation of the world seemed to be both inextricably connected and inevitably in opposition to each other.

[12] Schopenhauer makes the indemonstrable claim that music directly expresses the inner nature of the world. Cf. *WWR*, I, 264: "Supposing we succeeded in giving a perfectly accurate and complete explanation of music which goes into detail, and thus a detailed repetition in concepts of what it expresses, this would also be at once a sufficient repetition and explanation of the world in concepts, or one wholly corresponding thereto, and hence the true philosophy." It is this metaphysical view that Wagner appropriates in his "Beethoven" essay.

[13] For a very nice discussion of Schopenhauer's affinity with Rossini, cf. Michael Tanner, *Schopenhauer: Metaphysics and Art* (London: Phoenix, 1998), esp. 52.

his work. He describes a cultural crisis in which the domination of society by public opinion rules out any authentic forms of expression. We are all ruled by "Mode." Our heads have been turned by mass-produced fripperies and our talents squandered on worthless imitations of foreign cultures. It is tempting, he admits, to desire that this whole civilization be razed and something else built from the ruins, "an event to be conceived if all History went by the board as a result, let us say, of social Communism imposing itself on the modern world in the guise of a practical religion." But he himself has learned to resist this destructive urge, for he has glimpsed a coming redemption: "As Christianity stepped forth amid the Roman civilization of the universe, so *Music* breaks forth from the chaos of modern civilization."[14] Music, imbued now with metaphysical significance, will allow us to perceive in a vivid and immediate way that the things we currently value are merely trash.

The young Nietzsche, naturally feeling that he was one of the enlightened few who were capable of sharing this insight, felt some spontaneous sympathy with the project. But he knew that Schopenhauer's philosophy provided a slightly creaky foundation for it. He was aware, as we shall see, of some of the well-known objections to Schopenhauer's metaphysics and also of the related inconsistencies in Wagner's account of the metaphysical role of art. His own developing conception of the potential alliance between art and philosophy is indebted to the neo-Kantian critics of Schopenhauer and therefore incorporates a more explicit account of the limits to rational justification and of its relation to nonrational forms of persuasion.

THE AUTHORITY OF THE IDEAL

The turn away from the social and political hopes of the Left Hegelians, toward aesthetics, involved a transformation in the self-conception of the intellectual. The project of creating a substitute for religion was now premised on the idea of intellectual hierarchy; the generation of a general transformation in human consciousness came to be seen as the responsibility of an intellectual elite, as opposed to the product of social processes. The rehabilitation of aesthetic notions of cultural redemption, although they may be seen to be continuous with the romantic responses to Kant's third *Critique*, acquired an apolitical and, ultimately, antipolitical character. In his early work, Nietzsche, conceived of himself as the

---

[14] "Beethoven," in *Actors and Singers*, ed. and trans. William Ashton Ellis (Lincoln: University of Nebraska Press, 1995), 120.

"Arzt der Cultur."[15] He therefore helped to map the potential parameters of this new intellectual role and in doing so was inspired by F. A. Lange's conception of the "Standpoint of the Ideal."[16]

In his *History of Materialism*, Lange claims that critical philosophy can be properly employed both to discern the limits of reason, or the scope of its legitimacy, and to assess the limitations of its effectiveness as a means of influencing belief. In addressing both of these problems he proposes that people should be encouraged to submit to the authority of an overarching ideal, legislated by philosophers and elaborated by poets. This is intended to supply us with beliefs that are pragmatically or ethically necessary but which cannot, strictly speaking, be rationally justified.

His view of the need for such an ideal is in part derived from Kant and in part his own invention. Lange claims that people need a shared worldview; for pragmatic reasons they require shared beliefs; for ethical reasons they need the kind of worldview that supports common values. Even if reason were in principle capable of delivering consensus on such a fully coherent worldview, Lange doubts that the ordinary rational capacities of human beings could deliver it. He also doubts that even reason perfectly employed could supply it. But a shared and fully coherent view of the world is psychologically necessary, Lange holds, if we are to have a secure basis for ethical commitment.

Like many of his contemporaries, Lange fears, without fully spelling out his reasons, that a secular worldview is an inadequate basis for ethical life. He maintains that critical philosophy can deliver an entirely secular worldview, by eliminating religious and metaphysical dogmas that cannot be rationally justified, but that this worldview, entirely compelling as it is to philosophers, will not in itself be satisfying to the common intelligence. It will seem "inharmonious and full of perversities."[17] We will

---

[15] Cf. "Der Philosoph als Arzt der Cultur," *Nachgelassene Fragemente*, Sommer 1872 bis Ende 1874, *KGW* III-4.141.

[16] Various commentaries have been published on this early influence, including a monograph by George Stack: *Lange and Nietzsche* (Berlin: de Gruyter, 1983); two important essays by Jörg Salaquarda, one of which is cited below, the other being "Nietzsche und Lange," *Nietzsche Studien* 7 (1978): 236–53. Most recently, James Porter has examined this relationship in his *The Invention of Dionysus: An Essay on The Birth of Tragedy* (Stanford: Stanford University Press, 2000). Earlier works that discuss this relationship include H. Vaihinger's *The Philosophy of "As If,"* trans. C. K. Ogden (London: K. Paul, Trench, Trubner & Co. Ltd, 1924); and Walter Del Negro's *Die Rolle der Fiktionen in der Erkenntnistheorie Friedrich Nietzsches*, (München: Rösl, 1923). A very helpful and clear short introduction to Lange's thought may be found in Nadeem J. Z. Hussain, "Friedrich Albert Lange," *The Stanford Encyclopedia of Philosophy*, Fall 2006 ed., ed. Edward N. Zalta, URL = <http://plato.stanford.edu/archives/fall2006/entries/friedrich-lange/>.

[17] *The History of Materialism*, trans. Ernst Chester Thomas (London, 1950), 3:338. All Lange citations in English will be taken from this translation of the second edition (which is

reach for but not find ultimate reasons for what happens in the world. Lange seems to believe that for pragmatic and ethical reasons we need a fundamentally optimistic view of the world. This requires a more satisfactory fit between human purposes and the nature of the universe. It requires the authority of the ideal.

Unlike Kant, however, Lange does not believe that any ideal is naturally compelling for rational creatures. On Kant's view, reason itself, in both its practical and speculative uses, leads us quite naturally to fashion such an ideal for ourselves. The transcendental dialectic described in the first *Critique* presents us with an archetype for reason and its personification as God. The complete determination of the objects of our senses, Kant tells us, may only be conceived of in relation to a totality that permits comparison with all predicates in the field of appearance. Owing to "einer natürlichen Illusion," Kant tells us, we regard this principle as being valid, not only for objects of our senses, but for things in general.[18] Since it is the understanding that connects all phenomena, this totality is imagined to be a supreme understanding, an intelligence. Hence the inevitable personification of the ideal.[19]

We therefore arrive at an ideal that is legitimate insofar as it is a natural ideal of reason and is also, Kant points out, evidently effective in as much as it appeals to a basic and powerful intuition of human beings.[20] But Lange does not find this neat solution plausible. In his *History of Materialism*, he elaborates a naturalistic and developmental reconception (some might say misunderstanding) of apriority and rejects the idea that pure reason will naturally lead us to any universal ideal.[21] He also perceives that at the level of popular belief, traditional religious ideas are becoming incredible. They are being eroded by science, and particularly materialism. So in the absence of any naturally compelling authoritative ideal, Lange ventures, we will have to invent one.

---

divided into three volumes). All of the cited passages are also contained in the first edition of 1866, with which Nietzsche was familiar.

[18] Cf. *Immanuel Kant's Critique of Pure Reason*, trans. Norman Kemp Smith, (1929; Houndmills, Basingstoke, Hampshire and New York: Palgrave Macmillan, 1993, 2003), A582, B610.

[19] Ibid., A583, B611.

[20] Kant claims that "in all peoples, there shine amidst the most benighted polytheism some gleams of monotheism, to which they have been led, not by reflection and profound speculation, but simply by the natural bent [*natürlicher Gang*] of the common understanding, as step by step it has come to apprehend its own requirements." Ibid., A590, B618.

[21] Lange, *The History of Materialism*, 2:226: "As to the *necessity* of the ideas, it must, in the extent in which Kant maintains it, be decidedly controverted: Only for the idea of the soul, as a unitary subject for the multeity of sensations, may it be said to be probable. As to the idea of God, as far as a rational Creator is opposed to the world, there is no such natural disposition."

The Standpoint of the Ideal is available to us only if our perception of reality is aesthetically manipulated.[22] The poetic imposition of form on this reality permits us to "form a judgment as to the quality of the world" as the shared basis of our evaluations.[23] The authority of the ideal, which is required to provide us with an ethically secure worldview, must be reestablished through a form of poetic creativity.[24]

Lange's suggestion (and he is taking Schiller to be a model here) is that a certain kind of aesthetic apprehension of reality can supply what reason cannot. Criticism, on his view, can play the role of eliminating, albeit gradually, conflicting metaphysical dogmas, and at the same time the synthesizing function of poetry can represent reality to us in a way that makes it appear entirely harmonious and therefore conducive to moral evaluation.

His claims clearly caught Nietzsche's attention. Writing to his friend von Gersdorff in 1866, he summarizes the central insights of Lange's *History of Materialism*. They concern, he says, the confinement of knowledge to phenomena, conditioned by "our organization," and the simultaneous, structurally inevitable desire to know the *Ding an sich*, which nevertheless remains wholly unknowable.[25] In interpreting Nietzsche's famous statement that the world can be justified only as an aesthetic phenomenon, we must bear in mind this neo-Kantian conception of what the limits to justification are and how an aesthetic phenomenon might be called on to supply it.[26]

Lange's criticisms taught Nietzsche that Schopenhauer's boldest metaphysical claims are illegitimate.[27] But Lange's concept of the "Standpoint of the Ideal" also suggested to him that Schopenhauer's dramatically (if illicitly) vivid conception of the *Ding an sich* might be recovered as an aesthetic phenomenon.

---

[22] Lange writes, "The more freely synthesis exerts its function, the more aesthetic becomes the image of the world, the more ethical is its reaction upon our activity in the world. Not only poetry, but speculation too, however it may appear to be directed to knowledge only, has essentially aesthetic, and, through the attractive force of the beautiful, also ethical intent." Ibid., 3:338.

[23] Ibid., 3:337–38.

[24] Ibid., 3:336–37.

[25] *Nietzsche Briefwechsel*, I-2.160. For an interesting commentary on this letter, cf. Jörg Salaquarda, "Der Standpunkt des Ideals bei Lange und Nietzsche," *Studi Tedeschi* 12, no. 1 (Napoli, 1979): 138–64.

[26] *BT*, 5.

[27] Lange claims that we can have no knowledge of the nature of the "thing-in-itself." Invoking his naturalistic conception of apriority, he tells us: "The true essence of things, the last cause of all phenomena, is . . . not only unknown to us, but even the idea of it is nothing more and nothing less than the last outcome of an antithesis determined by our organisation, and of which we do not know whether, beyond our experience, it has any meaning at all." *History of Materialism*, 2:218.

The same strategy also seemed to Nietzsche to be suggested by another neo-Kantian critic of Schopenhauer, Rudolf Haym. In an unflattering 1864 review of Schopenhauer's *The World as Will and Representation*, Haym had insisted that the entire argument only seems to work at all because it conceals incoherence with metaphor.[28] It fails to make any sense of the relationship between Will and the world; and in fact Schopenhauer's conception of nature as a mirror of the Will is nothing more than a "fantastic-poetic anthropomorphization."[29]

Persuaded but unperturbed by this insight, Nietzsche congratulates Schopenhauer on making such a good job of the fantastic-poetic aspects of the project. On an artistic level, he assures von Gersdorff, Schopenhauer's philosophy provides a degree of edification that should provoke contrition even in Haym.[30] And given this predisposition to find an artistic interpretation of "Will" enthralling, it should be no surprise to us that Nietzsche took seriously, in these early years, Wagner's most grandiose philosophical claims about his own artistic enterprise. He thought that he had found a way of integrating the apparent cultural authority of this tremendous artistic figure into a critical philosophical framework that could transform it into a genuine form of intellectual authority.

Wagner had, all along, seen himself as a new Aeschylus, providing a mythic foundation for a national culture. He was uniquely equipped to do so, he thought, because he had seen that art is capable of expressing something that philosophy is not. In 1849, he perceived that Aeschylean tragedy was not the product of conscious reflection, but rather was inspired by the figures of two gods, Apollo and Dionysus, the one associated with

[28] Haym specifically points to the relationship between intellect, Will, and brain, as set out by Schopenahuer in chapter 20 of the second volume of *The World as Will and Representation*. The Will is individuated by space, time, and causality, which is in turn a function of the brain. However, the brain itself, as a part of nature, is understood to be an objectification of the Will. How, asks Haym, can the Will, in the absence of the category of causality, attain individuated objectification? Cf. "Arthur Schopenhauer," *Gesammelte Aufsätze von Rudolf Haym* (Berlin: Weidmann, 1903), 246. Sandro Barbera points out that from Eduard Zeller to Ernst Cassirer this was taken to be the *circulus vitiosus* of Schopenhauerean philosophy. Cf. "Eine Quelle der frühen Schopenhauer-Kritik Nietzsches: Rudolf Hayms Aufsatz 'Arthur Schopenhauer,'" *Nietzsche Studien* 24 (1995): 124–36. In his unpublished "On Schopenhauer" notes of 1868, Nietzsche singles out this problem as the most significant flaw in Schopenhauer's argument. Cf. Nietzsche's *Gesammelte Werke*, Erster Band (Munich: Musarion Verlag, 1922), 397–98. For a recent translation and commentary, cf. Christopher Janaway, ed., *Willing and Nothingness: Schopenhauer as Nietzsche's Educator* (Oxford: Oxford University Press, 1998).

[29] Haym, "Arthur Schopenahuer," 261.

[30] Ibid., 160: "Wenn die Philosophie Kunst ist, dann mag auch Haym sich vor Schopenhauer verkriechen; wenn die Philosophie erbauen soll, dann kenne ich wenigstens keinen Philosophen, der mehr erbaut als unser Schopenhauer."

ideal order and beauty, and the other with perfect spontaneity. Neither of these expressive needs could be fulfilled by philosophy, which, since its laying waste to the glories of the Tragic Age in Greece, had unfortunately been dominant for the last two thousand years.[31] In his prose works of the 1860s, Wagner had begun to integrate his new Schopenhauerean vision into this existing self-conception. The stage seemed set for a philosophical reinterpretation of his Aeschylean role.

Here was the young philologist's opportunity. And Nietzsche brilliantly seized the day with his *The Birth of Tragedy*. He elaborates the view that in Wagnerian music-drama, as in Greek tragedy, the Dionysian art of music reveals to us the inner nature of the world, the Will that rages beneath the shimmering veil of Apolline order. His own philosophical doubts about the Wagnerian project are quelled (though it cannot be said that the problems have really been finally resolved). The *Ding an sich* remains unknowable, but we can nevertheless generate for ourselves an aesthetically Ideal version of it. And what better medium than music to evoke hypnotically a feeling of its power while retaining a sense of its inscrutability? No wonder the religiously inclined nonbeliever found in Wagner's operas such an intoxicating mixture of emotion and philosophical intimation.

PHILOSOPHERS' FICTIONS

On both Lange's and Nietzsche's conception of aesthetic experience, art is not just supposed to sweep us up into its magical aura, like a popular piece of theatre, and then deposit us again in our ordinary lives. If the vision it presents to us is to seem genuinely meaningful, fulfilling a need that reason generates but cannot itself fulfill, then it must be the product of a genuine form of intellectual authority and not merely an appealing fantasy conjured up by the human imagination.

Lange, having rejected Kant's deduction of the transcendental ideas, is keen to point out that he is not recommending that we replace God, freedom, and immortality with just any artistic vision of life that takes our fancy. This sort of unconstrained individualism would, of course, set us entirely free from the moorings of critical philosophy and its expertise in human nature and human reason. "The individual," he tells us, "grows up from the soil of the species, and general and necessary knowledge forms the only safe basis for the elevation of the individual to an aesthetic apprehension of the world. If this basis is disregarded, speculation too

---

[31] Cf. "Art and Revolution," in *The Artwork of the Future and Other Works*, ed. and trans. William Ashton Ellis (Lincoln: University of Nebraska Press, 1993).

can no longer be typical, no longer be full of significance; it loses itself in fantasies, in subjective caprice and puerile frivolity."[32] Art as a nonrational means of persuasion must remain carefully linked to critical reason.

Nietzsche's reinterpretation of Schopenhauer certainly seems designed to avoid frivolity. Our justification of the world as an aesthetic phenomenon must be intrinsically related to our other forms of justification, that is, to what we can legitimately claim about the world. Nietzsche clearly believes that in spite of the shortcomings of Schopenhauer's metaphysics, the idea of the world as Will is legitimated by something more than poetic license. A certain kind of realism lies at the basis of its appeal to him.[33] Extravagant metaphysical claims aside, it is grounded in an appropriately disenchanted view of the world, one in which there is no ultimate purpose for anything, suffering is irremediably ubiquitous, and though we delude ourselves into thinking our lives are important we will each of us soon be dead.[34] Will, as a metaphor, allows us to confront this terrible reality in an aesthetically transfigured form which, like the Kantian sublime, is at once unfathomable and reassuring.

But it remains the case both for Lange and for Nietzsche that there is a gap between the secular worldview that philosophy delivers and the ideal presentation of the world that takes place in art. The former is rationally justified belief, in other words, reality so far as we know it. The latter is a fiction. The picture of the world presented to us in the form of the Ideal is both rationally underdetermined and artistically embellished. So philosophers, on this model, must exploit nonrational forms of persuasion to make their insights effective.

Lange seems to be uncomfortable with this idea. He introduces a distinction between "truth" and truth that obfuscates the distinction between justified and unjustified belief. He argues that the word *truth* is already popularly used to refer to religious convictions, supposed revelations, and other irrational but ethically significant convictions. Philosophers might then justifiably use it, if only in a figurative (*bildichen*) sense, to describe the standpoint of the Ideal.[35] He goes on to remind us that the Ideal is only "a *dogma* which not only is not proved, but which in fact, when logically tested, is *not true*, but which, if held as an *idea*, may, indeed,

[32] Ibid., 3:339.
[33] As we shall see in chapter 3, Nietzsche provides a naturalized (if still not fully coherent) reading of "Will" in *The Birth of Tragedy*.
[34] For an interesting discussion of the development of Nietzsche's pessimistic worldview, and especially of his criticisms of Schopenhauerian pessimism, cf. Joshua Dienstag, "Nietzsche's Dionysian Pessimism," *Pessimism: Philosophy, Ethic, Spirit* (Princeton: Princeton University Press, 2006), 161–200.
[35] *The History of Materialism*, 281.

like any other religious idea, edify mankind and raise him above the limits of sense."[36]

In claiming that his ideal is to be "held as an idea," he seems to imply that it may be consciously held to be an edifying fiction, in which case it will not subject us to the same infantilizing delusions as real belief. But given his pessimistic view about popular rational capacities, we would expect him to see this sophisticated form of commitment as unrealistic and unlikely. Since it has to supply a basis for our evaluations, it must surely be taken to have some epistemic standing. It is hard to imagine that anything other than real belief will do.[37]

Nietzsche's view of the role of art seems to come even closer to promoting straightforward delusions. For his view modifies, in an important way, Wagner's own uncritically Schopenhauerean view of the power of music. In his 1864 essay, "On State and Religion," Wagner argues that we are generally deluded into having a sense of purposefulness, in spite of the ultimate futility of their lives, by a benign *Wahn*. In his music-drama, the drama reproduces such a *Wahn*, while music provides an immediate experience of the Will that comprises the inner nature of reality. Music tears through the veil of illusion. Nietzsche, however, in the light of his critique of this metaphysical worldview, cannot make the same claims about the status of music. Both the Apolline plastic arts and the Dionysian art of music provide us with a worldview that is in some sense a fiction. In *The Birth of Tragedy*, Apolline illusion is compared to a dream state, but the Dionysian vision that rends this illusion is not sober, waking reality. It requires narcotic stimulation; it is an "intoxicated reality" that we experience through it. The form of artistic edification that he recommends is thoroughly nonrational.

So how, on this view, does the philosopher come to have effective authority over the ideals and fantasies that people adopt? Lange and Nietzsche both put an even greater distance than Kant does between themselves and existing religious belief. They are therefore faced with a more troubling question about how their ideals can become authoritative.

Lange's answer is a form of critical gradualism that exploits outstanding religious illusions and progressively modifies them to conform to the kind of worldview prescribed by philosophy. A combination of conservatism

---

[36] Ibid., 281.

[37] Even Kant's starkly denuded religion seems to require real faith if it is to serve its function, as Allen Wood argues convincingly in his "Rational Theology, Moral Faith, and Religion," *The Cambridge Companion to Kant*, ed. Paul Guyer (Cambridge: Cambridge University Press, 1992). He maintains that this remains a problem for Kant's ethics. Cf. 405: "Practical arguments by themselves cannot produce the belief whose indispensability they demonstrate. Such belief requires either theoretical evidence, which Kant regards as unavailable, or else nonrational motivating factors, which Kant wishes to eschew."

and strategic criticism might, then, be employed to mold popular belief into a form that is compatible with the Ideal. This places constraints on the way in which art might foster an "aesthetic apprehension" of the world, for it must be intimately related to existing beliefs, values, and cultural forms. This can best take place, Lange claims, in the context of a shared national culture.

If the outlines of this strategy still seem rather vague, at least compared to Kant's strict prescriptions in the *Religion*, this is because, Lange insists, the manipulation of popular belief is a complex affair; it must be sensitive to the nuanced forms of meaning in which ethical life is necessarily grounded. He tells us that "if we take the case of a particular community, e.g., that of the Germans in the present epoch, it is quite possible that the ethically most valuable combination of conceptions demands very many more ideas than Kant was willing to base his rational religion upon." It must also be extremely sensitive to the current state of national consciousness. The creation of authoritative ideals must, he says, take into account "the whole state of culture in a nation, the dominant forms of the association of ideas, and a certain fundamental disposition of mind, which is the result of innumerable factors."[38]

However, this appeal for sensitivity should not obscure the fact that the whole project is premised on a very unromantic view of popular belief. There is no Herderian celebration of cultural organicism here. People cannot be left to their own devices, to shape their cultures as they choose. Since the rational capacities of most human beings are pretty derisory, philosophical expertise is necessary as the only secure and legitimate foundation for our worldview.[39]

We can extrapolate from this view, then, a picture of the kind of epistemic advantage conferred on philosophers by their expertise. It may be seen to ensure not just valid insight but also a special purchase on popular belief. Philosophers are better at reasoning; they therefore have a clearer conception of the nature of reason; and this gives them special insight into the limits of reason. Hence their capacity to instill faith at the limits of reason through the promulgation of an aesthetic ideal. The kinds of popular superstitions that are detached from all intellectual authority might then be replaced with a genuine epistemic hierarchy, over which philosophers have legitimate and effective command.

It is certainly possible to see how Nietzsche might have been tempted to integrate this neo-Kantian conception of intellectual authority not only with Wagner's artistic enterprise, but also with the psychological

[38] *The History of Materialism*, 3:283.
[39] Ibid., 281: "The masses, poor in logic as in faith, hold the might of prophetic conviction as just as much a criterion of truth as the proof of a sum."

assumptions that ground Wagner's mythopoetic project. In his essays, Wagner shows that he has retained an important Feuerbachian attitude: religion is not simply a set of primitive errors but the expression of deep and powerful human drives.[40] It is this economy of drives that he sets out to identify and exploit. It seems plausible that Nietzsche might have aimed to combine these critical and psychological elements into a coherent strategy for belief-formation.

And yet this is not what Nietzsche accomplishes in *The Birth of Tragedy*. In assessing the nature of popular belief in secular societies, he undermines the idea that such an epistemic hierarchy can be established. It in fact becomes a struggle for him to hold on to any coherent set of ambitions as his conception of intellectual authority collides with his analysis of secularization.

FAITH IN SECULAR SOCIETIES

In 1872, Nietzsche, like Wagner, takes a dim view of cultures that thrive on the mere imitation of others. And, like Wagner, he seems at the same time to be recommending that we emulate the Greeks. For both of them this apparent contradiction may be resolved once we perceive that the coming revival of German culture will not involve a conscious imitation of Greek culture, but rather is emerging spontaneously from the same spirit—the spirit of music. With Wagner's messianic tone, Nietzsche sets out to defend the power of aesthetic experience and the need for an aesthetically generated myth as the beautiful horizon into which our reason recedes. But by the end of his first book he seems more impressed by the unstoppable power of secular rationalism than the revitalizing potential of *Tristan und Isolde*.

His assessment of the relevant problems turns out to be somewhat different from Lange's or Wagner's. He shares with them a very bleak view of popular rationality, but he also perceives that secularization places important restrictions on the form that popular belief can be made to take. If secularization is understood as an increasing commitment to rationalism, or the conviction that reason is the best guide to belief and action, the nature of popular belief must be severely constrained by this commitment.

Nietzsche does not confuse secularization with enlightenment. Since most people are bad at reasoning, they will demand reasons but in fact

---

[40] This view is implicit in his parallels between Christianity and the "new religion" of music, in the *Beethoven* essay, but it becomes most prominent in the 1880 essay, "Religion and Art."

content themselves with merely apparent rational justifications.[41] The result will be faith, but a kind of faith that looks more like an eclectic jumble of superstitions than a myth or religion. The rejection of prereflective myth in Alexandrian Greece and the rejection of the authority of revelation in post-Christian Europe both have the effect of disaggregating a common faith, replacing it with pragmatic attachments that masquerade as reasoned commitments. In much of his later work, Nietzsche continues to explore the uniquely problematic character of the secular belief produced by this process.

The Birth of Tragedy is his first important study of secularization. It is here that he first identifies a problem common to the secular culture of the Alexandrian Greeks and that of contemporary Europe. In each, he claims, faith fragments into "the same excessive lust for knowledge, the same unsatisfied delight in discovery, the enormous growth in worldliness, and alongside these a homeless roaming about, a greedy scramble to grab a place at the tables of others, frivolous deification of the present, or a dull, numbed turning away from it, all of this *sub specie saeculi*—of the here and now."[42] It is the specific nature of this new secular faith, and the mode of belief-acquisition that produces it, which complicates Nietzsche's account of the way in which intellectual authority might be exercised.

Tragic myth, Nietzsche tells us, had no power to halt the process of secularization once it had been initiated by Socrates. His narration of its decline presupposes that aesthetic experience is insufficient to impose order on this chaos. For the capacity of art to silence reason is precisely what secularization erodes: "Socratism condemns existing art and existing ethics in equal measure; wherever it directs its probing gaze, it sees lack of insight and the power of delusion, and it concludes from this lack that what exists is inwardly wrong and objectionable."[43] People demand reasons, even if what they unwittingly end up with actually falls short of them.

This analysis of secularization continues to inform Nietzsche's work long after his early aestheticism has been abandoned. He comes to see

---

[41] In *BT*, 11, Nietzsche tells us that Socratic rationalism does not promote genuine rational reflection, but rather is learned in a purely imitative fashion from Euripidean drama:

> The people themselves took lessons in oratory from Euripides, something of which he boasts in his contest with Aeschylus, where he claims that, thanks to him, the people have learned to observe, to negotiate, and to draw conclusions artfully and with the most cunning sophistication. . . . If the broad mass now philosophizes, conducts trials, and administers land and property with unheard-of cleverness, then this was his achievement, the successful result of the wisdom he had injected into the people.

[42] Ibid., 23.
[43] Ibid., 13.

that secular rationalism is not amenable to the kind of sculpting that Lange recommends. We have no grounds for supposing that Wagner's new religion will be any more capable of galvanizing a generation of true believers than Attic tragedy was of resisting the incoming tide of Socratism.

Given this analysis of secularization, we must therefore ask whether Nietzsche's conception of intellectual authority can take him any further. Does he provide himself with the resources to reformulate the way in which the valid insight of philosophers might be made effective in the absence of a genuine comprehension of their reasons?

It is certainly possible to imagine ways in which popular belief might still be manipulated. First, nonrational forms of persuasion might be made to masquerade as reasons. People might thereby be persuaded to take merely apparent reasons for genuine ones.[44] Second, people might be persuaded that they do not need reasons for certain kinds of beliefs. Faith might then be strategically directed by such meta-beliefs.

The problem with these strategies is that they can just as well be exercised by someone lower in the epistemic hierarchy. They do not confer any special effectiveness on those who genuinely have a superior understanding of the nature and limits of reason. Again, this insight is implicit in *The Birth of Tragedy*. Socratic reasoning is seen to be spread by Euripidean drama, through imitation of what is seen on the stage. But although they have genuinely internalized the normative constraint that they need reasons, people learn to supply them for themselves merely by parroting arguments which they have no real capacity to assess. Euripides' boast, according to Nietzsche, is that the people have learned from him how to negotiate and to argue.[45] But they do so through unreflective repetition.

This deflating realization is subsequently reinforced by Nietzsche's disgust at David Strauss's attempt to found a post-Christian religion in *The Old Faith and the New*. Strauss does so precisely by offering bad arguments in such a convoluted and confusing fashion that they might be taken for good ones by the undiscriminating reader.[46] In denouncing the banality of the resulting "faith" and Strauss's obvious pandering to public opinion, Nietzsche is also compelled to acknowledge that there is no

---

[44] This is in fact precisely what Ernest Gellner accuses Freud of doing. The "scientific" demeanor of psychoanalysis is, he thinks, crucial to the success of this secular "religion." Both Marx and Freud, he claims, employ rational standards for evidence but generate confusion about what counts as evidence. Gellner, *The Psychoanalytic Movement*, 111.

[45] *BT*, 11.

[46] The dilapidated state of the learned classes in Germany is shown, Nietzsche says, by the fact that "such superficial books as Strauss's are sufficient to meet the demands of their present cultural level." Such books contain a "casual, only-half listening accommodation with philosophy and culture and with the serious things of life in general." *UM*, i, 8.

reason why society should be less susceptible to this trite but reassuring nonsense than to the persuasive means available to real philosophers. The religion of the future, he admits, will be founded by philistines.[47]

THE LONELY PROPHET

This is not to say that all religiosity is extirpated from Nietzsche's work. Although he claims, by the time he writes *Ecce Homo*, that there is nothing in him of a founder of religions, the very title he chooses for this work indicates an ongoing comparison of himself to Christ. He clearly identifies still with the god Dionysus, a figure through whom he feels he can still express the affirmative vision of life that he endorses.[48] And most tellingly, it is his *Zarathustra* that he continues to consider the apex of his achievement.

Zarathustra is testament to Nietzsche's ongoing concern, after *The Birth of Tragedy*, not just to repudiate religion but to find some substitute for it. In particular, the central idea, that of eternal recurrence, seems to be intended to offer a form of secular redemption.[49] Lanier Anderson provides an especially compelling interpretation of the psychological role that it is supposed to play. It is, on Anderson's view, a thought-experiment through which the "fragmentary, accidental, puzzling, or regrettable aspects of a person's life or character can be redeemed by being brought into a whole that the person can affirm."[50] In recognizing the significance of some troubling event in the overall context of a life that we can affirm,

[47] Ibid., 4.

[48] *EH*, "Preface," 2; and *EH*, "Thus Spoke Zarathustra," 6 and 8. Cf. also *TI*, "What I Owe to the Ancients," 4: "[The Dionysian] gives religious expression to the most profound instinct of life, directed towards the future of life, the eternity of life, —the pathway to life, procreation, as the *holy* path."

[49] Several readers have convincingly argued that eternal recurrence as it appears in the published works (though there is a discrepancy here with the unpublished writings) cannot be taken to be a cosmological doctrine. Cf. esp. Nehamas, *Nietzsche: Life as Literature* (Cambridge, Mass.: Harvard University Press, 1987), 141–69; Lanier Anderson, "Nietzsche on Truth, Illusion, and Redemption," *European Journal of Philosophy* 13, no. 2: 182–225. Bernard Reginster, *The Affirmation of Life: Nietzsche on Overcoming Nihilism* (Cambridge, Mass.: Harvard University Press, 2006), 205–6.

[50] Lanier Anderson, "Nietzsche on Truth, Illusion, and Redemption," 200. The first statement of the thought-experiment can be found in *GS*, 341:

> *The heaviest weight.* —What if some day or night a demon were to steal after you into your loneliest loneliness and say to you: "This life as you now live it and have lived it, you will have to live again and innumerable times again; and there will be nothing new in it, but every pain and every joy and every thought and sigh and everything unutterably small or great in your life you will have to return to you, all in the same succession and sequence, —even this spider and this moonlight between the trees, and even this moment and I myself. The eternal hourglass of existence is turned over again and again, and you

its weight in our lives can be reassessed. It will acquire a new meaning and hence a new value.[51] It provides, then, a real form of redemption in this life as opposed to a postponed hope of redemption in the next.

The idea of eternal recurrence, whether or not we find it to be successfully redemptive, seems to be an attempt to re-create a form of religious consolation.[52] And Nietzsche clearly sees it as one of his greatest insights. In what sense, then, has he renounced the task of founding a secular religion? Although he himself seeks a way of reconciling himself with the secular view of human existence, he no longer, he claims, wants any believers.[53] He no longer has any means of communicating philosophical insights to those who are not already capable of arriving at them.

When Zarathustra comes down from his mountain, no one understands him. His disciples disappoint him. The "highest men" disappoint him. Humanity is not ready for his thoughts. Only in imagination does he does he find followers.[54] Throughout the narrative, we are presented with a vivid depiction of the loneliness that comes with insight.[55]

The work is supposed to supply its own music.[56] Nietzsche no longer has the company of great artists, to assist in communicating his vision.

---

with it, speck of dust!" Would you not throw yourself down and gnash your teeth and curse the demon who spoke thus? Or have you once experienced a tremendous moment when you would have answered him: "You are a god and never have I heard anything more divine." If this thought gained power over you, as you are, it would transform and possibly crush you. The question in each and every thing, "Do you desire this once more and innumerable times more?" would lie upon your actions as heaviest weight. Or how well disposed would you have to become to yourself and to life *to long for nothing more fervently* than this ultimate eternal confirmation and seal.

[51] Ibid., 202.

[52] For a skeptical view of the coherence of the thought-experiment, cf. Michael Tanner, *Nietzsche: A Very Short Introduction* (Oxford: Oxford University Press, 2001).

[53] *EH*, "Preface, 'Why I am Destiny,'" 1.

[54] F. A. Lea identifies Nietzsche with Zarathustra, in this longing for company: "Thus, in imagination, the childless Nietzsche, the master without pupils, the professor without students, shoulders the responsibility for an entire succeeding generation; and once more appeals for a band of dedicated souls—'lonely ones of today, seceding ones'—to share the responsibility with him." F. A. Lea, *The Tragic Philosopher: Friedrich Nietzsche* (London: Athlone Press, 1957), 200. In his 1886 preface to *Human, All Too Human*, Nietzsche tells us: "When I needed to I once . . . *invented* for myself the 'free spirits' to whom this melancholy-valiant book with the title *Human, All Too Human* is dedicated: 'free spirits of this kind do not exist, did not exist, but as I have said, I had need of them at that time.'"

[55] Cf. e.g. *TSZ*, part III, 9, "The Return Home": "O Zarathustra, I know all: and that among the many you were *lonelier*, you singular one than you ever were with me! Loneliness is one thing, solitude another: *that* you have learned now. And that among humans you will always be wild and strange."

[56] *EH*, "Thus Spoke Zarathustra," 1: "Perhaps the whole of *Zarathustra* can be considered music—certainly, a rebirth in the art of *hearing* was one of its preconditions."

Even Shakespeare and Goethe, he claims, would not be able to breathe this air; Dante and the poets of the Veda are not worthy of this company.[57] His writings, he thinks, stand on their own, in seeking to communicate ideas which have never previously been anticipated, for which we have previously not even had concepts, and which still no one is acute enough to appreciate.[58]

His fundamental insight, he claims in *Ecce Homo*, remains unintelligible.[59] This is the tragedy of *Zarathustra*. It portrays a prophet whom no one understands and yet who cannot bear the thought of the future of humanity unless it is shaped by his prophecy.[60] It is a work for everyone and no one.

So it seems that even if Nietzsche continues to feel he has special insights into how we should adjust our worldview to compensate for the absence of religious belief, and even if he retains the ambition to transform humanity with these insights, he never resolves the question of how they might have effective authority. With the abandonment of his aestheticism, he abandons any account of how philosophers might have this persuasive power.

NEITHER RELIGION NOR ENLIGHTENMENT

Nietzsche comes to reject the idea that philosophers can establish for us, through some nonrational means, a single, shared, and normatively correct worldview. The only persuasive means at our disposal that unerringly links correctness and persuasiveness is reason. In a context in which pragmatic demands masquerading as reasons compete to influence belief, and where the crudest of these apparent reasons often succeed, any popular simplifications propounded by philosophers will have no special status or effectiveness. The necessary conclusion would seem to be that the only way in which philosophers can secure their effectiveness is through the promotion of rationality, or enlightenment.

But Nietzsche remains troubled by the fact that in the absence of an egalitarian account of our rational capacities, such as Kant's, we cannot assume that there will be any way of making the legitimate insights of philosophers available to all. Every area of philosophy would have to yield a categorical imperative in order for us to have equality before the

---

[57] Ibid., 6.

[58] Ibid., 6.

[59] *EH*, "Why I Write Such Good Books," 1.

[60] Cf. *EH*, "Thus Spoke Zarathustra," 8: "Zarathustra has control over the *great disgust* at people: people are for him something unformed, matter, an ugly stone that needs a sculptor."

laws of reason. Our most complex forms of justification would have to be reducible to simple, useable principles, which were themselves uncontroversially valid.[61] And philosophy by its very nature deals with the nonobvious, the controversial, the outer limits of our comprehension of rational justification.

Even if we had an optimally confident view of the capacity of philosophy to deliver objectively valid reasons that were in principle comprehensible to any rational person, they could in fact only be authoritative over those capable of assessing them. Since intellectual authority just is the authority of reason, this is necessarily limited in scope for imperfectly rational beings. Yet if philosophy offers something in lieu of reasons it must risk losing either legitimacy or its effectiveness. It seems that philosophers must, as Nietzsche finally acknowledged, give up on the hope of having "believers."

Nietzsche, like Feuerbach and Schopenhauer, lived most of his life on the margins of the academy. And like these thinkers he did not see intellectual life as consisting in a shared enterprise that takes place in a community of reasoners. In the academy, ideally understood, this enterprise might be connected to and continuous with the various forms of justification that different spheres of human thought and endeavor require. The academy might therefore be conceived of as an institution that permits intellectual authority to benefit society more broadly without requiring any direct manipulation of popular belief. But for historical as well as personal reasons, this was not the model of intellectual authority that Nietzsche endorsed.

In the era of Bismarck's *Kulturkampf*, the enterprise was failing in important ways. The academic freedoms that Humboldt had defended were being eroded. German politics and German culture, as Nietzsche often complained, were becoming severed from any genuine intellectual authority. In the absence of a functioning institutional framework, the problems with which Nietzsche grappled concerning the effectiveness of valid insight were pressing and important. His later philosophical work, I hope to show, only deepens his pessimism about the possibility of finding a solution.

---

[61] Jerome Schneewind has demonstrated the centrality to the history of modern moral philosophy of this question concerning how we might arrive at a "method of ethics," that is, a procedure for settling normative issues that anyone can employ. Cf. *The Invention of Autonomy: A History of Modern Moral Philosophy* (Cambridge: Cambridge University Press, 1998); and Schneewind, "Natural Law, Skepticism, and Methods of Ethics," *Journal of the History of Ideas* 52, no.2 (April–June 1991): 289–308. I shall return to this issue in chapter 5.

CHAPTER 3

Laws of Agreement

INTRODUCTION

Nietzsche identifies a general problem concerning our need for both agreement and correctness. Philosophers, he thinks, are most likely to have the correct views but hardly anybody agrees with them. Others can generate broader social agreement but the views on which they converge are not very likely to be correct. In some areas of life this matters more than in others. In politics it seems to matter rather a lot, since the issue is of fundamental importance to our notions of legitimacy and authority.

As we shall see in chapters 4 and 5, Nietzsche identifies a particularly acute problem in the normative realm, where there is an apparently irremediable lack of recognized expertise. But a similar problem presents itself in the case of factual knowledge, and in this chapter I will sketch out the kind of case that he makes for this concern.

If we examine Nietzsche's views on factual, metaphysical, or normative beliefs, in each case we are presented with some serious interpretive difficulties. As we shall see, there are skeptical and nonskeptical elements that seem to be in conflict with one another in his thinking in each of these realms. It appears that there is an unstable oscillation in his thought. Different interpreters, we shall see, have tried to resolve the conflict in different directions. I will suggest that it is difficult to arrive at an interpretation that renders his thought absolutely consistent on each of these issues. An incompatibility thesis seems like a plausible interpretation in each case, but especially in the normative case.[1]

But I will argue that in the case of factual claims, whether we can defend a consistent skeptical reading, a consistent nonskeptical reading, or concede that there are incompatible elements, we will still have to attribute to Nietzsche a commitment to the discovery of truth in some sense. And his concerns about intellectual authority and political self-justification will remain relevant so long as we acknowledge him to be seeking truth.

In the case of normative beliefs, as we shall see in subsequent chapters, more serious doubts have been raised about whether Nietzsche is seeking

---

[1] On the "incompatibility thesis," cf. the introduction to this book.

truth at all. And the kind of political skepticism that we attribute to him will depend on what we make of these worries. If we view him as a consistent moral antirealist, the concerns that he has about intellectual authority will turn out to be very different from any that would follow from moral realism.

But in each area of belief, we shall see, Nietzsche's later work raises interesting questions about intellectual authority, deepening his insights into the problems that arise in *The Birth of Tragedy*. Insofar as he remains a political skeptic, I shall claim, it is on account of his insistence that we have no plausible solution to these problems.

Nietzsche clearly never fully gives up the aspiration to wield some kind of intellectual authority, but after the failure of his most ambitious aesthetic project, we see a gradual narrowing of these aspirations. As we saw in chapter 1, in the *Untimely Meditations* of the early 1870s, Nietzsche argues that the intellectual classes in contemporary Germany, who one might expect to be best able to differentiate between truth and ideology, have in fact largely been co-opted by the secular state. Powerful pragmatic interests have prevented them from criticizing politically expedient beliefs. But he holds onto the hope that there will be individuals who set out "to apply the scalpel of truth to all things, including the body of the state."[2]

The *Untimely Meditations* reveal a shift from the early aestheticism to a focus on criticism of existing belief. When he embarks on this critical project he seems optimistic about the capacity of philosophy, or *die philosophische Wissenschaft*, to reshape popular belief.[3] This optimism is at its height in *Human, All Too Human*. But as Nietzsche uncovers the powerful pragmatic constraints that govern belief-acquisition and inhibit criticism, he gradually loses his hope that the majority of people might benefit from the critical insights of philosophers.

As we have seen, in *The Birth of Tragedy*, Nietzsche characterizes secular societies (such as ancient Greece or contemporary Europe) as those in which reason is accepted to be the only reliable guide to belief. But he also holds that people cannot always fulfill the demand for justification that secular rationalism imposes on them. Belief-acquisition is generally an unreflective process, constrained by various pragmatic demands as well as the intellectual limitations of individual intellects. One of these pragmatic demands is the need for the minimal forms of agreement that facilitate social cooperation and communication.

Nietzsche sees in secular societies a competition between fragmentation and a powerful drive toward consensus. As we shall see, he thinks that

[2] *UM*, iii, 7.
[3] *HTH*, I, 2.

this latter drive is promoted largely by pragmatic needs and so consensus is often not the product of rational convergence. It is evidence instead of our need for a "law of agreement." The unknowing replication of merely expedient belief is facilitated by a general acceptance of merely apparent justifications.

In the middle-period works in particular, Nietzsche frequently insists that the psychological security and certainty that unreflective acceptance of inherited belief guarantees is a powerful disincentive to critical reflection.[4] He therefore comes to see that this must place serious constraints on any potential receptiveness to the critical insights of philosophers, thereby limiting the possible intellectual authority that they might wield.

Furthermore, a general lack of critical reflection makes us extremely vulnerable to the encroaching ideological power of the secular state. The state has a strong interest in promoting specific forms of agreement, as well as the means of instituting them, through its potential control of the press and higher education. It is also capable, as Nietzsche was vividly aware, of co-opting or eradicating competing sources of authority.

In the absence of a priestly caste there can be no bulwark against this ideology. The state's hegemony appears to Nietzsche to be challenged by no reliable extra-political source of authority. In a political culture that appears to accept unquestioningly state control of higher education, he fears that unconditional obedience is becoming the norm.[5]

Nietzsche cannot grant the state absolute authority to determine beliefs and values. But it is hard to see how this ideological capacity can be constrained if those few capable of discovering truth have no effective authority. His case for this concern about an absence of recognized expertise seems to me to be strongest in the normative realm, as we will see in chapter 5. As a claim about factual knowledge it seems weaker, since as he himself acknowledges, scientific knowledge does seem to become widely suffused in society, sufficiently in fact to erode religious beliefs. The victory of atheism is itself an important case of epistemic success.[6] But there are problems that arise even in this realm. Although it may often be rational for us to defer to experts, it is not always obvious when we should do so, since it is often so difficult to recognize expertise.

---

[4] Ruth Abbey has emphasized the strongly rationalist element in Nietzsche's middle works, particularly *Human, All Too Human*. Cf. *Nietzsche's Middle Period* (Oxford: Oxford University Press, 2000), esp. ch.1.

[5] Cf. Nietzsche's 1872 lectures entitled, "Über die Zukunft unserer Bildungsaltalten," where he claims that, contrary to the Humboldtian ideal of intellectual freedom, education has been placed entirely in the service of the state. *KGW* III-2.139. Also, cf. *UM*, iii, 8.

[6] Cf. *GS*, 357.

Even in areas such as the natural sciences, where criteria such as predictive success establish clear expertise, it is often difficult for nonexperts to modify their beliefs in ways that are appropriate to scientific knowledge. Many scientific theories are just too complex. Nietzsche's own half-digested understanding of various scientific ideas, including his forays into Lamarckian biology, illustrates this problem.

Another area in which we might think we will clearly have to defer to experts over the facts is history. Much of our historical learning will inevitably have to be accepted on authority. But although it may be obvious to us that historical scholars can teach us salient facts, there will always be a remaining problem concerning the analysis and interpretation of these facts. It is less obvious what constitutes expertise in these areas. We do not have to conclude that this is because there is no truth of the matter, only that it is much harder to know it, since these kinds of belief are so closely bound up with human interests and emotional investments.[7]

Nietzsche's deepening understanding of the problem of intellectual authority, then, contributes to his political skepticism. In his later writings he abstains from developing any theory of political legitimacy. An important intellectual motivation for this abstention is his insight that the consensus required by political life cannot readily be achieved, except through unacceptable forms of political manipulation.

Nietzsche's Skepticism about the Truth

There are two aspects of Nietzsche's views about truth that will be of most interest for our general argument. First, he makes claims about the difficulty of discovering it. Second, he points out that it will be difficult to wield authority over the beliefs of others even if one does. But his work also clearly raises epistemological and metaphysical issues that throw interpretive difficulties in the way of any straightforward exposition of these claims.

A prominent and perplexing feature of Nietzsche's work is the fact that he often appears to doubt the existence of factual truths, and yet he also appears to make truth-claims about facts. We have different options for making sense of this apparent conflict. First, we might attribute to Nietzsche

---

[7] Nietzsche establishes, in *UM*, ii, that historical interpretation is subject to extensive manipulation. Whereas he seems to imply in that essay that philosophers might exploit this manipulability, even in contemporaneous writings such as the "Lectures on the Future of our Educational Institutions," he acknowledges that the state has hegemonic power in this area.

a consistently "common sense" view of truth, one that does not involve any radical skepticism.[8] This will make sense of Nietzsche's apparent truth-claims, though it will require some hermeneutic effort to explain the persistence of his apparently skeptical theses. Second, we might insist that Nietzsche is a consistent skeptic about truth (this was for a long time the dominant view and, as we shall see, sophisticated versions of it have recently been defended), in which case the apparent truth-claims will have a special character. Third, we might accept that Nietzsche makes either incoherent or incompatible claims.

On the incoherence view, he will be simply confused. On the incompatibility view, there will be powerful strains in his work, which are coherent in themselves, but which are incompatible with one another. This might involve, for example, his making interesting cases for both epistemological skepticism (there are facts, but we cannot find out what there are) and metaphysical skepticism (there are no facts).[9] Or it might involve his expressing certain epistemological views about our criteria for recognizing the truth, but in fact employing different criteria in his own criticism.

The "party of common sense," to use Bernard Williams's expression, has recently garnered much support.[10] Maudemarie Clark has claimed that although Nietzsche's early work expresses more radically skeptical views, an important transition occurs in *Human, All Too Human*, owing to Nietzsche's renunciation of Schopenhauerean metaphysics.[11] The repudiation

---

[8] I am taking this schema from Lanier Anderson's "Nietzsche on Truth, Illusion, and Redemption."

[9] This is the claim that Peter Poellner makes about Nietzsche's views on metaphysics. Cf. Peter Poellner, *Nietzsche and Metaphysics* (Oxford: Clarendon Press, 1995), 137–38. Poellner claims that Nietzsche develops skeptical arguments about the justification of various metaphysical views that are in tension with his own anti-essentialist assertion that denies the intelligibility of such views.

[10] Cf. Lanier Anderson, "Nietzsche on Truth, Illusion, and Redemption," 185.

[11] Cf. Maudemarie Clark, "On Knowledge, Truth, and Value: Nietzsche's Debt to Schopenhauer and the Development of his Empiricism," in *Willing and Nothingness*, 47–52, 63. A particularly important passage indicating a transition may be found in *HTH*, i, 3, where Nietzsche writes:

Estimation of unpretentious truths. —It is the mark of a higher culture to value the little unpretentious truths which have been discovered by means of rigorous method more highly than the errors handed down by metaphysical and artistic ages and men, which blind us and make us happy. At first the former are regarded with scorn, as though the two things could not possibly be accorded equal rights: they stand there so modest, simple, sober, so apparently discouraging, while the latter are so fair, splendid, intoxicating, perhaps indeed enrapturing. Yet that which has been attained by laborious struggle, the certain, enduring and thus of significance for any further development of knowledge is nonetheless the higher; to adhere to it is manly and demonstrates courage, simplicity and abstemiousness.

of the metaphysical aspects of Schopenhauer's philosophy leads to an empiricism and naturalism that is already inherent in Schopenhauer's thought, owing, according to Clark, to his admiration for Hume. She points out that

> Schopenhauer recognizes that empiricism and naturalism go together and he clearly believes that these doctrines, which he resists, must be accepted if one denies the possibility of metaphysical knowledge.[12]

On this view, in rejecting the possibility of metaphysical knowledge in *Human, All Too Human*, Nietzsche is permitted to retain the essentially Humean assumptions that are present in Schopenhauer's thought. Clark tells us that

> To get from Schopenhauer's philosophy to empiricism and naturalism, Nietzsche had only to reject Schopenhauer's claim that metaphysical knowledge is possible and necessary for the intelligibility that science seeks.[13]

Clark perceives a significant and lasting change of orientation in Nietzsche's thought: a strongly empiricist and naturalist strain, she claims, is evident throughout the later works.[14]

Clark does find an epistemologically skeptical position, or "falsification thesis," in the early writings. It is clearly articulated in the essay "On Truth and Lying in a Non-Moral Sense." But Clark claims that this thesis presupposes some confused claims that are entirely overcome by the time Nietzsche writes the *Genealogy*. According to Clark, the thesis involves two problematic premises: first, the representational theory of perception defended by Schopenhauer, and second, the idea that truth must involve correspondence to "things-in-themselves." The first claim rules out the strong, metaphysical notion of correspondence presupposed in the second. Our linguistic conventions, on this view, cannot possibly correspond to things-in-themselves.

---

[12] Ibid., 57.

[13] Ibid., 58.

[14] Clark argues that the empiricist criterion for knowledge is central to *The Gay Science* and also finds evidence for a continuing adherence to naturalism in *Beyond Good and Evil*, 230, and *Antichrist*, 13–14. Brian Leiter also endorses this view of the mature works, citing in particular, *Beyond Good and Evil*, 134, and *Twilight of the Idols*, 3:3. Cf. also Brian Leiter, "Perspectivism in Nietzsche's *Genealogy of Morals*," in *Nietzsche Genealogy, Morality, Essays on Nietzsche's Genealogy of Morals*, ed. Richard Schacht (Berkeley: University of California Press, 1994), 336–37. Cf. also Simon May, *Nietzsche's Ethics and his War on "Morality,"* 144–45: "What warrants our truth-claims, for Nietzsche, is . . . something like an empirical determination supplied by subject-independent reality (whatever that would precisely be)."

So the falsification thesis that Clark attributes to Nietzsche in his early work is incoherent, as Nietzsche soon realizes. Clark asks:

> Once Nietzsche reverts to Kant in his denial that we can know anything about transcendent reality, how can he know that the empirical world fails to correspond to the transcendent? How can he know that the subservience of the will to practical interests distorts the true world or precludes such correspondence?[15]

Clark argues that the representational theory of perception in which this falsification thesis is grounded is repudiated by the time of *Human, All Too Human*.[16] The idea of the "thing-in-itself" is seen to be abandoned by the time Nietzsche writes *Beyond Good and Evil*. And any skepticism about the existence or knowability of truth is thereafter absent from his work.

This "common-sense" view, defended by both Clark and Leiter, is supposed to rule out both the epistemological and metaphysical forms of skepticism that have been attributed to the later Nietzsche under the general label "perspectivism."[17] The epistemological version of Nietzsche's perspectivism may be seen to originate with Arthur Danto. It consists in the claim that our ideas and concepts necessarily falsify reality, for they are always merely contingent constructions whose aim is to help us to survive.[18] It has also been exploited outside Nietzsche studies to provide a Nietzschean straw man for those who wish to refute a certain species of epistemological skepticism.[19]

But the "common-sense" view is also intended to rule out another form of perspectivism, one that rests on a metaphysical skepticism about

---

[15] Maudemarie Clark, *Nietzsche on Truth and Philosophy*, 90.

[16] Clark, "On Knowledge, Truth and Value," 52.

[17] Nietzsche frequently employs perspective as a metaphor. But he does not himself claim to have formulated a doctrine called "perspectivism"; he uses the term (*Perspektivismus*) only once in the published works, in *GS*, 354.

[18] Cf. Arthur Danto, *Nietzsche as Philosopher*, 75: "In the interests of life and survival, we are constrained to affirm the body of beliefs which passes for common sense and reject whatever conflicts with this."

[19] Cf., eg., Adrian Moore, *Points of View* (Oxford: Oxford University Press, 1997), 103–7. Moore characterizes Nietzsche's position thus:

> In any act of representation, some agent, some centre of force, imposes an interpretation—an interpretation that, in part, it would like to compel other centres of force to accept. This interpretation is not just a passive response to something that is antecedently given, in which meaning is to be found. It is rather a creation of meaning. It is an act of the will to power. The world is a dramatic text whose interpretation is part of acting out a particular life, creatively adopting a particular style, telling a particular story: the story that will become the narrator's autobiography. The interpreted world and the interpreting agent are constituted together. (104–5)

the nonexistence of facts.[20] This version of the doctrine, Brian Leiter claims, constitutes the "received view" of Nietzsche. He summarizes it in the following way:

i. the world has no determinate nature or structure;
ii. our concepts and theories do not "describe" or "correspond" to this world because it has no determinate character;
iii. our concepts and theories are "mere" interpretations or "mere" perspectives (reflecting our pragmatic needs, at least on some accounts);
iv. no perspective can enjoy an *epistemic* privilege over any other, because there is no epistemically privileged mode of access to this characterless world.

For the defenders of the "common-sense" interpretation, this view is simply based on a mistake concerning the import of Nietzsche's perspectival metaphors.

These metaphors are, Clark and Leiter claim, entirely consistent with Nietzsche's empiricist views about truth. They imply a nonskeptical view of the way in which we acquire knowledge. According to the version of perspectivism that they attribute to Nietzsche, affects and interests generate perspectives by calling our attention to aspects of reality.[21] Perspectivism in this sense is merely an inevitable feature of our acquisition of knowledge of a mind-independent reality.[22]

There are certainly significant passages in the later works that seem to support the "common-sense," empiricist reading. In *Twilight of the Idols*, Nietzsche writes:

We have science these days precisely to the extent that we have decided to *accept* the testimony of the senses, —to the extent that we have learned to sharpen them, arm them, and think them through to the end. Everything else is deformity and pre-science: I mean metaphysics, theology, psychology, epistemology. *Or* formal science, a system of signs: like logic

[20] Danto sometimes seems to be attributing this metaphysical skepticism to Nietzsche, cf. e.g. *Nietzsche as Philosopher*, 72, where he says that for Nietzsche our ideas are "arbitrary structurings of chaos." Cf. also 76 and 86.

[21] Clark, "On Knowledge, Truth, and Value," 76. "Different affects make different aspects of reality salient and focus our attention on them, so that other features disappear from view—that is why perspectives are partial or 'one-sided.' But that gives us no basis for denying that our affects give access to truth, that the features to which they call our attention are really there, are 'objective' features of the world whether we notice them or not." Cf. also Brian Leiter, "Perspectivism in Nietzsche's *Genealogy of Morals*," 345–46.

[22] Cf. also Simon May, *Nietzsche's Ethics and his War on Morality*, 141: "There is no inherent incompatibility between a statement's being empirically warranted and its being ineluctably a partial viewpoint, which is not necessarily more 'correct' than other viewpoints and is itself motivated by interests of preservation or power."

and that application of logic, mathematics. They do not have anything to do with reality, not even as a problem.[23]

However, critics of the "common-sense" view have pointed out that in the very same works in which Nietzsche is seen to rule out the falsification thesis, there are passages in which he seems to defend some version of it. Lanier Anderson, in particular, has drawn attention to passages that indicate its persistence.[24]

Clark points out that Nietzsche rejects the Kantian idea of the "thing-in-itself," and with it, the metaphysical correspondence theory of truth in section 16 of *Beyond Good and Evil*.[25] But in this same work, Anderson notes, Nietzsche claims that "the *erroneousness* of the world we think we live in is the most certain and solid fact that our eyes still grab hold of. We find reason after reason for it, reasons that might lure us into speculation about a deceptive principle in 'the essence of things.'"[26] And he also explicitly claims that the "perspective optics of life" demands belief in the truth of false judgments.[27] So his perspectivism seems to imply falsification.

If the skeptical arguments persist, we have to ask whether or not they are compatible with the empiricist views cited by those who defend the "common-sense" interpretation, or whether Nietzsche is in fact committed to incompatible claims. The published works in themselves seem to provide an insufficient basis for any systematic view about truth, even a nuanced and developmental view such as that defended by Clark. But some commentators have recently attributed to Nietzsche, on the basis of the unpublished writings and their relation to the published works, sophisticated forms of skeptical arguments that purportedly yield a single, coherent position on truth.

Lanier Anderson attributes to Nietzsche a consistent position rooted in what he calls the "subtraction argument." This holds that "cognition is supposed to falsify because subjective perspectives have a positive influence on the content of our representations which cannot be

[23] *TI*, "Reason in Philosophy," 3.
[24] Lanier Anderson, "Overcoming Charity: The Case of Maudemarie Clark's *Nietzsche on Truth and Philosophy*," *Nietzsche-Studien* 25 (1996): 307–41, and "Nietzsche on Truth, Illusion, and Redemption." On the persistence of the falsification thesis in *TI*, cf. "Overcoming Charity," 317, citing *TI*, III, 2, and *TI*, III, 5.
[25] Clark, *Nietzsche on Truth and Philosophy*, 113.
[26] *BGE*, 34.
[27] Ibid., 11. Anderson also cites *BGE*, 24; *WP*, 567; *WP*, 584; *GS*, 57; *GS*, 354. On Nietzsche's continued adherence to the falsification thesis, cf. also Nadeem Hussain, "Nietzsche's Positivism," *European Journal of Philosophy*, 12, no. 3: 326–68, at 327. For a reply to Hussain on this issue, cf. Maudemarie Clark and David Dudrick, "Nietzsche's Post-Positivism," *European Journal of Philosophy* 12, no. 3: 369–85.

subtracted out."[28] Cognition orders experience according to our needs. It therefore falsifies what is given to us independently.[29]

The skepticism here is not located at the epistemological level (concerning knowledge of facts), or at the metaphysical level (concerning the existence of facts). What is falsified, on this reading is *another kind* of phenomenal world," the content of which is supplied by the "chaos of sensations."[30] Anderson sees this account of the "contents carried by the sensory 'elements' of experience" as reminiscent of Ernst Mach's sensualism, a view that is also defended by Nadeem Hussain.[31]

This view, it is claimed, permits us to make sense of Nietzsche's empiricism, while acknowledging that he has a nonstandard view of sensory experience.[32] It also allows us to make sense of Nietzsche's pursuit of truth, by attributing to him a "theory-internal" view of what this involves, according to which we employ various criteria (such as adequacy to underlying sense-contents, or satisfaction of cognitive values such as simplicity and explanatory power) to assess cognitive superiority or relative truth.[33]

However, problems still seem to arise for the consistently skeptical view even in this modified form. Peter Poellner, who accepts the persistence of the falsification thesis in the later writings, insists that there is inconsistency in the *Nachlass*. He finds there two distinct arguments for falsification. First, the objects represented by a subject are seen to be in some sense "created" by that subject. Poellner quotes the following passage from the *Nachlass* in support of this view:

> The entirety of the organic world is the juxtaposition of beings [*Wesen*] surrounded by fabricated [*erdichteten*] small worlds: in that they project [*setzen*] their strength, their appetites, their habits of experience outside themselves, as their *external world*. The capacity to create (shape, invent, fabricate) is their basic capacity.[34]

He points out that this view seems to presuppose a picture of the subjects that "create" the objects they experience as "uncaused quasi-monadic entities, unaffected by anything genuinely external to—ontologically independent of—them."[35]

Secondly, Poellner claims, we find elements of the view that we are confronted with an external reality that is in endless flux. On this view

[28] Anderson, "Nietzsche on Truth, Illusion, and Redemption," 189.
[29] Ibid., 191.
[30] Ibid., 190, citing *WP*, 569.
[31] Hussain, "Nietzsche's Positivism."
[32] Cf. Ibid., 355.
[33] Lanier Anderson, "Nietzsche on Truth, Illusion, and Redemption," 193.
[34] *KGW* VII.3.34.247. Cited by Poellner, *Nietzsche and Metaphysics*, 190.
[35] Poellner, 196.

"reality in itself does not consist of 'objects' quantitatively identical over periods of time long enough for us to attribute 'being' in the sense of qualitative persistence to them."[36] This would mean that Nietzsche's argument presupposes the existence of an external reality that is independent of us as subjects of knowledge.

Poellner also finds inconsistency in Nietzsche's denial that there are "facts" that make our statements true or false, while helping himself to various psychological theses that seem to presuppose that there are facts.[37] In sum, then, it looks as though it will be very difficult to retrieve from Nietzsche a coherent and consistent view, and there will be a much greater burden of interpretive labor placed on those who hope to defend a consistent view than those who accept the prima facie inconsistencies.[38]

But these questions do not have to be resolved, for the purposes of our argument, so long as we can reliably conclude that Nietzsche is in some sense or other seeking factual truth. This element seems to me to be stable across the range of interpretations, even where "truth" is understood in a special sense, or where it is deemed inconsistent with his own avowed skepticism about the truth.[39]

THE DIFFICULTY OF DISCOVERING TRUTH

Whatever Nietzsche's criteria for the recognition of factual truth are, he seems committed to recognizing it.[40] And he thinks that this will be very difficult. In *The AntiChrist*, he writes:

> We have had to wring the truth out of ourselves every step of the way, had to give up almost everything that our heart, our love, our trust in life relied on. It requires greatness of soul: the service of truth is the hardest service. —So what does it mean to be *upright* in spiritual matters?

[36] Ibid., 197. Poellner attributes this interpretation to Richard Schacht (*Nietzsche*, 178, 185, 198).

[37] Ibid., 199.

[38] Michael Steven Green also views Nietzsche as inconsistent, claiming that there are several conflicting epistemologies in his work, deriving from his commitments to both naturalism and to transcendental theories of cognition. Cf. Michael Steven Green, *Nietzsche and the Transcendental Tradition* (Urbana: University of Illinois Press, 2002), 14.

[39] Cf. Lanier Anderson, "Nietzsche on Truth, Illusion, and Redemption," 194: "Few virtues or projects get as much unqualified endorsement in the Nietzschean corpus as honesty and the pursuit of truth."

[40] Cf. *HTH*, II, "Assorted Maxims," 3 "He who finally sees how long and how greatly he has been made a fool of embraces in defiance even the ugliest reality." Also, *HTH*, I, 34: "A question seems to lie heavily on our tongue and yet refuses to be uttered: whether one *could* consciously reside in untruth? or, if one were *obliged* to, whether death would not be preferable?"

That you are strict with your heart, that you look down on "beautiful
feelings," that you make your conscience from every yes and no![41]

Knowledge of the truth, then, requires extraordinary critical effort. Nietzsche seems to hold that this is the case for at least three reasons.

First, our inherited beliefs manifest a great deal of error. "Through im-
mense periods of time," Nietzsche tells us, "the intellect produced nothing
but errors."[42] He maintains that "erroneous articles of faith, which were
continually inherited . . . became almost part of the basic endowment of
the species."[43] A great deal of work is devoted to the excavation of these
errors, particularly insofar as they have had a religious character, and to
analyzing the causes of error.[44]

Second, Nietzsche worries that criticism of these erroneous beliefs is
pragmatically inadvisable. Many of our errors have become entrenched
because they have served some important pragmatic function. The reflective individuals who question and criticize these errors will therefore
place themselves at a pragmatic disadvantage. Nietzsche suggests that

Compared with him who has tradition on his side and requires no reasons for his actions, the free spirit is always weak, especially in actions;
for he is aware of too many motives and points of view and therefore
possesses an uncertain and unpractised hand.[45]

In *The Gay Science*, this point is incorporated into Nietzsche's speculative account of the development of the human intellect. He claims
that

every great degree of caution in inferring, every skeptical disposition, is
a great danger to life. No living being would be preserved had not the
opposite disposition—to affirm rather than suspend judgement, to err
and make things up rather than to wait, to agree rather than deny, to

[41] AC, 50.
[42] GS, 110.
[43] Ibid., 110.
[44] He seems sometimes to imply that an analysis of our motivations for a belief can play
a role in refuting it. Cf., e.g., *HTH*, I, 9: "All that has hitherto made metaphysical assumptions *valuable, terrible, delightful* to [people], all that has begotten these assumptions, is
passion, error, and self-deception; the worst of all methods of acquiring knowledge, not the
best of all, have taught belief in them. When one has disclosed these methods as the foundation of all extant religions and metaphysical systems one has refuted them!" However,
elsewhere he corrects this genetic fallacy, saying, "In the case of the knowledge of truth the
point is whether or not one *possesses* it, not from what motives one sought it or along what
paths one found it" (225). We will come back to the issue of the genetic fallacy in relation
to normative beliefs, in chapter 4.
[45] Ibid., 230.

pass judgement rather than to be just—been bred to become extraordinarily strong.[46]

The reflective pursuit of truth therefore seems to be a privilege of those
who already have basic existential security. Even then, it shatters one's
faith in many consoling and reassuring illusions.[47]

The thinker, Nietzsche tells us, must now be understood as "the being
in whom the drive to truth and those life-preserving errors are fighting
their first battle, after the drive to truth has *proven* itself to be a life-
preserving power, too."[48] Nietzsche's most difficult questions about the
value of truth surface with this insight.[49]

Third, the philosophical criticism that exposes error seems to itself
contain seductions into further error. He frequently warns us of these
dangers. In *Human, All Too Human*, Nietzsche describes the analysis
that sees through all those erroneous conclusions that have been drawn
only on the basis of utility (e.g. "an opinion makes us happy, therefore it
is a true opinion" and "an opinion causes pain and agitation, therefore it
is false"), but he adds the warning:

> The free spirit, who is all too often acquainted with the erroneousness
> of this kind of reasoning and has to suffer from its consequences, often
> succumbs to the temptation to draw the opposite conclusions, which
> are of course equally erroneous: a thing cannot prevail, therefore it is
> good; an opinion causes pain and distress, therefore it is true.[50]

He also warns us of the danger that overcoming difficulty will become a
source of self-congratulation which inhibits critical reason:

> One person retains an opinion because he flatters himself that it was
> his discovery, another because he acquired it with effort and is proud
> of having grasped it: thus both do so out of vanity.[51]

---

[46] *GS*, 111.

[47] *HTH*, I, 34: "The whole of human life is sunk deeply in untruth; the individual cannot
draw it up out of his well without thereby growing profoundly disillusioned about his own
past, without finding his present motives, such as that of honour, absurd, and pouring
mockery and contempt on the passions which reach out to the future and promise happiness in it."

[48] *GS*, 110.

[49] Bernard Williams has argued that the formulation of this problem is one of Nietzsche's
most important and original contributions to philosophy. Cf. Bernard Williams, *Truth and
Truthfulness: An Essay in Genealogy* (Princeton, N.J.: Princeton University Press, 2002).

[50] *HTH*, I, 30. In the second volume of *Human, All Too Human*, Nietzsche warns, "It is
not to everyone's taste that truth should be called pleasant. But at least let no one believe
that error becomes truth when it is called *unpleasant*" (*HTH*, II, "Assorted Maxims," 349).

[51] Ibid., I, 527.

The properly critical philosopher, on his view, has to engage in constant self-overcoming, to avoid the smug belief that he has arrived at true knowledge when he has merely reassured himself about his own errors.[52]

This demanding critical process, then, is not one that Nietzsche thinks can be undertaken by just anybody. Most people are simply not "predestined for knowledge." They are incapable of undertaking the rigorous criticism and constant self-overcoming that it demands.[53] Nietzsche therefore holds that his "free spirits" will be few and that they will be largely alienated from society on account of their heresies.

LAWS OF AGREEMENT

In an important passage from *The Gay Science*, Nietzsche explicitly connects the need for social consensus to the inhibition of critical reasoning. He writes:

> *The greatest danger.* —Had there not always been a majority of men who felt the discipline of their heads—their "rationality"—to be their pride, their obligation, their virtue, and who were embarrassed or ashamed by all fantasizing and debauchery of thought, being the friends of "healthy common sense," humanity would have perished long ago! The greatest danger that hovered and still hovers over humanity is the outbreak of *madness*—that is, the outbreak of arbitrariness in feeling, seeing, and hearing; the enjoyment in the lack of discipline of the head, the joy in human unreason. The opposite of the

---

[52] Cf. *GS*, Preface for the second edition, 2: "After such self-questioning, self-temptation, one acquires a subtler eye for all philosophizing to date; one is better than before at guessing the involuntary detours, alley-ways, resting places, and *sunning* places of thought to which suffering thinkers are led and misled on account of their suffering." Also, *HTH*, I, 609: "Young people love what is strange and interesting, regardless of whether it is true or false. More mature spirits love in truth that which is strange and interesting in it. Heads fully mature, finally, love truth also where it appears plain and simple and is boring to ordinary people: they have noticed that truth is accustomed to impart its highest spiritual possessions with an air of simplicity."

[53] *GS*, 25:

> *Not predestined for knowledge.* —There is a stupid humility that is not at all rare, and those afflicted with it are altogether unfit to become votaries of knowledge. As soon as a person of this type perceives something striking, he turns on his heel, as it were, and says to himself: "You have made a mistake! Where were your senses? This cannot be the truth!" And then, instead of looking and listening more keenly again, he runs away from the striking thing, as if he had been intimidated, and tries to shake it from his mind as fast as possible. For his inner canon says: "I do not want to see anything that contradicts the prevalent opinion. Am *I* made to discover new truths? There are already too many old ones." (cf. also *GS*, 293; and *BGE*, 30)

world of the madman is not truth and certainty but the generality and universal bindingness of a faith; in short, the nonarbitrary in judgement. And man's greatest labour so far has been to reach agreement about very many things and to lay down a *law of agreement*—regardless of whether these things are true or false. This is the discipline of the head which has preserved humanity—but the counter-drives are still so powerful that it is basically with little confidence that one may speak of the future of humanity. The picture of things still moves and shifts continually, and perhaps more and faster from now on than ever before; continually, the most select minds bristle at this universal bindingness— the explorers of *truth* above all! Continually this faith, as a commonplace belief shared by everyone, breeds nausea and a new lust in subtler minds.[54]

He is claiming here both that shared beliefs are necessary for social cooperation and that they guarantee what is for most people a necessary form of psychological security.

Nietzsche's legal metaphor for the role of shared beliefs has its origins in the "On Truth and Lying" essay.[55] This essay describes the social obligation as "the obligation to use the customary metaphors, or, to put it in moral terms, the obligation to lie in accordance with firmly established convention, to lie *en masse* and in a style that is binding for all."[56] In later works, Nietzsche subtly revises this view. The simplistic conceptions bequeathed to us by primitive errors are seen to produce easily comprehensible and communicable beliefs, thereby permitting "laws of agreement" without there ever being any conscious decision to establish such regulatory faiths. Once these false beliefs are incorporated into a mode of existence, criticism of them becomes less and less feasible.[57]

The role that education plays in our societies, on this view, is primarily to socialize us. Nietzsche maintains that "the environment in which he is

[54] GS, 76.
[55] OTL, 143:

That which is to count as "truth" from this point onwards now becomes fixed, i.e. a way of designating things is invented which has the same validity and force everywhere, and the legislation of language also produces the first laws of truth, for the contrast between truth and lying comes into existence here for the first time. . . . Human beings do not so much flee from being tricked as from being harmed by being tricked. Even on this level they do not hate deception but rather the damaging, inimical consequences of certain species of deception. Truth, too, is only desired by human beings in a similarly limited sense. They desire the pleasant, life-preserving consequences of truth; they are indifferent to pure knowledge if it has no consequences, but they are actually hostile towards truths which may be harmful and destructive.

[56] Ibid., 146.
[57] GS, 110.

educated seeks to make every man unfree, inasmuch as it presents to him the smallest range of possibilities. The individual is treated by his educators as though, granted he is something new, what he ought to become is a *repetition*."[58] The critical pursuit of truth therefore requires a rejection of the powerful social pressure to conform.[59]

Nietzsche clearly holds that most of the "fettered spirits," "the herd," will be unable to resist this pressure. Their beliefs will be formed by habituation rather than rational reflection.[60] In *The Gay Science*, Nietzsche states the point in a more general way.[61] He says,

> I keep having the same experience and keep resisting it anew each time; I do not want to believe it although I can grasp it as with my hands: *the great majority lacks an intellectual conscience* . . . I mean: *to the great majority of people* it is not contemptible to believe this or that and to live accordingly *without* first becoming aware of the final and the most certain reasons pro and con, and without even troubling themselves about such reasons afterwards.[62]

Most people, he insists, will be averse to thinking through the rational justifications of their beliefs themselves.[63] And even in the absence of this aversion, most people would not have sufficient intellectual capabilities or self-discipline to accomplish it.[64]

[58] *HTH*, I, 228.

[59] Women, Nietzsche thinks, rightly avoid the affront to social mores that scientific knowledge would involve: "All proper women find something shameful about science. They think it is too forward, as if it would let people peek under their skin—or worse!—under their dress and finery." *BGE*, 127.

[60] Cf. *HTH*, I, 226: "The fettered spirit takes up his position, not for reasons, but out of habit; he is a Christian, for example, not because he has knowledge of the various religions and has chosen between them; he is an Englishman, not because he has decided in favour of England: he encountered Christianity and Englishness and adopted them without reasons, as a man born in wine-producing country becomes a wine drinker." Familiarity is seen to play an important role in the construction of "common sense." In *GS*, 355, Nietzsche writes: "*The origin of our concept of 'knowledge'* —I take this explanation from the street. I heard one of the common people say, 'he knew me right away' —and I asked myself: what is it that the people actually take knowledge to be? What do they want when they want 'knowledge'? Nothing more than this: that something unfamiliar is traced back to something more *familiar*."

[61] Cf., eg., *GS,* 21.

[62] Cf., e.g., Ibid., 2.

[63] Cf. Ibid., 293.

[64] Even such revision of belief as does take place, will, for most people, involve only the appearance of rational revision. Cf. Ibid., 307: "Something you formerly loved as a truth or a probability now strikes you as an error; you cast it off and believe your reason has made a victory. But maybe that error was as necessary for you then, when you were still another person—you are always another person—as are all your present 'truths,' like a skin that concealed and covered many things you weren't allowed to see yet. It is your new life, not your reason, that has killed an opinion for you: *you don't need it any more*."

Secular societies, as we have seen, are characterized by the conviction that reason is the only legitimate authority over belief. But people are eminently capable of satisfying themselves with merely apparent reasons. The desire for faith and the capacity for self-delusion that, on Nietzsche's view, we find on religious societies, are equally present in secular ones. In a further section, entitled "*Believers and their need to believe*," Nietzsche describes to us "that impetuous *demand for certainty* that today discharges itself among large numbers of people in a scientific-positivistic form," claiming that

> the demand that one *wants* by all means that something should be firm (while owing to the fervour of this demand one treats the demonstration of this certainty more lightly and more negligently): this is still the demand for foothold, support, in short, the *instinct of weakness* that, to be sure, does not create sundry religions, forms of metaphysics, and convictions but does—preserve them.[65]

In spite of his own conviction that he is overturning some of the most cherished beliefs of modern societies, Nietzsche retains a deep pessimism about the potential for popular enlightenment. This pessimism is rooted in the perception that expertise in many of its forms will simply not be recognized by those societies.

The Failure to Recognize Expertise

Nietzsche's concern about philosophical expertise seems most obviously to apply to the model of the philosopher as a critic of religion. It is not easy to expunge from our belief-system all our inherited religious prejudices. And since many of them are bound up with emotionally significant aspects of our worldview, their critical extirpation by philosophers is bound to meet with psychological resistance even amongst atheists.

But Nietzsche's work also retains something of the neo-Kantian model, on which philosophy polices the *Wissenschaften*. He criticizes both historical and natural scientific claims. His critique of philology, for example, does not derive simply from historical or scholarly insights, but derives from deeper questions about historical understanding, as evidenced by his famous "History" essay, from the *Untimely Meditations*, but also contemporaneous writings on "Wir Philologen." And his engagement with Darwinism plainly does not involve any simple appropriation of Darwinian claims, but rather a criticism and refinement of them.[66]

[65] Ibid., 347.
[66] John Richardson has brought out the sophistication of this critical project in *Nietzsche's New Darwinism*, esp. ch.1.

In each of these cases, Nietzsche's concerns about the recognition of expertise are limited (particularly, as we shall see, by contrast with the normative case, where even "experts" fail to agree), since he acknowledges at least that the insights of scientists and historians tend to become broadly accepted in society; hence their role in the destruction of popular religious belief.[67] But nevertheless, his critical approach to historical and natural *Wissenschaften* implies that many beliefs that are taken to be rationally justified are in fact merely pragmatically expedient errors. And criticism of these errors is bound to engender wariness of the "debaucheries of thought" that are repellent to "friends of 'healthy common sense.'"

The very idea of philosophical expertise being relevant to factual belief seems to go against the legal model of belief-regulation that Nietzsche sees as a pervasive feature of secular societies. This involves prejudice that the pursuit of knowledge involves the apprehension and application of simple rules. This prejudice then discourages people from demanding of themselves more complex forms of justification. The faith that is taken for truth is "everybody's faith." It is faith in "a 'world of truth' that can be grasped entirely with the help of our four-cornered little human reason."[68]

Nietzsche claims, in *Beyond Good and Evil*, that this inherently democratic prejudice has been adopted even by scientists and scholars:

> The scientific [*wissenschaftlich*] man's declaration of his independence, his emancipation from philosophy, is one of the more subtle effects of the democratic way of life (and death): the self-glorification and presumptuousness of scholars is in the full bloom of spring, flowering everywhere you look—which is not to say that this self-importance has a pleasant smell. "Away with all masters!"—that is what the rabble instinct wants, even here.[69]

The egalitarian hope of enlightenment is that the inherent lawfulness of *Wissenschaft* will permit the government of belief by law rather than by masters, or a clerisy.

According to Nietzsche the hope for this kind of self-governance is a mistaken one. But it nevertheless discourages intellectual deference. Far from establishing themselves as a secular clerisy, philosophers promulgate insights that sound "like follies and sometimes like crimes."[70]

---

[67] Cf. *GS*, 357: "One can see *what* it was that actually triumphed over the Christian god: Christian morality itself, the concept of truthfulness that was taken ever more rigorously; the father confessor's refinement of the Christian conscience, translated and sublimated into scientific conscience, into intellectual cleanliness at any price."

[68] Ibid., 373.

[69] *BGE*, 204.

[70] Ibid., 30.

In contravening common sense they commit themselves to being unpersuasive even where their propositions are true.

Belief in secular societies therefore seems to Nietzsche to be characterized by first, acceptance that reason is the only legitimate guide to belief; second, the valuing of rational autonomy, or the view that we must each make up our minds on the basis of our assessment of the relevant reasons; and third, a widespread failure to reflect adequately on our reasons for belief or to distinguish genuine epistemic reasons from merely apparent ones.

In this situation, it seems that although deference to authority is discouraged, there is a special vulnerability to ideological manipulation. The lack of genuine critical capacities makes people especially manipulable. Since the acquisition and preservation of beliefs is so deeply interwoven with pragmatic interests, it seems that surreptitious forms of manipulation will be available to those who have power in relation to these interests. The state, in particular, has an unparalleled degree of ideological power. And those philosophers who can liberate themselves from ideological control have no special capacity to manipulate belief and thereby to confer effective authority on reason.

CHAPTER 4

Nietzsche as a Moral Antirealist

INTRODUCTION

Nietzsche's political skepticism, I have argued, derives from the following set of arguments: stable political authority requires normative consensus; this consensus must be manufactured ideologically; and although Nietzsche wants to preserve political authority in some form, he cannot concede to the state this ideological power, for he wants to preserve evaluative freedom. His skepticism, then, can be seen to derive from a perceived conflict between the requirements of political authority and the requirements of normative authority.

The commitment to evaluative freedom implies what we have called a "transcendental" argument for limiting state power.[1] So long as the fundamental determinant of our values is held to be something other than the state's dicta, we cannot coherently cede total ideological control to the state. We must preserve whatever independent source of normative authority we recognize.

However, a broad range of views has been attributed to Nietzsche concerning what this evaluative independence should consist in. It is easy enough to make sense of on a moral realist view. It would consist in the free pursuit of normative truth. But in spite of the fact that his value-criticism often looks very much like a quest for normative truth, most of Nietzsche's meta-ethical suggestions have an antirealist character. He is therefore generally read as a consistent moral antirealist, where the claim about consistency has to involve a special explanation of the character of the value-criticism.

In this chapter I shall aim to set out the problems that arise for the antirealist in trying to make sense of Nietzsche's objection to political self-justification. If we want to make sense of his position, I shall argue, we have to see his antirealist tendencies as being in tension with it.

There are several possible models of evaluative independence the antirealist might adopt. As we shall see, some readers have emphasized the more deterministic elements of Nietzsche's moral thought, which stress the role of physiological and psychological factors in determining our values.

---

[1] Cf. introduction of this book.

Independence will then consist in a form of authenticity, which rules out some forms of constraint but not others. Others have emphasized the more constructivist elements that are seen to underlie his exhortation to create new values. The most plausible antirealist reading, it seems to me, will be one that can accommodate both elements.[2] But there is no antirealist reading that can render his concern for independence completely coherent.

If evaluative freedom or independence does not involve the discovery of truth, we cannot expect others to converge freely on the same norms. Nor do we have at our disposal any rational means of persuading them. Any convergence, unless it is just accidental, will have to be the result of some form of coercion. As an antirealist, Nietzsche can only coherently be recommending that he himself should have evaluative independence and that his own values should, if they are to be effective in societies, be coercively imposed on others.

As we saw in chapters 2 and 3, Nietzsche perceives that philosophers in fact possess no such effective authority. They do not have available to them any special means of rational or nonrational persuasion. So his hopes for revaluation, on this model, will already begin to look fantastical. But further trouble for this view arises from the fact that he seems to pin these hopes not simply on his own capacity for and freedom to engage in revaluation but on the capacities and freedom of others. But how could he grant others that freedom and the same time aim to coerce them into agreement with the results of his own revaluations?

It might be thought that this problem could be solved if just a few others were given license to generate their own norms and values, whilst everyone else is ideologically manipulated. And, after all, Nietzsche does not think that more than a few people will ever be capable of independent thought. But even the extension of evaluative independence to a few others will be problematic on the antirealist model.

In this chapter I will defend the view that we must take this model, on the antirealist reading, to assume the following form: free or independent valuers will be those who generate value judgments in a way that is self-conscious about any physiological and psychological determinants, that is uninhibited by ideology, and that is unconstrained by any need for rational justification.[3] The model raises the following problem. If I set out to generate a set of principles around which I think society ought to be organized, any form of organization I come up with will preclude the

---

[2] Though I shall argue in chapter 5 that only the realist reading of his value-criticism can in fact accommodate them both.

[3] This is the model defended by John Richardson, in *Nietzsche's New Darwinism*. As we shall see, it does make sense of important elements in Nietzsche's thought, though I shall claim that it is inconsistent with other elements.

possibility of organizing that society around the multiple other possible principles and values that other free value-creators might come up with. The implementation of my values would necessarily inhibit the capacity of other value-creators, however few or many them there were, to implement their own.

So the antirealist strain in his work, as we shall see, turns out to produce problems of coherence. These are most evident at the political level where the basic principles of political organization are at stake and where any of the principles chosen will require the instilling of a supporting ideology.

The antirealist reading thereby reveals an interesting set of questions about moral antirealism and politics. If the antirealist wants to sustain normative independence (even, as we shall see, for only a few) this will conflict with the political demand for normative convergence. In constituting a ruling ideology, we have to give up on preserving the evaluative independence of others. And this may not be something that the antirealist wants to give up.

Assessing Nietzsche's Meta-Ethics

So what motivations do we have for reading Nietzsche as an antirealist? For some readers the answer might seem obvious. His later writings contain a great deal of speculation about meta-ethical questions, much of which points us in an antirealist direction. We will examine it in detail below. But Nietzsche's value-criticism is complex, and there are several different features of it that we have to take into account in ascribing to him an overall view.

We can identify three forms of value-criticism in his work. First of all, he seeks to expose moral hypocrisy. He does so by asking descriptive questions about the extent to which we live up to our own values. This form of criticism becomes prominent in *Human, All Too Human,* where Nietzsche's cutting psychological observations are influenced by la Rochefoucauld.[4] He sets out to expose the existence of morally discreditable motives where purely moral motives are generally imputed. He tells us, for example, that seeking to evoke pity in others involves a malicious desire to hurt them, this being the only means that the weak can employ to exercise their power to harm.[5]

---

[4] Cf. *HTH*, I, 35.

[5] Ibid., 50. Maudemarie Clark and Brian Leiter point out that Nietzsche is trying to debunk the idea of unegoistic actions in such passages. They also attribute to him the Schopenhauerean view that moral actions cannot be egoistic and hence the view that there are no moral actions. Introduction to *Daybreak*, ed. Clark and Leiter (Cambridge: Cambridge University Press, 1997), xxii–xxiii.

Second, Nietzsche asks normative questions about whether the values we hold are the right values. In *Daybreak* he starts to go beyond the psychological criticism associated with la Rochefoucauld and embark on this project of normative assessment.[6] It culminates in his *On the Genealogy of Morality*, where he sets out to assess the value of morality. He tells us in his preface to this work that he not only aims to answer the descriptive question, "Under what conditions did man invent the value judgements good and evil?" but also the normative question, "What value do [these evaluations] themselves have?"[7]

Leiter and Clark point out that Nietzsche claims to have begun this project of evaluation in *Human, All Too Human*, but that it is really only in *Daybreak* that he explicitly addresses the question of the value of unegoistic actions and moves away from the earlier psychologism.[8] Certainly from this point on his primary concern seems to be with normative assessment of the moral worldview that has been formed by Christianity.[9]

Nietzsche attacks certain kinds of values. He judges them from the point of view of his own. He is not, then, rejecting values or even moral values per se. As Leiter points out, he employs the terms *Moral* and *Moralität* to refer to the values he affirms as well as those he criticizes.[10]

Whether we take Nietzsche to be assessing the objective correctness of value judgments, or merely expressing his own evaluative perspective on them, will depend on what we take the implicit meta-ethical assumptions motivating this form of value-criticism to be. And this is not a straightforward issue in Nietzsche interpretation, hence the plurality of views that we will have to survey in this chapter and the next.

Nietzsche's third form of value-criticism involves asking meta-ethical questions about the status of values. It is here that we find Nietzsche to be fairly eclectic in his views, considering different options at different times. But some of them are more compatible with his value-criticism than others, and we will assess them along these lines.

The reader who takes seriously Nietzsche's antirealist suggestions is confronted with the problem of assessing the extent to which these explicit remarks really describe his implicit assumptions in the second, normative form of value criticism described. Defenders of an overall antirealist reading of Nietzsche have to offer some explanation of the fact that his

---

[6] Though his descriptive claims concerning the origins of moral judgments, as he points out in the preface to the *Genealogy* (*GM*, Preface, 4), originate in *Human, All Too Human*.

[7] *GM*, Preface, 3.

[8] Clark and Lieter, "Introduction," *Daybreak*, xxiv–xv.

[9] Cf. *D*, 132.

[10] Leiter, *Nietzsche on Morality*, 74.

objectivist-sounding value judgments and his anti-objectivist meta-ethics seem prima facie to conflict.[11]

Different accounts of the antirealist meta-ethics will take different views of how this apparent conflict can be explained. Nietzsche's antirealist remarks point us in several different directions. As we shall see, in his arguments for antirealism, he seems to waver between an error theory, based on a cognitivist view of moral judgment, and a noncognitivist view of moral claims.

His later work, since it contains different suggestions about what valuing consists in, also contains different accounts of value-criticism and what it entails. The secondary literature, as we shall see, brings out two strains of thought concerning how we should go on valuing and how his reflective project can facilitate greater freedom in our modes of evaluation. One strain emphasizes evaluative freedom as a form of creativity. Nietzsche sees his project, and that of other "free spirits," as the "creation of values." This strain is particularly prominent, we shall see, in *Beyond Good and Evil*.

The other strain emphasizes his naturalistic analyses of the physiological and psychological determinants of our evaluative commitments. On this more deterministic view, valuing is not fundamentally amenable to conscious, reflective control. Moral reflection is a process of discovery, not creation, whereby we uncover the roots of our own values and free ourselves from "false consciousness" in relation to them. His genealogies aim at discovery of this kind. The independence that they confer might be seen to consist in a form of authenticity, allowing us to live according to our predetermined values.

I shall argue that the most compelling view of Nietzsche as a consistent antirealist will be one that can account for both of these strains in his work. It must account for the persistence in his value-criticism of both the theme of freedom as innovation and the theme of freedom as authenticity. Since the antirealism in all its forms seems to be motivated by Nietzsche's naturalism, this will provide a further interpretive constraint.

---

[11] As Brian Leiter puts it, "Nietzsche simply does not write like someone who thinks his evaluative judgments are merely his idiosyncratic preferences. . . . He takes sides with such force, such polemical ferocity, that it seems hard to think of Nietzsche as believing . . . that the evaluative judgments he thrusts on his readers reflect no objective fact of the matter, that they admit of no objective grounding for those who do not share what simply happens to be Nietzsche's idiosyncratic evaluative tastes." He goes on to say: "The difficulty is that there seems to be a substantial amount of Nietzschean rhetoric that cannot be reconciled with this metaethical view, and that cries out for some sort of realist construal." *Nietzsche on Morality*, 153. Cf. also Richardson, *Nietzsche's New Darwinism*, 68, and Nadeem Hussain, "Honest Illusion: Valuing for Nietzsche's Free Spirits," forthcoming in *Nietzsche and Morality*, edited by Brian Leiter and Neil Sinhababu (Oxford: Oxford University Press).

This means that we must first rule out an implicitly theistic and hence nonnaturalistic basis for antirealism that has been widely, if surprisingly, attributed to Nietzsche.

THEOCENTRISM

In assessing Nietzsche's relevance to political thought, some prominent commentators have taken his most alarming insight to consist in the view that moral relativism and nihilism necessarily result from the death of God. Leo Strauss, a pioneer of this view of Nietzsche, takes Nietzsche's purported relativistic insight to be "shown most simply by the true doctrine that God is dead."[12] Relativism consists, for Strauss, in the view that in the absence of theistic faith, "our ultimate principles have no other support than our arbitrary and hence blind preference for them."[13] Assuming that we have no reason to prefer one thing to another, he sees this relativistic insight as debilitating and nihilistic; all we have by way of evaluative capacities is choice, and we have no basis for making choices. The rejection of faith in objective values is, he thinks, "identical with nihilism."[14] Strauss also claims that Nietzsche's atheism "is not unambiguous, for he has doubts whether there can be a world, any world whose center is not God," and that his work might be read as a "vindication of God, if a decidedly nontheistic vindication of God."[15]

The view of Nietzsche is echoed by Bruce Detwiler, who insists that "the death of God means more than the demise of all absolutes and all ultimate sources of authority; it means the demise even of our faith in the possibility of absolutes."[16] He similarly connects atheism to a "devaluation

---

[12] Cf. Leo Strauss, *Studies in Platonic Political Philosophy*, ed. Thomas Pangle (Chicago, University of Chicago Press, 1983), 176–77:

> If we may make a somewhat free use of an expression occurring in Nietzsche's *Second Meditation out of Season*, the truth is not attractive, lovable, life-giving, but deadly, as is shown by the true doctrines of sovereign Becoming, of the fluidity of all concepts, types, and species, and of the lack of any cardinal difference between man and beast (*Werke*, ed Schlechta, 1:272); it is shown most simply by the true doctrine that God is dead. The world in itself, the "thing-in-itself," "nature" (aph.9) is wholly chaotic and meaningless. Hence all meaning, all order originates in man, in man's creative acts, in his will to power.

On Strauss's indebtedness to Nietzsche, cf. Laurence Lampert, *Leo Strauss and Nietzsche* (Chicago: University of Chicago Press, 1996).

[13] Strauss, *Natural Right and History* (1950; Chicago: University of Chicago Press, 1965), 4.

[14] Ibid., 5.

[15] Ibid., 181.

[16] Bruce Detwiler, *Nietzsche and the Politics of Aristocratic Radicalism*, 69.

of all values"[17] and to nihilism.[18] It is not just moral value, or a corrupt, ascetic subset of moral values, that are implicated.[19] According to this radical thesis all forms of value are delegitimated by the death of God.[20]

It already looks as though such a view will be too radical, if it disallows any values at all. It will not be able to make sense of Nietzsche's value-criticism, since he is clearly criticizing some values in the name of others. But there is a deeper reason that it is unlikely he could have held such a view.

I have described the view as implicitly theistic because it seems to rely on the claim that the only sound justification for our values is a theistic one. As Ronald Dworkin has pointed out, if atheism is seen to delegitimate all values, this counterfactual has to be presupposed.[21] This would be a strange assumption for an atheist to make. It also seems to lead to incoherence. Once we assume the nonexistence of God, we are caught in a self-undermining argument. To say that no values are legitimate is in itself to make a normative claim, so we are making a normative claim that denies the validity of any normative claims. The atheist, then, cannot coherently endorse the claim that the only basis for legitimate normative claims is a theistic one.

If it seems odd that such a view should have been attributed to Nietzsche, it is interesting to note that the origins of this approach to Nietzsche can be traced back to Karl Löwith, who was in fact explicitly trying to vindicate a theistic view by showing that we have to choose between theism and nihilism.[22] He tells us that "Nietzsche foresaw the

---

[17] Ibid., 70.

[18] Ibid., 69.

[19] Brian Leiter, by contrast, distinguishes between the moral values that motivate Nietzsche's own normative critique and "morality in the pejorative sense," or the form of morality (arising from *ressentiment*) that Nietzsche condemns. *Nietzsche on Morality*, 74–75.

[20] In assessing the political significance of this apparently momentous event, Detwiler claims, with Strauss, that it calls the whole tradition of political theory that began with Plato into question. *Nietzsche and the Politics of Aristocratic Radicalism*, 84.

[21] Ronald Dworkin, "Objectivity and Truth: You'd Better Believe It," *Philosophy and Public Affairs* 25, no.2 (spring 1996): 87–139, at 91.

[22] Strauss himself engaged in a well-known correspondence with Löwith about Nietzsche. Cf. "Correspondence of Karl Löwith with Leo Strauss," trans. George Elliott Tucker, *Independent Journal of Philosophy/Unabhängige Zeitschrift für Philosophie* 5, no. 5 (1988): 177–92. There are clear similarities in their accounts of Nietzsche, particularly in the way in which they both trace a trajectory of secularization from Hegel to Nietzsche. Strauss claims that "Nietzsche is *the* philosopher of relativism," and he defends this view by offering the same narrative as Löwith, claiming that "relativism came to Nietzsche's attention in the form of historicism—more precisely, in the form of a decayed Hegelianism." Through Hegel, he claims, Christianity "had become completely secularized, or the *saeculum* had

future appearance of that 'European nihilism' which declares that after the downfall of the Christian belief in God, and thus also of morality, 'nothing is true,' but 'everything is permitted.'"[23] He further contends that "Nietzsche's actual thought is a thought system, at the beginning of which stands the death of God, in its midst the ensuing nihilism, and at its end the self-surmounting of nihilism in eternal recurrence."[24] Through the doctrine of eternal recurrence, on this account, Nietzsche is attempting to deify our earthly life once more.[25]

Nietzsche's work is seen as precisely the nihilistic counterpart of Christian faith.[26] On Löwith's view, Nietzsche implicitly endorses the Christian account of what conditions would have to hold for moral values to be valid, but first of all denies that these conditions do in fact hold, then embarks on a failed attempt to reconstruct them.[27] Löwith himself denies that such reconstruction is necessary, since Christian faith has not and cannot be refuted.[28]

---

become completely Christian." Nietzsche is then seen to demonstrate the irreconcilability of secular history and Christian theology—that history reveals to us the relativity of all beliefs and values, necessitating the re-creation of myth. Cf. "Relativism" in *The Rebirth of Classical Political Rationalism* (Chicago: University of Chicago Press, 1989), 24–25. Compare Karl Löwith, *From Hegel to Nietzsche*, trans. David E. Green (New York: Holt, Rinehart and Winston, 1964). Peter Berkowitz notes the underlying similarity of Strauss and Löwith's views. Cf. *Nietzsche: The Ethics of an Immoralist* (Cambridge, Mass.: Harvard University Press, 1995), 276n8. Berkowitz himself sees Nietzsche's work (as Strauss does) as a "vindication of God" and although his account seems broadly Straussian (bearing striking similarities, in argument and vocabulary, to Strauss's "Preface to Spinoza's Critique of Religion"), Löwith is clearly also an influence. Cf. Berkowitz, *Nietzsche*, 289n1, 290n6, 293n12, 296n5, 299n20.

[23] Löwith, *From Hegel to Nietzsche*, 189.

[24] Ibid., 193.

[25] Cf. Löwith's review of *What Nietzsche Means*, by George Allen Morgan, *Philosophy and Phenomenological Research* 2, no. 2 (December 1941): 240–242: "To integrate eternity in time, identifying 'Werden' with 'Sein,' is the pinnacle of Nietzsche's speculation and therefore has to be also the starting-point for any fundamental criticism of his Dionysian deification of our earthly life."

[26] Ibid., 373.

[27] Michael Allen Gillespie expresses a similar view in his *Nihilism before Nietzsche* (Chicago: University of Chicago Press, 1995). Cf, e.g., xxi, where he tells us that Nietzsche's "Dionysian will to power" is "not an alternative to the Christian God but only his final and in a sense greatest modern mask."

[28] Löwith, *Meaning in History* (1949; Chicago: University of Chicago Press, 1970) v–vi:

Nietzsche was right when he said that to look upon nature as if it were a proof of the goodness and care of God and to interpret history as a constant testimony to a moral order and purpose—that all this is now past because it has conscience against it. But he was wrong in assuming that the pseudo-religious makeup of nature and history is of any real consequence to a genuine Christian faith in God, as revealed in Christ and hidden in nature and history.

If, like Löwith, we take Nietzsche to be trying to accommodate atheism from within the parameters of a basically Christian worldview his thought will turn out to be fundamentally incoherent. But the conclusion (drawn also by Strauss and Berkowitz) that Nietzsche's work is a "vindication of God" seems to have been illicitly built into the premises on this interpretation of his project.

Perhaps a less controversial formulation of the "death of God" antirealist thesis can be found, though, if we express it in the form of an error theory. If we take moral claims to express factual propositions, we might take the view that the truth-conditions for such propositions would have to include facts about God's will. This would be the case if semantic analysis showed that all moral claims implicitly refer to God's will. Atheism would then entail the view that they are all false.

Nietzsche does tell us that the moral beliefs of Christians can have this form. To them, the value judgment "x is right" means simply "God wills x" and it will be true if and only if God does actually will x. In *Twilight of the Idols*, Nietzsche points out that "Christianity presupposes that man does not know, *cannot* know, what is good for him, what evil: he believes in God, who alone knows it. Christian morality is a command; its origin is transcendent; it is beyond all criticism, all right to criticism; it has truth only if God is the truth—it stands or falls with faith in God."[29] These kinds of moral beliefs must certainly be held to be in error if atheism is true. But does Nietzsche think that all values, even all moral values, even just all the moral values of Christians, must take this form?

In the book where he announces the death of God, *The Gay Science*, he does tell us that few people have as yet realized what has happened, and "much less may one suppose that many people know as yet *what* this event really means—and how much must collapse now that this faith has been undermined because it was built upon this faith, propped up by it, grown into it; for example, the whole of our European morality."[30] But it seems natural to read this not as a global skepticism about value, or even specifically moral value, but rather a culturally specific comment about

---

More intelligent than the superior vision of philosophers and theologians is the common sense of the natural man and the uncommon sense of the Christian believer. Neither pretends to discern on the canvas of human history the purpose of God or of the historical process itself. They rather seek to set men free from the world's oppressive history by suggesting an attitude, either of skepticism or faith, which is rooted in an experience certainly nurtured by history but detached from and surpassing it, and thus enabling man to endure it with mature resignation or with faithful expectation.

[29] TI, "Skirmishes of an Untimely Man," 5.
[30] GS, 343.

the Europeans, whose value judgments have been in error owing to their religious heritage.

Even within the Christian worldview that Nietzsche thinks is collapsing, it is not clear that moral claims depend directly on theological claims. In his preface to the *Genealogy*, Nietzsche tells us that at a young age he learned "to separate theological from moral prejudice." In that work he does make clear that belief in God has played an important role in the development of the form of morality he is criticizing. He tells us that

> the advent of the Christian God as the maximal God yet achieved, . . . brought about the appearance of the greatest feeling of guilt on earth. Assuming that we have now started in the *reverse* direction, we should be justified in deducing, with no little probability, that from the unstoppable decline in faith in the Christian God there is, even now, a considerable decline in the consciousness of human guilt. . . . Atheism and a sort of *second innocence* belong together.[31]

But theistic belief and morality are here seen to be related as part of a complex psychological structure and feelings of moral guilt are clearly expected to outlive, for some time, belief in God.[32] That state of affairs, the persistence of Christian morality after the demise of belief in the Christian God, is in fact what necessitates his critique in the first place. So even Nietzsche's critique of narrowly Christian morality seems to be independent of his rejection of theism.

If Nietzsche did want to make the strong semantic claim that all value judgments implicitly invoke God, most of this critique of morality would look pretty redundant. He would have to do no more than expose the implicit reliance on theism and then state that "God is dead" in order to debunk any value. And if his critique were intended to debunk all forms of value, rather than some subset of moral values, his normative value-criticism would look hopelessly self-contradictory. It would involve a reliance on standards that are implicated by its own critique.

The argument from atheism, then, seems to attributed to Nietzsche either an implausible substantive claim about theism as the sole valid justification for values, or an implausible semantic claim about the implicit theistic content of value judgments. In addition, it fails to do justice to the rich array of arguments that he does actually deploy in support of his antirealist views. Recent work on Nietzsche's antirealism has explored this array of arguments in more depth. Attention has been focused, in particular, on Nietzsche's naturalism as a basis for his meta-ethical views.

[31] *GM*, ii, 20.
[32] Cf. Ibid., 27.

And it seems plausible to suggest that instead of his antirealism being motivated by his atheism, both the antirealism and the atheism can be seen to be motivated by his naturalism.

FICTIONALISM

As we saw in chapter 4, empiricism and naturalism become central orientations in Nietzsche's work from *Human, All Too Human* on. This development clearly influences his approach to meta-ethics, as he tries to comprehend how it is that natural, merely human creatures might be subject to moral norms.[33] He aims to "translate man back into nature."[34] His naturalistic analysis of values incorporates diverse suggestions about what is going on when we accept moral norms. These in turn yield diverse suggestions about whether we can still end up having moral values at the end of a reductive analysis of them. The range of views about these issues in the secondary literature seems to me to reflect a real eclecticism in Nietzsche's texts.

However, we do have to rule out some moves that Nietzsche is not making. He does not take a direct route to relativism via some false inferences from empirical claims about our evaluative practices. He does not, for example, hold that diversity implies relativism. In *The Gay Science*, he criticizes the historians of morality who "see the truth that among different peoples moral valuations are *necessarily* different and then infer from this that *no* morality is binding."[35]

---

[33] This naturalistic impetus in Nietzsche's thought has recently been emphasized by Maudemarie Clark, "On Knowledge, Truth, and Value"; Brian Leiter, esp. *Nietzsche on Morality*, and "The Paradox of Self-Creation and Fatalism in Nietzsche, in *Nietzsche*, ed. Leiter and Richardson (Oxford: Oxford University Press, 2001); Bernard Williams, *Making Sense of Humanity* (Cambridge: Cambridge University Press, 1995), and *Shame and Necessity*; and John Richardson, *Nietzsche's New Darwinism*. Leiter sees Nietzsche primarily as a methodological naturalist, where this implies that philosophical inquiry "should be continuous with empirical inquiry in the sciences." Limited substantive naturalism, or an incorporation of the results of the natural sciences, is also evident in his work, but only insofar as he rejects supernaturalism. Cf. *Nietzsche on Morality*, 6–11. Williams, concerned not to fall into a hopeless physicalistic reductionism, claims that the interest of Nietzsche's naturalism lies in his demand for moral psychological minimalism, which in answer to the question "How much should our accounts of distinctively moral activity add to our accounts of other human activity," replies, "As little as possible." It especially casts suspicion on materials such as the will that are invoked especially to "serve the purposes of morality" ("Nietzsche's Minimalist Moral Psychology," *Making Sense of Humanity and Other Philosophical Papers* [Cambridge: Cambridge University Press, 1995], 65–79).

[34] *BGE*, 230.

[35] *GS*, 345.

Neither does he falsely infer conclusions about the status of value judgments from accounts of their origins. He explicitly warns us against the genetic fallacy.[36] He criticizes historians of morality who fall prey to this:

> The mistake of the more subtle among them is that they uncover and criticize the possibly foolish opinions of a people about their morality, or of humanity about all human morality—opinions about its origin, its religious sanction, the myth of free will and such things—and then think they have criticized the morality itself. . . . A morality could even have grown *out of* an error, and the realization of this fact would not as much as touch the problem of its value.[37]

This is quite an important warning, since one of Nietzsche's primary descriptive concerns is with the origins of moral judgments and his descriptive claims clearly play an important role in his value-criticism.[38]

However, there are certainly other arguments deriving from his naturalism that he does take to support moral antirealism. Amongst them is the view that morality is essentially propositional and that moral claims, like religious claims, can only be true by virtue of correspondence to some nonnatural facts. It looks as though this is what Nietzsche is saying in *Twilight of the Idols*, when he writes:

> *There are absolutely no moral facts.* What moral and religious judgements have in common is belief in things that are not real. . . . Moral

---

[36] Brian Leiter has noted that Nietzsche's identification of the genetic fallacy here must warn us against simplistic readings of the *Genealogy* that would read this error into his account of the origins of ascetic morality. Cf. *Nietzsche on Morality*, 173–74.

[37] *GS*, 345.

[38] I will say more about what I take that role to be in chapter 5. Many recent commentators have defended Nietzsche's claims about the genesis of values as having some force that does not involve the genetic fallacy. The critical force of the claim that moral values originate in *ressentiment*, for example, has been construed in several different ways. It has been seen as part of an internal critique of moral judgments. Cf., e.g., Walter Kaufmann, *Nietzsche: Philosopher, Psychologist, Antichrist*, 113. Brian Leiter criticizes this view, claiming that Nietzsche's concern is to free "higher types" from the constraints of morality in the pejorative sense. On this view the account of the origins of these value judgments is inessential to the critique of them but nevertheless "has a special *evidential* status as to the *effects* (or causal powers) of that morality, for example, as to whether morality obstructs or promotes human flourishing." Cf. *Nietzsche on Morality*, 177. Bernard Reginster has argued that Nietzsche's analysis of *ressentiment* is not intended to constitute a critique of values that this psychological phenomenon supports, but rather identifies a psychological problem on the part of the agent who has this motivation (specifically deriving from a form of self-deception and hence a loss of the integrity of the self). Cf. "Nietzsche on Ressentiment and Valuation," *Philosophy and Phenomenological Research* 57, no.2 (June 1997): 281–305.

judgements, like religious ones, presuppose a level of ignorance in which even the concept of reality is missing and there is no distinction between the real and the imaginary; a level where "truth" is the name for the very things that we now call "imaginings" [*Einbildungen*].[39]

Nadeem Hussain takes this passage to be an instance of a more general error theory about value. He states the overall view in the following form: "Nothing has value in itself and therefore all claims of the form '*X* is valuable' are false."[40] The passage from *Twilight* is taken to be an application of this view to narrowly moral values.

Hussain finds support for his generalized error theory view in passages such as the following remark from *The Gay Science*:

Whatever has *value* in the present world has it not in itself, according to its nature—nature is always value-less—but has rather been given, granted value, and *we* were the givers and granters![41]

He takes such passages to imply an error theory, rather than either a noncognitivist account of morality, or a subjective realist view, on which the truth-conditions of moral claims would refer to some subjective states of an agent. He does so on the grounds that Nietzsche also insists that value judgments involve an "intellectual loss."[42] This loss is to be accounted for by the fact that when we value we take things to be valuable in themselves, when in fact they are not.

This kind of error theory, then, can be seen to be rooted in Nietzsche's naturalism insofar as it presupposes a metaphysical claim about the nonexistence of the kinds of nonnatural properties on which goodness would have to supervene. Of course, there are contemporary moral realists who would deny that realism requires this apparatus of nonnatural properties.[43] But Nietzsche could scarcely have been expected to formulate

---

[39] *TI*, " 'Improving' Humanity," 1. I have followed Hussain in translating *Einbildungen* as "imaginings" (rather than "illusion," as Judith Norman has it), since this captures the active and voluntaristic element that *Einbildung* incorporates, distinguishing it from the terms *Illusion* and *Wahn* that he frequently uses.

[40] Hussain, "Honest Illusion."

[41] *GS*, 301. Hussain also cites *HTH*, I, 4; *D*, 3; *GS*, 115; *BGE*, Preface, 107; *TSZ*, 1: "On the thousand and one goals," 1: "On the Afterworldly," *WP*, 428.

[42] He cites *HTH*, I, Preface, 6.

[43] Cf., e.g., Ronald Dworkin, "Objectivity and Truth"; Geoffrey Sayre-McCord, "Introduction: The Many Moral Realisms," in *Essays on Moral Realism*, ed. Geoffrey Sayre-McCord (Ithaca: Cornell University Press, 1988); Richard Boyd, "How to Be a Moral Realist," (105–36) and Peter Railton, "Moral Realism," (137–66) in *Moral Discourse and Practice: Some Philosophical Approaches*, ed. Stephen Darwall, Allan Gibbard, and Peter Railton (New York: Oxford University Press, 1997).

these very recent arguments, so it is perfectly reasonable to assume that he construed realism in a metaphysically richer way, and one that seemed to him to be rendered implausible by naturalism.

The trouble with such an error theory is that it presents Nietzsche with some pretty tricky problems in explaining how it is that he goes on valuing himself. Any interpreter who takes this to be Nietzsche's basic meta-ethical view will have to find somewhere in his work the resources to provide such an explanation. Hussain finds the solution in Nietzsche's notion of value-creation.

The project of "creating new values" is suggested in several places in Nietzsche's work, but repeatedly in *Beyond Good and Evil*.[44] Of course, the error theorist will need a special construal of these passages, since if value can only mean intrinsic value, and this is a nonexistent, nonnatural property, philosophers cannot very well be expected to create it. Nietzsche does not specify what exactly is supposed to be "created," so we can only infer this in the broader context of views that we are attributing to him. It would not make sense, on this antirealist view, to suppose that objectively existing values are being created. But the idea of value-creation can be made comprehensible if we suppose that it is value judgments that we can create. On the cognitivist view, this means that we must invent propositional claims about intrinsic value.

Since Nietzsche uses a constructivist vocabulary in describing previous valuations by philosophers, it might seem natural to interpret his own project as being analogous. In *The Gay Science*, he claims that "it is we, the thinking-sensing ones, who really and continually *make* something that is not yet there: the whole perpetually growing world of valuations, colours, weights, perspectives, scales, affirmations, and negations."[45] On this fictionalist construal, valuing does not simply involve projecting our given and unalterable affects onto the world, but rather generating ways of valuing through some intentional human activity.[46]

The intended object of that activity has not previously been value-creation. The generation of ways of valuing has formerly been a by-product of the illusory quest for normative truth. Nietzsche, however, has had (on this reading) the insight that all value judgments are in fact false, so he will not be able to do something precisely analogous. We cannot

[44] Cf., e.g., *TSZ*, 1, "On the three metamorphoses," *GS*, 335; *BGE*, 203, 211, 260.
[45] *GS*, 301, 242; *KGW* V-2.220.
[46] Bernard Reginster sees both strands in Nietzsche. He maintains that "on some occasions [Nietzsche] suggests that . . . evaluative projection is guided by our affects. . . . On other occasions, Nietzsche considers a different model, according to which our evaluative projections are no longer guided by our affects, but are full-fledged creations that in fact shape them." Cf. *The Affirmation of Life: Nietzsche on Overcoming Nihilism* (Cambridge, Mass.: Harvard University Press, 2006), 87.

knowingly believe falsities.[47] According to Hussain's reading, what we can do is create a "fictionalist simulacrum of valuing."[48]

On Hussain's view, Nietzsche sees that fiction allows us to participate in an illusory or imaginary reality while at the same time acknowledging it to be such. Hussain suggests that we can construe this on Kendall Walton's conception of make-believe.[49] Art and imaginative play, on this view, "show us the psychological possibility of regarding things as valuable when we know that they are not." Art can provide us with a source of techniques for simulating valuing.

If we engage in this kind of make-believe about values, our value judgments can take the following fictionalist form: "S values X by regarding X as valuable in itself while knowing that X is not in fact valuable in itself."[50] If this reading is right, in exhorting philosophers to participate in the creation of new values, Nietzsche would be asking them to create fictions of a certain sort, that is, to invent new judgments of value and to behave as if they were true, while knowing them not to be.

Hussain takes Nietzsche's suggestions about our need for art to support this reading. Art can be employed to generate knowingly an illusory view of the world. Many of the important passages occur in *The Gay Science*, where Nietzsche writes, for example:

> What means do we have for making things beautiful, attractive, and desirable when they are not? And in themselves I think they never are! Here we have something to learn from physicians, when for example they dilute something bitter or add wine and sugar to the mixing bowl; but even more from artists, who are really constantly out to invent new artistic *tours de force* of this kind. To distance oneself from things until there is much in them that one no longer sees and much that the eye must add *in order to see them at all*, or to see things around a corner and as if they were cut out and extracted from their context, or to place them so that each partially distorts the view one has of the others and allows only perspectival glimpses, or to look at them through rose coloured glass or in the light of the sunset, or to give them a surface and skin that is not fully transparent; all this we should learn from artists while otherwise being wiser than they. For usually in their case this delicate power stops where art ends and life begins; *we*, however,

---

[47] Nietzsche makes this point with his usual hyperbole in *HTH*, I, 34: "A question seems to lie heavily on our tongue and yet refuses to be uttered: whether one *could* consciously reside in untruth? or, if one were *obliged* to, whether death would not be preferable?"

[48] Hussain, "Honest Illusion."

[49] cf. Kendall Walton, *Mimesis as Make-Believe: On the Foundations of the Representational Arts* (Cambridge: Harvard University Press, 1990).

[50] Hussain, "Honest Illusion."

want to be poets of our lives, starting with the smallest and most commonplace details.[51]

The trouble is that in most of these later passages, Nietzsche is talking about how we can perceive the world in such a way that it would seem valuable to us, where the norms for what would be valuable are already presupposed. Art can beautify the world. But this project of beautification takes for granted existing norms for the way the world ought to be.[52]

It is, of course, conceivable that Nietzsche also intends philosophers to construct these underlying norms. And if we are only engaging in a simulacrum of valuing, we might expect this to be a fairly unconstrained creative process. It might not be the case that we can make-believe just anything, since we may be subject to psychological limitations and coherence constraints. But the exhortation to create new judgments of value seems to suggest that this process can, in the light of our insight into the fictional character of all value judgments, be subject to the will.[53]

But when Nietzsche engages in revaluation himself it is not at all clear that the process he undertakes is subject to the will in the way that he himself suggests in his fictionalist-sounding passages.[54] Even his aesthetic judgments seem to impose themselves on him with the force of necessity.[55] It is in spite of himself that he loves Wagner's ability to draw "from the very bottom of human happiness—as it were, from its drained cup, where the bitterest and the most repulsive drops have merged in the end, for better or for worse, with the sweetest.[56] And in the *Genealogy*, he says of philosophers: "Our ideas, our values, our yeas and nays, our ifs and buts, grow out of us with the necessity with which a tree bears fruit."[57] This phenomenon has been analyzed by Harry Frankfurt: although modern individuals value the freedom to choose their

---

[51] *GS*, 299. Hussain also cites *GS*, Preface, 4; *GS*, 107; *GS*, 301; *TI*, "Skirmishes," 24.

[52] Cf. also *GS*, Preface, 4; *GS*, 107.

[53] Bernard Reginster describes the process in terms of "imagining in a belief-like way," and claims that such imagining can (for example, in the case of the make-believe that children engage in) generate real emotions and induce motivation. Cf. Reginster, *The Affirmation of Life*, 93.

[54] Nietzsche's question about the value of truth (*BGE*, 1) implies that we cannot simply accommodate our values to whatever beliefs we hold true.

[55] In *Beyond Good and Evil*, he claims that this is generally true of artists. Cf. *BGE*, 213.

[56] *GS*, 87. This sense that our aesthetic judgments are not subject to the will is reinforced in several places; he implies that they rely on sensibilities that are beyond conscious control. For example, in *BGE*, 245, he says of Mozart: "How fortunate *we* are that his rococo still speaks to us," and he laments the fact that this capacity is destined to disappear. And in *The Case of Wagner*, Preface, he writes: "I understand perfectly when a musician says today 'I hate Wagner, but I can no longer endure any other music.'"

[57] *GM*, Preface, 2.

own ideals, the very espousal of ideals seems to involve a submission to necessity.[58]

While we can imagine formulating any number of value judgments of the form "*X* is valuable in itself," it is harder to imagine how we could really adopt them at will, so that they would guide our behavior in the way that values ordinarily do. For this would require us to care about them. And as Frankfurt points out, we can only care about what we believe is worthy to be cared about.

Robert Pippin has examined the psychological complexity of Nietzsche's account of what it is for us to "love our ideals." He does so by analogy with romantic attachments, telling us that although such attachments are not the result of a reflective process of normative evaluation, we nevertheless think of them "as expressive, revelations of the more important and worthy aspects of ourselves—and so as also partly evaluative, at least in this expressive sense."[59] Who and what we love, in other words, is constrained at some deep psychological level by what we take to be valuable in ourselves and others.

There are, no doubt, a few situations in which love can trump any considerations of moral worthiness, for example, with regard to one's children.[60] But in many aspects of our lives (our friendships, our political allegiances, our artistic preferences) our patterns of caring are deeply entwined with our normative judgments. It is hard to imagine how we could have pretense all the way down.

It is difficult to imagine, then, that Nietzsche believes that all his own values are simply "fictionalist simulacra" and that his emphasis on authenticity and integrity refers ultimately to values that are held only through make-believe.[61] As John Richardson puts it, if this were the case,

[58] Cf. Harry G. Frankfurt, "On the Necessity of Ideals," in *Necessity, Volition, and Love* (Cambridge: Cambridge University Press, 1999), 108–16.

[59] Robert Pippin, "Morality as Psychology, Psychology as Morality: Nietzsche, Eros, and Clumsy Lovers," in *Nietzsche's Postmoralism: Essays on Nietzsche's Prelude to a Philosophy's Future*, ed. Richard Schacht (Cambridge: Cambridge University Press, 2001), 79–99, at 86.

[60] I am grateful to Lanier Anderson for suggesting this.

[61] This would seem to come close to the kind of self-conscious, ironic culture that Nietzsche denounces in *UM*, ii, 5:

The oversaturation of an age with history seems to me to be hostile and dangerous to life in five respects: such an excess creates that contrast between inner and outer which we have just discussed, and thereby weakens the personality; it leads an age to imagine that it possesses the rarest of virtues, justice, to a greater degree than any other age; it disrupts the instincts of a people, and hinders the individual no less than the whole in the attainment of maturity; it implants the belief, harmful at any time, in the old age of mankind, the belief that one is a latecomer and epigone; it leads an age into a dangerous mood of irony in regard to itself and subsequently into the even more dangerous mood "we would need to hear scare quotes" in all Nietzsche's value judgments.[62] It is hard to read his condemnation of Christian values, or even of *Parsifal*, in this way. So although there are passages where Nietzsche sounds like a fictionalist, they do not seem to be the ones where he is expressing his best judgment about his own normative project. And, as we shall see, the set of issues raised here concerning freedom and necessity turn out to be the trickiest to deal with on any antirealist reading.

DETERMINISM

Nietzsche's naturalism leads him to repudiate any view of valuing that involves correspondence to nonnatural properties. But it also provokes him to attempt to supply a naturalistic account of the way in which evaluative judgments are motivated. He is particularly concerned to uncover the prereflective or unconscious determinants of our values, in phenomena such as desires, interests, and instincts. Some have taken this to imply a noncognitive view of moral judgments, though it is consistent with a cognitive view, and Nietzsche does not seem to take a consistent line on that issue.

Maudemarie Clark finds in his mature work a noncognitivist strain that is basically Humean. And there are certainly passages where Nietzsche employs the Humean analogy with color in describing a projectivist view of evaluation.[63] He also sometimes seems to view this projection in emotivist terms, saying, "moralities are also merely a *sign language of the affects*."[64] Clark suggests that this Humean tendency stems from the empiricism that Nietzsche espouses after his repudiation of Schopenhauerean metaphysics. Stripping the "Will" of its poetic, metaphorical aspects, she argues, reduces it to a naturalized description of the noncognitive aspects of

---

of cynicism: in this mood, however, it develops more and more a prudent practical egoism through which the forces of life are paralyzed and at last destroyed.

Authenticity (*Ächtheit*) is an important theme in the *Untimely Meditations*. Cf., e.g., UM, i, 1, on "authentic German culture" (*ächte deutsche Bildung*) as opposed to mere "cultivatedness" (*Gebildetheit*); and UM, i, 2, on the authentic man of culture (*ächter Kulturmensch*) as contrasted with the "cultural philistine" (*Bildungsphilister*). Nietzsche laments the loss of genuine culture because it erodes the preconditions for the authentic self: UM, ii, 4; and UM, iii, 1. We might see this preoccupation as being continuous with his later concern with integrity, as stressed by Bernard Reginster in "Nietzsche on Ressentiment and Valuation."

[62] Richardson, *Nietzsche's New Darwinism*, 127.

[63] *GS*, 301, 242; *KGW* V-2.220.

[64] *BGE*, 187.

human life. The cognitive side of human beings then comes to be seen as "an instrument of the affective side" and antirealism naturally seems to follow from this view.[65]

Leiter also finds continuity with Hume in Nietzsche's naturalism.[66] He claims that "Nietzsche's central argument for anti-realism about value is *explanatory*: moral facts don't figure in the 'best explanation' of experience, and so are not real constituents of the objective world."[67] Leiter eschews the distinction between cognitive and noncognitive views as a means of classifying Nietzsche's meta-ethics, on the grounds that the semantic issue is not a focused concern of Nietzsche's and he has no stable view about it.[68] But he attributes to Nietzsche the view that we can explain the different value judgments that people make with reference to physiological and psychological type-facts about the agent.[69]

John Richardson also brings out Nietzsche's emphasis on the non-rational determinants of value judgments and particularly his neo-Darwinist, evolutionary explanation of them. Richardson claims that valuing, for Nietzsche, is the product of natural and social selection, which has instilled in us various drives. "A person's overall valuing," Richardson says, "is the synthetic product of these drives. And a person's explicit or conscious values are an indirect expression of those valuings in drives."[70]

Each of these interpretations tries to make sense of Nietzsche's concern with moral psychology and the causal determinants of our values. This is a prominent theme in his naturalistic project. There are passages where Nietzsche unambiguously expresses a biologistic view of these determinants, for example in *Daybreak*, where he says that our "moral judgements and valuations are only images and fantasies upon a physiological process unknown to us."[71] Much of his analysis in the "Natural History of Morals" in *Beyond Good and Evil* bears out this preoccupation. His often overlooked concern about the mixing of races as a source of moral

---

[65] Maudemarie Clark, "On Knowledge, Truth, and Value: Nietzsche's Debt to Schopenhauer and the Development of his Empiricism," in *Willing and Nothingness*, 60.

[66] *Nietzsche on Morality*, 4–5.

[67] Ibid., 148.

[68] Leiter claims that although Nietzsche asks the metaphysical question, "Is there any fact of the matter about ethical issues?" he does not ask the semantic questions about the meaning of moral language that lies behind this distinction between cognitive and noncognitive views of morality. Cf. "Nietzsche's Metaethics: Against the Privilege Readings," *European Journal of Philosophy* 8 no. 3 (2000): 277–97, at 278.

[69] Ibid.,148.

[70] Richardson, *Nietzsche's New Darwinsim*, 74. On these views of valuing as a drive toward some end or goal, even animals are capable of valuing, Richardson claims (73).

[71] D, 119; cited by Richardson, ibid., 74n.

decadence derives from this preoccupation with biological determinism.[72] And at the end of the first essay of his *Genealogy*, he writes:

> Every table of values, every "thou shalt" known to history or ethnology, needs first and foremost a *physiological* elucidation and interpretation, rather than a psychological one; and all of them await critical study by medical science.[73]

Neither Leiter nor Richardson takes these biological phenomena to be, for Nietzsche, the sole determinants of valuations. But they take them to indicate the kind of explanation of valuations that Nietzsche thinks we need, that is, one on which we are not ultimately moved by reasons.

If we take Nietzsche to presuppose antirealism, then he must hold that we cannot be genuinely moved by reasons, as opposed to being subject to the mere illusion of a justifying reason. We are then confronted with the puzzle concerning what is going on in Nietzsche's highly reflective value-criticism. Leiter's solution to this puzzle is to insist that the reasoning we see here is ultimately instrumental or prudential in character. Objectivity, such as we find it in Nietzsche's work, is relational; it pertains to "what is good and bad *for a person*" rather than "what is good and bad *simpliciter*."[74] These norms for what is good and bad for persons are not themselves objective; they are perspectival and are determined by "type-facts," or immutable physiological and psychological characteristics.[75]

[72] Cf. *BGE*, 200: "In an age of disintegration where the races are mixed together, a person will have the legacy of multiple lineages in his body, which means conflicting (and often not merely conflicting) drives and value standards that fight with each other and rarely leave each other alone. A man like this, of late cultures and refracted lights, will typically be a weaker person: his most basic desire is an end to the war that he *is*." Cf. also *BGE*, 242, 251. Interestingly, although *D*, 119, implies epiphenomenalism, *BGE*, 200, seems to imply a different picture of value-standards as basic drives that are not presented as distinct from the physical and on which view the causation problem is not raised. It may be that the biologistic strain in Nietzsche's work is not fully coherent. Steven D. Hales and Rex Welshon provide an interesting discussion of Nietzsche's views about the relationship between the mental and the physical in *Nietzsche's Perspectivism* (Urbana: University of Illinois Press, 2000). The different possible interpretations that they examine offer different solutions to the causation problem. They claim (172–74) that there is some ambiguity in Nietzsche's work concerning whether the mental is to be identified with the physical, whether it supervenes on the physical, or whether the terms *mental* and *physical* do not refer to distinct ontological realms at all. They find the rejection of substance dualism the most plausible interpretation but suggest that Nietzsche nevertheless "cannot make up his mind about whether to reduce the mental/physical contrast to will to power or to replace the mental/physical contrast with will to power."
[73] *GM*, i, 17n.
[74] Cf. Leiter, "Review of Peter Berkowitz, *Nietzsche: The Ethics of an Immoralist*," *Mind* n.s., 105, no. 419 (July 1996): 487–91, 489.
[75] Cf. Leiter, *Nietzsche on Morality*, 91: "The claim . . . is that each person has certain largely immutable physiological and psychic traits, that constitute the 'type' of person he or she is." These type-facts are, on Leiter's reading, held to be causally primary over the course

The point of Nietzsche's apparently normative value-criticism, or his revaluation of values, is, on this reading, to free the "higher-types" from the constraints of ascetic morality, so that they might better attain their own authentic ends. Leiter writes:

Like Marx, Nietzsche conceives of particular systems of value as in the "interests" of particular classes or *types* of people. (Unlike Marx, he believes this because he thinks it is fundamentally natural, not socio-economic facts, that determine one's interests.) So although "morality" is, in Nietzsche's view, well-suited to the great "herd" of mankind, it is, in fact, a danger to those potentially higher human beings, who mark any great historical or cultural epoch. Nietzsche's real aim, then, is to free these nascent higher types from their "false consciousness," i.e., their false belief that the predominant morality is in fact *good for them*.[76]

For Leiter, Nietzsche's higher types have a set of determinate characteristics, which can to a certain extent be read off the representatives of the type he admires (Goethe, Beethoven, Napoleon).[77] Those others who have the potential to develop these qualities should be freed to "become who they are."

It is in this way that Leiter makes sense of the "paradox of fatalism and self-creation" in Nietzsche's work, that is, the apparent conflict between a deterministic view of valuing and the ideal of self-creation and value-creation that he seems to advocate.[78] A passage that is important from the point of view of these considerations can be found in *The Gay Science*:

Let us ... *limit* ourselves to the purification of our opinions and valuations and to the *creation of tables of good that are new and all*

---

of a person's life, determining the possible trajectories that such a life can take (81–83). The passage that seems to me to best support Leiter's reading occurs in *BGE*, 231: "Learning changes us; it does what all nourishment does which also does not merely 'preserve'—as physiologists know. But at the bottom of us, really "deep down," there is, of course, something unteachable, some granite of spiritual *fatum*, of predetermined decision and answer to some predetermined questions."

[76] Leiter, *Nietzsche on Morality*, 28.

[77] Ibid., 115–22.

[78] Cf. Leiter, "On the Paradox of Fatalism and Self-Creation in Nietzsche," in *Willing and Nothingness*. Cf. also *Nietzsche on Morality*, 82–83, where Leiter tells us that Nietzsche's determinism consists only in "causal essentialism," the view that "for any living substance . . . that substance has 'essential' properties that are causally primary with respect to the future history of that substance, i.e., they non-trivially determine the space of possible trajectories for that substance." This is distinguished from "classical determinism" ("for any event *p* at a time *t*, *p* is necessary given the totality of facts prior to *t*, together with the actual laws of nature"); and from "classical fatalism" ("whatever happens had to happen, but not in virtue of the truth of Classical Determinism").

our own, and let us stop brooding about the "moral value of our actions"! ... We ... *want to become who we are*—human beings who are new, unique, incomparable, who give themselves laws, who create themselves! To that end we must become the best students and discoverers of everything lawful and necessary in the world: we must become *physicists* in order to be able to be *creators* in this sense—while hitherto all valuations and ideals have been based on *ignorance* of all physics or were in *contradiction* to it. So long live physics! And even more so that which *compels* us to it—our honesty![79]

Leiter takes this passage to be evidence that Nietzsche's exhortation to create new values is compatible with his view that valuing involves submission to necessity.[80] Higher types free themselves from the "false consciousness" of a morality fitting for lower types in order to ensure the realization of their own predetermined potential. They are not called on to create new values ex nihilo. A literal reading of Nietzsche's claims about human types is, then, essential to this reading.

The view that humanity can, for Nietzsche, be divided into these types is seen to be supported by the characterizations of them that occur in the *Genealogy*, the central text examined by Leiter in his *Nietzsche on Morality*. Nietzsche's narrative, in the work, involves masters, priests, and slaves. Leiter takes these categories to refer to both class positions and typical character states of human beings.[81] Nietzsche's rhetorical project in the work, then, has to be that of encouraging higher types to repudiate the morality of the slaves. If this reading is correct, it allows us to reconcile Nietzsche's value-criticism and his project of revaluation with a deterministic form of antirealism.

However, I am not sure that we can make sense of the rhetorical project of the *Genealogy* in this way. Nietzsche uses the figures of the slaves, masters, and priests to tell a story about how ascetic morality came to be the dominant form of valuing. This story is part of a *Streitschrift*, a polemic against narrowly moral values. But the rhetoric does not seem to me to encourage readers to recognize themselves as one type or another, but rather to view moral value judgments from each of these perspectives. By demonstrating to us that we are capable of adopting any of these perspectives, he encourages us to make fresh assessments of our own

---

[79] *GS*, 335.

[80] This resolution in terms of self-conscious submission to necessity, grounded in an apprehension of what one is determined to be is also seen to be supported by Nietzsche's preoccupation with *amor fati*. The idea first occurs in *GS*, 276. Cf. also *EH*, II, 10. Leiter emphasizes Nietzsche's development of this idea in *Ecce Homo*, where he represents his own life in fatalistic terms (*Nietzsche on Morality*, 85–86).

[81] *Nietzsche on Morality*, 200–1.

inherited values.[82] He aims to replace unreflective allegiance with moral reflection. In doing so (as I shall argue in more detail in chapter 5) he is looking for a way of transcending the conflicting perspectives that he describes.

In the first essay, he provides us with a speculative history in which an original ruling caste that united strength and "truthfulness" divides into two distinct castes. Each represents a different way of valuing, one that supports distinct kinds of human attributes and activities. The priests, who pursue intellectual and spiritual goals, become alienated from power in the physical and material sense. So they devise a way of valuing that supports their own way of life by converting the necessarily ascetic means to their end into an ideal, the ascetic ideal.

Nietzsche then describes the resulting types of evaluation in terms which, I think, discourage us from identifying ourselves completely with either group—the dancers and jousters, or the intelligent haters:

> You will have guessed how easy it was for the priestly method of valuation to split off from the chivalric-aristocratic method and then to develop further into the opposite of the latter; this receives a special impetus when the priestly caste and warrior caste confront one another in jealousy and cannot agree on the prize of war. The chivalric-aristocratic value-judgments are based on a powerful physicality, a blossoming, rich, even effervescent good health which includes the things needed to maintain it, war, adventure, hunting, dancing, jousting and everything else that contains strong, free, happy action. The priestly-aristocratic method of valuation—as we have seen—has different criteria: woe betide it when it comes to war! As we know, priests make the most *evil enemies*—but why? Because they are the most powerless. Out of this powerlessness, their hate swells into something huge and uncanny to a most intellectual and poisonous level. The greatest haters in world history, and the most intelligent, have always been priests: —nobody else's intelligence stands a chance against the intelligence of priestly revenge.[83]

---

[82] Cf. *GM*, iii,12:

As knowers, let us not be ungrateful towards such resolute reversals of familiar perspectives and valuations with which the mind has raged against itself for far too long . . . : to see differently, and to *want* to see differently to that degree, is no small discipline and preparation of the intellect for its future "objectivity"—the latter understood not as "contemplation without interest" . . . but as *having in our power* our "pros" and "cons": so as to be able to engage and disengage them so that we can use the *difference* in perspectives and affective interpretations for knowledge.

[83] Ibid., i, 7.

The ascetic ideal becomes the more broadly accepted way of valuing amongst those who possess neither strength nor intelligence because it appeals to the weak and the dispossessed as a means of justifying their own powerlessness. According to this way of valuing, the rich and powerful are wicked and will be punished. It seems unlikely that anyone has ever read the *Genealogy* and identified wholeheartedly with these "slaves," seething with *ressentiment*. But equally, it seems implausible that anyone (particularly anyone engaged by Nietzsche's highly reflective and introspective project of revaluation) would identify with the simple-minded jousters.

Instead of soliciting identification with these types, it seems to me that Nietzsche is trying to get us to see ascetic values from the point of view of nonascetic values. He is drawing our attention to an important inconsistency and source of conflict in our system of values. He tells us that,

> the two *opposing* values "good and bad", "good and evil" have fought a terrible battle for thousands of years on earth; and although the latter has been dominant for a long time, there is still no lack of places where the battle remains undecided. You could even say that, in the meantime, it has reached ever greater heights but at the same time has become ever deeper and more intellectual: so that there is, today, perhaps no more distinguishing feature of the *"higher nature"*, the intellectual nature, than to be divided in this sense and really and truly a battle ground for these opposites.[84]

Although he states that it is only those who possess a "higher nature" who are divided in this sense, the more plausible reading seems to me to be that his general rhetorical purpose is to get each of his readers to recognize such a conflict in themselves. The use of categories such as "higher natures" makes the same kind of rhetorical appeal as a realty listing that says "Only for the discerning buyer." It encourages an aspiration to be part of this constituency. It does not necessarily involve the assumptions that membership of this constituency is preordained. And neither does it seem to presuppose that the conflict can obviously be resolved in one direction or another for any given reader.

In attempting to evoke this internal struggle in his reader, Nietzsche seems to me to be trying to co-opt his readers in the project of transcending the conflicting evaluative perspectives. I will argue in chapter 5 that he aims to assess the value of these valuations from the point of view of the overall development of humanity. The *Genealogy* plays a part in an ongoing process of criticism that aims to liberate us from established perspectives, rather than vindicate any particular one of them.

[84] Ibid., i, 16.

At several points in the *Genealogy*, Nietzsche indicates that the work is a preface to this larger undertaking, rather than its finally achieved form.[85] The project of revaluation always remains, for Nietzsche, a promise for the future. He often reminds us that the "free spirits" for whom he writes do not yet exist.[86] Even when they do, their task will be experimental.[87] The results of their revaluation are not predetermined. In 1888, when he had already completely the first volume of his projected work, *The Revaluation of All Values*, (he refers to *The Anti-Christ* as the first volume of this work), Nietzsche still saw his task as that of addressing a great question hanging over him, rather than as that of persuading specific readers to accept a preestablished answer.[88]

So whereas Hussain's reading seemed to give too much weight to freedom in evaluation, Leiter's seems to give too much weight to necessity. The latter, in particular, seems to provide too deterministic a reading to do justice to the sense, evoked by his value-criticism, of deep normative conflict. To the extent that we are engaged by Nietzsche's value-criticism it seems to me to be through identification with the apparently irresolvable conflict that he evokes, and through the aspiration to overcome it. The question, then, is whether a weakening of the deterministic claim can provide us with an antirealist reading that does justice both to the felt necessity that defines the problem and the aspiration to freedom inherent in the will to overcome it.

VALUE-CRITICISM AS INNER CONFLICT-RESOLUTION

John Richardson has recently proposed an antirealist reading that tries to account for both the forms of necessity that have been described, and the assumption of freedom that motivates Nietzsche's project of revaluation. The latter element is given a constructivist reading. The deterministic arguments yielded by Nietzsche's naturalistic analyses seem, prima facie, to conflict with constructivist suggestions that he makes. Richardson argues that

[85] Cf. e.g. Ibid., iii, 27, where Nietzsche refers us to a future work: *The Will to Power: Attempt at a Revaluation of All Values*. At the end of the first essay, Nietzsche suggests that some faculty of philosophy promote a series of prizes on the history of morality, saying that "*all* sciences must, from now on, prepare the way for the future work of the philosopher: this work being understood to mean that the philosopher has to solve the *problem of values* and that he has to decide on the *hierarchy of values*." And in *Ecce Homo*, he describes the *Genealogy* as a "psychologist's three crucial preparatory works for a revaluation of all values." *EH*, "The Genealogy of Morality."

[86] *HTH*, I, Preface, 2; *GM*, ii, 24; *AC*, Preface.

[87] *BGE*, 42: the philosophers of the future will be "Versucher" (attempters).

[88] *TI*, Preface: "A *revaluation of all values*: this question mark is so dark and so huge that it casts a shadow over anyone who puts it forward."

these different elements can be reconciled with one another if we properly understand both the critical project that uncovers the determinants of conflicting values and the creative project that aims to overcome this conflict.

Richardson's suggestion is that Nietzsche's analysis of the way in which our values have previously been selected by both natural and social mechanisms is part of a critical project that aims to free us from these determinants so that we might self-select our values. Selective mechanisms, on this reading, furnish us with goals or ends.[89] Natural selection promotes the ends of survival and reproduction for an organism. Social selection, on the other hand, works against these inherited drives, inculcating in us values that serve society, or "the herd."[90] These different ends, or "valuings," inevitably come into conflict with one another. Nietzsche, on this view, claims to have discovered a means by which we can free ourselves from this internal conflict by selecting our own values.[91]

For Richardson this project is, in the first instance, primarily epistemic: genealogical investigations allow us to gain insight into the determinants of our values. Through this insight, Nietzsche hopes, we can generate critical distance from these values.[92] We can then incorporate this insight by adopting ends that we ourselves consciously select. To do so is to achieve the freedom, which, for Richardson, is Nietzsche's highest value.[93] So we can understand the exhortation to "become who we are" not in terms of a rigid doctrine of types, but in terms of developing our capacity for evaluative freedom:

> The key to becoming myself is to select my values, i.e., the goals of the dispositions that—in making my behavior—specify "who I am." It is to make myself the cause of these decisive bodily aims. Initially and as a matter of course, these aims are set by selection in the species' or societies' past: how my body aims was selected—"became"—before I was born, within the natural and social processes that formed my drives and habits. To become myself is to make my values *during* my life, as well as by and for that life. I revise these drives and habits, selecting them to serve my individual will.[94]

This reading makes sense of some important elements in Nietzsche's work, in particular, the aspiration to independence that we described in chapter 1.

[89] Richardson, *Nietzsche's New Darwinism*, 7.
[90] Ibid., 84.
[91] Ibid., 95: "[Nietzsche] insists that we stand before the possibility of a new way of making values, feasible now as never before."
[92] Ibid., 100.
[93] Ibid., 106.
[94] Ibid., 96.

The idea that rational criticism can be a means to attaining an important form of freedom originates in Nietzsche's middle period. There he comes to see that our drives, rather than being immutable determinants of our behavior, can be brought under reflective control. In *Human, All Too Human,* he repudiates any philosophy that "sees 'instincts' in man as he now is and assumes that these belong to the unalterable facts of mankind."[95] Critical reasoning is now seen to be capable of altering the constitution of unconscious drives. This important theme has been emphasized by Alexander Nehamas, who points out that Nietzsche comes to see instincts as culturally acquired and as mutable.[96] We are not, pace Leiter, simply stuck with the basic determinants of our values being what they are. We can come to understand them and modify them.

Some problems arise, however, when we try to understand the imperative to select our values in antirealist terms. Richardson sees this as a universal prescription (even though few will actually be able to accomplish it). On an antirealist reading, it cannot have the status of an objective norm. But Richardson holds that self-selection can be derived, for Nietzsche, from existing values and can be accepted for internal reasons as superior to our current predicament of inner conflict.[97] Richardson attributes to Nietzsche, then, a minimal universalism, consisting in the demand that we self-select our values, and by implication, that we preserve the necessary conditions for self-selection.[98] But it is difficult to see what such a universal prescription could mean.

On this view, everyone should be free to select (insofar as they are able) their own values, with the exception of the value of self-selection itself. In other words, in selecting our own values we are subject to one constraint: that we should leave others free to select their own values (in case they are capable of so doing).[99] So we are free to select values only to the extent that we do not impair the ability of others to do so. But this universalism no longer looks very minimal. For it seems that anything we select will impair the ability of others to select something incompatible.

[95] *HTH,* I, 2.

[96] Cf. Alexander Nehamas, "A Reason for Socrates' Face: Nietzsche on 'The Problem of Socrates,'" in *The Art of Living: Socratic Reflections from Plato to Foucault* (Berkeley: University of California Press, 1998), 128–57, at 140.

[97] Richardson, *Nietzsche's New Darwinism*, 107, 120–21.

[98] Ibid., 124: "Nietzsche's view, as I read him here, has some affinity to (what have been called) 'practical reasoning theories' in recent metaethics. These argue that (a kind of) objectivity in ethics is indeed feasible, but depends not on theory's matching independently real goods, but on the proper exercise of practical reason. There are certain 'universal demands' imposed by reasoning over reasons for acting."

[99] Richardson claims that Nietzsche's own values demonstrate his respect for this constraint. Ibid., 135: "His principal purpose . . . is to teach the method of freedom by genealogy—to spread the capacity to choose one's ethical and political values oneself."

We should bear in mind here that "valuing" on Richardson's view does not refer to mere beliefs and attitudes but to the actual ends that our life processes serve.[100] So evaluative conflict would not involve simply conflicts of beliefs or attitudes, but incompatible ways of life. Any chosen value would have to be compatible with any way of life that might be chosen by another free selector. It is hard to imagine that we could, under these constraints, value anything at all. Any valuation would impair the ability of others to value something different.

So although Richardson's reading pulls together some very important strands in Nietzsche's work, the attribution of an overall moral antirealism still generates problems when we try to assess how Nietzsche thinks we should go on valuing from here. These problems are exacerbated at the political level, where it seems particularly hard to make sense of Nietzsche's concerns on an antirealist construal.

Antirealism about Political Values

I have claimed so far in this chapter that Nietzsche makes various antirealist meta-ethical claims. It is difficult to reconcile any of them entirely with Nietzsche's project of normative value-criticism, and it may be that no reading can yield any absolute overall coherence (we will return to this issue in chapter 5). But whether or not he is read as a consistent antirealist, he will still turn out to be committed to the view that those of us who are capable of it should have the freedom to determine our own values. The human beings whom Nietzsche values will be those "who are new, unique, incomparable, who give themselves laws, who create themselves."[101] Human dignity still seems to him to consist in independence or self-determination. This free self-determination will, of course, include the capacity to determine our own political values. But it is not obvious that this freedom is something the antirealist can coherently hold on to.

In part, the political problem is simply a natural extension of the one discussed in the previous section, concerning the difficulties with a universal imperative to create our own values. This purportedly minimal universalism

[100] Ibid., 262.

[101] GS, 335. Hussain and Richardson's readings clearly retain an appreciation of this commitment to independent evaluation, in the imperative to create new values. But even Leiter's "types" incorporate some sense of autonomy or independence. In freeing us from "false consciousness," on this view, genealogy permits reflective endorsement of the values that we are intended by nature to have. It generates a form of authenticity. The "higher types" who are capable of achieving this will value independence as one of their virtues: they will not be used instrumentally by others (Nietzsche on Morality, 116).

causes stark problems in the realm of political values because these must specify the basic principles around which a polity should be organized. If Nietzsche freely chooses one set of values and wills their effectiveness, he will be willing their imposition on those who might choose something else.

An individual who is called on to "create values," that is, to determine through some rationally arbitrary process what their values will be, cannot do so in a way that is consistent with respecting the freedom of others to do the same thing.[102] Nietzsche cannot coherently hold both that we should organize a polity around the principles that he chooses, and that we should organize it around ones that are inconsistent with his choices but which have been freely chosen by someone else. Any choice will compromise the freedom of other potential self-selectors.

It might be objected that Nietzsche is concerned, above all, with fostering competition between different value-creators, that conflict and resistance are precisely what he desires. Bernard Reginster builds into his view of "will to power" the idea that it inherently involves the willing of resistance, in order that we might have the satisfaction of overcoming obstacles.[103] But even this view attributes to Nietzsche an ultimate ideal, that of the agonistic society, which would be incompatible with the imposition by others of a social order that erases competition. Willing this end necessarily involves the aspiration to constrain the freedom of others to realize an alternative state of affairs.

The political case also presents us with a special problem concerning the means through which such values would have to be made effective. Their effectiveness could only be secured through the generation of a supporting ideology. This would have to involve convergence either around these values themselves, or at least around ones that indirectly promote

---

[102] Contra Richardson. Cf. *Nietzsche's New Darwinism*, 135: "What he wants for his favored readers is that *they* self select their ethical and political values as well. So he does not, after all, want those readers simply to take those values over from him." And: "His principal purpose is not to transmit [his] values of hardness and so on, but to teach the method of freedom by genealogy—to spread the capacity to choose one's ethical and political values oneself. . . . His most polemical and outrageous assaults on morality function chiefly to "free" us from our sedimented values and to enable us to self select new values. . . . Nietzsche expects each other 'free spirit' to choose somewhat *different* valuings from his own."

[103] On Reginster's view this generates what he calls "the paradox of will to power." He tells us that: "The will to power will not be satisfied unless three conditions are met: there is some first-order desire for a determinate end, there is resistance to the realization of this determinate end, *and* there is actual success in overcoming this resistance. But then, the conditions of the satisfaction of the will to power do indeed imply its dissatisfaction. The overcoming of resistance eliminates it, but the presence of such resistance as a necessary condition of satisfaction of the will to power implies its own dissatisfaction, in the sense that it necessarily brings it about." Cf. *The Affirmation of Life*, 136.

the same ends. For example, if Nietzsche values an order of rank in society, this might be achieved through competition over some valued social good, such as honor or esteem, rather than through conscious espousal of an ideal of rank ordering. But either way, some appropriate norms and practices would have to be widely inculcated in a society in order for it to display the right characteristics, or support the right forms of rule. The necessary convergence, on the antirealist picture, could only be achieved through manipulation and coercion.

Neither is it clear how Nietzsche, on the antirealist reading, imagines that we could generate the kind of ruling ideology that would be required to sustain his political values. As we have seen in previous chapters, he is aware that he has no nonrational means of persuasion in his power that would be sufficient to compete with the existing state hegemony. So on the antirealist view, according to which his political prescriptions have no normative standing, we would have to read them as mere hypothetical remarks about what he would do if he were in control of a state apparatus. But reading them thus exacerbates the problem.

John Richardson seems to read Nietzsche in something like this way. He takes Nietzsche to be advocating an extensive program of social transformation and ideological control. He concedes that Nietzsche is not a political theorist in the conventional sense, but attributes to him political ends that could only be accomplished by political rulers.[104] Nietzsche, on his view, would have philosophers seize the opportunity made available by genealogical insight to reprogram, through breeding, economic reorganization, and reeducation, people's basic values.[105]

If Nietzsche's political wishful thinking has to involve a fantasy of state control, he can only be recommending the very form of political self-justification that he himself condemns. If his political values are intended to have no genuine normative standing, if they are not being offered as justified views that might be legitimately accepted by others, they can only be read as an aspiration to the very kind of ideological authority that Nietzsche exhorts his readers to resist.

As we shall see, this political incoherence is an idiosyncrasy of the antirealist reading of Nietzsche. He certainly encourages an antirealist

[104] Ibid., 188.

[105] In defense of the view that Nietzsche advocates eugenics, Richardson cites many passages from *The Will to Power* on breeding, including *WP*, 862 [1884]; *WP*, 462 [1887]; *WP*, 1053 [1884]; *WP*, 734 [1888]. This reading has the virtue of trying to accommodate the biologistic claims about miscegenation and degeneration that we noted previously. However, it seems to me to be too programmatic an interpretation, particularly given the lack of supporting evidence in the published works. There are passages in the published works, however, where Nietzsche suggests that ideological manipulation would be necessary to accomplish his goals. Cf., e.g., *BGE*, 61, and *BGE*, 203.

interpretation of valuing. But insofar as he does he generates significant problems for his own position. For the antirealist cannot coherently recommend that others arrive at value judgments independently and at the same time recommend the imposition of political values that would require their ideological subordination.

CHAPTER 5

Nietzsche as a Moral Realist

INTRODUCTION

The readings evaluated in chapter 4 take seriously Nietzsche's antirealist meta-ethical claims and therefore read his objectivist-sounding value-criticism as having a peculiar character. In this chapter, I hope to show that a case can also be made for taking the value-criticism at face value, and thus for viewing the antirealist meta-ethical suggestions as a misdescription of the value-criticism. The scattered remarks that imply a more realist meta-ethics can be more coherently related to the overall evaluative project. And the realist reading of this project allows us to comprehend more clearly the political predicament that Nietzsche seems to be concerned about.

If we want to take Nietzsche's moral philosophy seriously in its own right, it would, of course, be nice to find in his work an anticipation of the most sophisticated contemporary meta-ethical views.[1] But the incompatibility reading that I will defend (which sees a tension between his most prominent meta-ethical claims and what is actually going on his value-criticism) suggests to us that his most penetrating philosophical insights are not likely to be found in the realm of meta-ethics. His naturalistic project certainly seems compatible with some contemporary realist views, but it does not look as though he could himself see a way of reconciling his naturalism with objectivism.

But whether or not his work contains special insights into meta-ethics, the realist reading of his value-criticism still generates interesting insights concerning the nature of normative authority. And these insights will have an important bearing on how we think about political authority.

In this chapter I will claim that Nietzsche's value-criticism is universalist in scope and realist in its basic orientation. The primary object of Nietzsche's concern, throughout the later writings, is the fate of mankind. He does not simply regret that the advancement of some particular type of human being, his own type, has been inhibited. As we shall see, his

---

[1] As we saw in chapter 3, some readers have adopted this kind of interpretive strategy regarding Nietzsche's epistemological views, assimilating his ideas to those of Wittgenstein, Quine, and Davidson. Michael Tanner comments on this phenomenon in his *Nietzsche: A Very Short Introduction*, 3. Cf. also Peter Poellner, *Nietzsche and Metaphysics*, 3.

criticism is oriented around a broader concern for humanity as such, or for the type "man" (*Mensch*). In this respect, then, it is universalist.

This universalism supplies the necessary context for Nietzsche's claims about evaluative diversity and differentiation. The overall development of humanity will best be served, he thinks, if different people value different things. As we shall see, he recommends hierarchy, differentiation, and perspective, but the normative context for these recommendations is universalist. So while such claims sometimes appear, prima facie, to be anti-universalist they are in fact examples of what T. M. Scanlon has called parametric universalism.[2]

But the universality of Nietzsche's ultimate judgments about humanity does not in itself imply objectivity. Mere preferences can have a universal scope. If Nietzsche took value judgments to be reducible to preferences, he could apply them universally, while still holding that they are just his own values rather than ones that are valid for everyone. He could, for instance, think that every human being is implicated in his order of rank, and also that every human being has an obligation to behave in a way that befits their rank, but still hold that both the rank ordering and the universal imperative are expressions of his own personal preferences, or the preferences of people like him.

He will only turn out to be a moral realist if he thinks that we can arrive at value judgments that are universally valid. The reasons that he offers us for his revaluations will have to be offered as valid reasons for anyone. So in analyzing the nature of his value-criticism I will discuss first his explicit aspiration to make value judgments that are universal in scope, and then his implicit aspiration to objectivity, or universal validity.

I shall claim that Nietzsche presupposes that there are facts about what is good for humanity, so our judgments about this (and hence our evaluations of values) can be universally valid. But he does not suppose that everyone will be capable of arriving at these valid judgments. He is an anti-universalist about moral capacities. He believes that there are inequalities in people's intellectual capacities that entail inequalities in their

---

[2] Scanlon uses the term *parametric universalism* to describe any view that upholds ultimate standards, but allows for context-dependent variations in what is right. It is distinguished from relativism ("the thesis that there is no single ultimate standard for the moral appraisal of actions, a standard uniquely appropriate for all agents and all moral judges; rather, there are many such standards"). It involves instead "applying a fixed set of substantive moral principles to varying circumstances." He gives the following example: "Failing to help a person whose car has broken down . . . would be a serious wrong in a place where someone who is stranded overnight is likely to freeze to death, but not a serious wrong in a safe country with a mild climate." Cf. T. M. Scanlon, *What We Owe to Each Other* (Cambridge, Mass.: Harvard University Press, 1998), 328–29.

moral capacities. It is this claim that generates the distinctive set of problems that he formulates concerning normative authority.

For Nietzsche, the moral beliefs that most people hold are simply wrong and are bound to be. They have been distorted, in particular, by false religious beliefs. Even secular evaluative practices betray their origins in an erroneous worldview. It takes extraordinary critical effort to rid ourselves of these distorting influences. Most people do not possess the required intellectual capabilities.

As in the case of ordinary beliefs (as we saw in chapter 4), the pressure to reach a "law of agreement" will inevitably lead to convergence on value judgments that are not rationally justified. Most people simply do not possess the intellectual skills that are required for the critical examination of their beliefs. Rational justification in the moral realm is intellectually demanding. The revaluation of values will inevitably, Nietzsche holds, be the preserve of only a few "free spirits."

Furthermore, even though Nietzsche thinks that philosophers might possess the required expertise, other people will have no capacity to recognize this and hence reason to accept the results of their revaluations. Religions have promoted a model of recognized normative expertise, whereby a priestly caste is accepted as having special authority in normative matters. But secularism admits no such possibility, since people who do not have the capacity to reason correctly themselves will equally have no capacity to discriminate between those whose views are or are not likely to be rationally justified. And the absence of rational convergence amongst those who would claim to be experts exacerbates this problem.

As we noted earlier, Nietzsche does not articulate an explicit view of the extent to which this situation is remediable should human capacities develop beyond their present state. But since he remains unconvinced that popular enlightenment is a potential solution to the problem of normative agreement, we have to infer that he is pessimistic about the future intellectual development of most human beings.

This set of claims about normative authority has an important bearing on how we think about political authority and legitimacy. Since states and governments need to be accepted as legitimate, they require normative convergence. We might expect that the moral realist could hope for genuinely uncoerced convergence, but even on the realist reading, it looks as though Nietzsche must be pessimistic about this possibility. Most people, he thinks, have no means through which they can reliably access moral truth. So he can envisage no way in which a genuine and independent form of normative authority can serve as a foundation for political life.

At the same time, the moral realist cannot cede to the state the authority to promote convergence coercively. Moral realism involves a commitment to an independent source of moral authority, which states cannot be

permitted to override. We might imagine a moral realist conceding ideological authority to the state only if that state were held to be intrinsically
and necessarily constrained by the correct moral norms. But as we saw in
chapter 1, in his descriptive account of the state, Nietzsche discerns no
such capacity for moral self-regulation.

Hence Nietzsche's political skepticism. Insofar as he is a moral realist,
he cannot give up the demand that political life be governed by the correct norms. But equally he cannot imagine how normative truth could
ever be made the basis of political authority. In other words, the demands
of normative authority and political authority cannot be reconciled.

UNIVERSALIST VALUE JUDGMENTS

Although Nietzsche claims that his normative value-criticism begins in
Daybreak, he does not in fact offer us all that much normative evaluation
of values there. The work consists mainly in descriptive, psychological
claims. But he does introduce at least one important claim. He tells us
that current forms of moral judgment should be overcome because, when
viewed from the point of view of the overall development of humanity,
they have to be seen as a retardant. Owing to the morality of custom, the
"rarer, choicer, more original spirits" have felt themselves to be a danger
and have been perceived so by their contemporaries. Every form of orig-
inality has thereby "acquired a bad conscience."[3] This theme is reiterated
in all the subsequent works.

The evaluation of values that he undertakes in the later writings is oriented around a single universalist commitment: that of the improvement,
and ultimately self-overcoming, of humanity.[4] His interest in the category
of the human (*menschlich*) becomes prominent, of course, in *Human, All*

---

[3] *D*, 9.

[4] Cf. *BGE*, 257, on "the enhancement of the type 'man,' the continual 'self-overcoming
of man,' to use a moral formula in a supra-moral sense." Although the idea of "will to power"
has been taken by some as a reductively universalist basis for Nietzsche's value-criticism
(notably Martin Heidegger, in his *Nietzsche* volumes, Richard Schacht, in *Nietzsche*, and
John Richardson, in *Nietzsche's System* [New York: Oxford University Press, 1996]), it
does not play a central role in the later published works. Insofar as it does play a role it is
in specifying the conditions under which humanity can flourish. The latter remains the guiding orientation in all the works that postdate *Zarathustra*. The interpretations that hold will
to power to be central, place a great deal of weight on the unpublished notebooks. But as
Brian Leiter has pointed out, "in the two major self-reflective moments in the Nietzschean
corpus—*Ecce Homo*, where Nietzsche reviews and assesses his life and work, including
specifically all his books predating *Thus Spoke Zarathustra*—Nietzsche says *not a word*
about 'will to power.'" Leiter, "Review of *Nietzsche and Metaphysics; Nietzsche's System*,"
Mind n.s., 107, no. 427 (July 1988): 683–90, at 690.

Too Human.[5] His assessment of the role of morality in the development of humanity begins here.[6] But it is in *Thus Spoke Zarathustra* that the advancement or enhancement of this type becomes an object of normative commitment. Zarathustra, when he comes down from his mountain, claims that he loves humanity and wants to bring it a gift.[7] The gift, of course, is the means to its own self-overcoming.[8]

Zarathustra does not claim that he can create new values. He claims that he can create freedom and "seize the right to new values."[9] He means to free humanity from the value judgments that are promoting its degeneration. In *Beyond Good and Evil*, similarly, he tells us that philosophers, by "applying the knife vivisectionally to the chest of the very *virtues of their time*" can show the way to "a *new* greatness of man, . . . a new untrodden way to enhancement."[10]

Nietzsche's work from this time on is clearly oriented around this central ambition. He asks what kinds of values have served the enhancement of the type "man."[11] And he asks what kinds of values should prevail in future if we are to flourish.[12] In the preface to his most sustained critique of values, his *Genealogy of Morality*, he writes: "Let us articulate this *new demand*: we need a *critique* of moral values, *the value of these values themselves must first be called into question*—and for that there is needed a knowledge of the conditions and circumstances in which they grew, under which they evolved and changed." He then goes on to tell us

---

[5] Though already in the *Untimely Meditations*, he tells us that the kind of philosopher he admires "desires truth, not as cold, ineffectual knowledge, but as a regulating and punishing judge; truth, not as the egoistic possession of the individual, but as the sacred right to overturn all the boundary-stones of egoistic possessions; in a word, truth as the judgment of humanity." *UM*, ii, 6.

[6] Cf., e.g., *HTH*, I, 40: "The beast in us wants to be lied to; morality is an official lie told so that it shall not tear us to pieces. Without the errors that repose in the assumptions of morality man would have remained an animal. As it is, he has taken himself for something higher and imposed sterner laws on himself."

[7] *TSZ*, I, "Prologue," 2.

[8] Ibid., 3.

[9] Ibid., "Speeches," 1: "To create new values—that even the lion cannot do; but the creation of freedom for oneself for new creation—that is within the power of the lion."

[10] *BGE*, 212.

[11] Ibid., 257 and 262. Cf. also Ibid., 44: "We, who are quite the reverse, have kept an *eye* and a conscience open to the question of where and how the plant 'man' has grown strongest, and we think that this has always happened under conditions that are quite the reverse. . . . We think that harshness, violence, slavery, danger in the street and in the heart, concealment, Stoicism, the art of experiment, and devilry of every sort; that everything evil, terrible, tyrannical, predatory, and snakelike in humanity serves just as well as its opposite to enhance the species 'humanity.'"

[12] Ibid., 202: "*Morality in Europe today is the morality of herd animals*: —and therefore, as we understand things, it is only one type of human morality beside which, before which, and after which many others (and especially *higher*) moralities are or should be possible."

that his ambition is to show the extent to which different valuations have inhibited or promoted the enhancement of the type "man," asking:

> What if a symptom of regression were inherent in the "good," like-wise a danger, a seduction, a poison, a narcotic, through which the present was possibly living *at the expense of the future? . . .* So that precisely morality would be to blame if the *highest power and splendor* actually possible to the type man was never in fact attained? So that precisely morality was the danger of dangers?[13]

His evaluation of values consists therefore in an assessment of the instrumental value of different modes of evaluation in relation to his ultimate value of improving on humanity's present state.

The assessment of the value of values requires, he tells us, a thorough knowledge of their nature. In order to understand fully the role that different evaluative beliefs and practices play in human life we must understand the many different dimensions of life to which they are related.[14] For Nietzsche, this must include knowledge of the physiological determinants of value judgments.[15] More obviously, it must include a nuanced grasp of their social and cultural meanings, as revealed by genealogical inquiry.

An important indication of what the latter would involve, if rigorously pursued, can be found in the second essay of the *Genealogy*. Nietzsche points out to us what would be involved in understanding the concept of punishment and the multiple meanings that it has held in different contexts, with its festive as well as deterrent aspects, its mnemonic usefulness and its cathartic power.[16] It is only by uncovering the origins and significance of our evaluations that we can assess the role they have played in the development of the human type.[17]

---

[13] *GM*, Preface, 6.

[14] *BGE*, 186: "In Europe these days, moral sentiment is just as refined, late, multiple, sensitive, and subtle as the 'science of morals' (which belongs with it) is young, neophyte, clumsy, and crude. . . . We should admit to ourselves with all due severity exactly *what* will be necessary for a long time to come and *what* is provisionally correct, namely: collecting material, formulating concepts, and putting into order the tremendous realm of tender value feelings and value distinctions that live, grow, reproduce, and are destroyed, —and, perhaps, attempting to illustrate the recurring and more frequent shapes of this living crystallization, —all of which would be a preparation for a *typology* of morals."

[15] Cf. *GM*, i, 17n.

[16] Ibid., ii, 13.

[17] If we bear in mind the epistemic role that Nietzsche's genealogies play in his project of revaluation we can avoid attributing to him the genetic fallacy. As Leiter puts it (*Nietzsche on Morality*, 177): "The point of origin of a morality has a special *evidential* status as to the *effects* (or causal powers) of that morality, for example, as to whether morality obstructs or promotes human flourishing."

The set of ultimate standards that inform his conception of enhancement or progress are not systematically laid out. They have to be inferred from his evaluations.[18] He does not just provide us with a typology of values, he ranks them. His rankings reveal his implicit commitments. But these are complex. The evaluative practices that he assesses, most importantly, those associated with ascetic morality, are seen to have been good for humanity in some respects even if they have been disastrously bad in others.

We can see this complexity in the *Genealogy*, where Nietzsche exercises judiciousness in assessing the ascetic ideal. He tells us that ascetic morality is "the most terrible sickness that has ever raged in man."[19] He says that his aim is to protect us "against the *great nausea at man!* Against *great pity for man!*"[20] But the work ends on a note of deep ambivalence about the ascetic ideal. Nietzsche acknowledges that "apart from the ascetic ideal, man, the human *animal*, had no meaning so far." The ascetic ideal gave man's suffering a purpose and "man was *saved*, thereby, he possessed a meaning, he was henceforth no longer like a leaf in the wind, a plaything of nonsense—the 'sense-less'—he could now *will* something, no matter at first to what end, why, with what he willed: *the will itself was saved*."[21]

Nietzsche's assessment is that ascetic morality has been in some ways beneficial to humanity. In spite of the fact that the priestly form of human existence is dangerous, it is nevertheless through these means that "man first became *an interesting animal*." He tells us: "Only here did the human soul in a higher sense acquire *depth* and become *evil*—and these are the two basic respects in which man has hitherto been superior to other beasts!"[22] His ambivalence does not simply derive from the fact that the ascetic ideal has been good for some kinds of people and bad for others.[23] It derives from his global assessment of its benefits and costs to humanity as such.

This is not to say that Nietzsche is uninterested in what serves the interests of different types of human beings. He is certainly interested in dividing

---

[18] When Nietzsche addresses the topic of his new ideal for humanity explicitly, particularly in *Zarathustra* and *The Gay Science*, he is often frustratingly vague. Cf. Michael Tanner, *Nietzsche*, 99–100. But a complex picture of his guiding values is generated by the critical project, particularly as it is developed in the *Genealogy*.

[19] *GM*, ii, 22.

[20] Ibid., iii, 14.

[21] Ibid., iii, 28.

[22] Ibid., i, 6. Cf. also ibid., i, 7: "Human history would be altogether too stupid a thing without the spirit that the impotent have introduced into it."

[23] Leiter emphasizes the concern with types of human being, but not the concern for the human as such, which provides the universalist context for Nietzsche's judgments. Cf. *Nietzsche on Morality*, 105: "Nietzsche's central worry . . . is that MPS, which may be good for the herd, is *harmful* for higher types of human beings."

humans into subtypes, particularly with respect to their evaluative practices.[24] And he is committed to preserving various subtypes, detailing, for example, the qualities of the noble type that he values.[25] He also repeatedly emphasizes the need for nonnobles, the labourers who will anchor the social and economic structures that facilitate great human achievements.[26]

Lack of differentiation, he fears, will lead to the degeneration of the human type. In *Beyond Good and Evil* he tells us that

> every enhancement of the type "man" has so far been the work of an aristocratic society—and it will be so again and again—a society that believes in the long ladder of an order of rank and differences in value between man and man.[27]

He therefore opposes any moral or political views that seek to impose uniformity. His rejection of egalitarianism and his opposition to democracy are rooted in the concern that they promote a uniformity that can only be achieved by leveling down.[28] He even claims that any enduring legal order, according to which everyone is subject to the same laws, will eliminate aspects of the competition between men that furthers the species.[29]

---

[24] *BGE*, 194: "The difference among men becomes manifest not only in the difference between their tablets of goods—in the fact that they consider different goods worth striving for and also disagree about what is more and less valuable, about the order of rank of the goods they recognize in common—it becomes manifest even more in what they take for really *having* and *possessing* something good."

[25] Cf. Ibid., part 9.

[26] Cf., e.g., *Twilight of the Idols*, "Skirmishes," 40:

What is stupid (basically, the degeneration of instinct that is the cause of *all* stupidity today) is that there is a labour question at all. Certain things *should not be called into question*: first imperative of the instinct. —I have no idea what people intend to do with the workers now that they have been called into question. . . . Workers were enlisted for the military, they were given the right to organize, the political right to vote: is it any wonder that workers today feel their existence to be desperate (expressed morally—to be an *injustice*)? But what do people *want*? We ask once more: what do they *will*? If you will an end, you have to will the means too: if you want slaves, then it is stupid to train them to be masters.

[27] *BGE*, 257.

[28] Cf. Ibid., 203, where Nietzsche addresses those who, like him, "consider the democratic movement to be not merely an abased form of political organization, but rather an abased (more specifically a diminished) form of humanity, a mediocritization and depreciation of humanity in value"; and also *BGE*, 242, on the physiological process that lies behind democratic movement, leading to "leveling and mediocritization of man."

[29] *GM*, ii, 11: "From the highest biological standpoint, legal conditions can never be other than *exceptional conditions*, since they constitute a partial restriction of the will to life, which is bent upon power. . . . A legal order thought of as sovereign and universal, not as a means in the struggle between power-complexes but as a means of *preventing* all struggle in general . . . would be a principle *hostile to life*, an agent of the dissolution and destruction of man, a sign of weariness, a secret path to nothingness.—" He is here echoing *GS*, 376.

When Nietzsche claims, then, that it is immoral to say "what is right for one is fair for the other," he means that differentiation and rank are what is ultimately most valuable for humanity.[30] He insists that we recognize that "what helps feed or nourish the higher type of man must be almost poisonous for a very different and lesser type."[31] But his various specific claims about what is good for one type being bad for another are examples not of relativism but of parametric universalism.[32]

The ultimate goal of enhancing the human type will, for example, best be served if some people value strength and mastery and some weakness and subordination. Women, specifically, should value the latter. It is a terrible retrogression for women, Nietzsche claims, when they aspire to be "masters" and desire "progress."[33] They should aim to be agreeably submissive.[34]

The same kind of parametric universalism can be found in Nietzsche's discussion of the meaning of ascetic ideals, in the third essay of the *Genealogy*. He wants to comprehend the different evaluative significance that they have for artists, for philosophers, for scholars, for priests, for women. But his overall concern is the universalistic one of assessing the way in which they have either served or hindered the development of humanity.[35] This can only be achieved if we understand the different

[30] *BGE*, 221. Brian Lieter has taken the following passage (*WP*, 332) as evidence of skepticism about normative theory: "A man as he *ought* to be: that sounds as insipid as 'a tree as it ought to be.'" It sounds to me as though Nietzsche here wants to stress the value of diversity—we would not want trees to conform to some single norm, since the very beauty of a tree lies in its uniqueness—and that such judgments are made in the context of ultimate, universalistic normative judgments about what is good for humanity or for trees. Cf. Brian Leiter, Review of "*Nietzsche and Metaphysics*," 683–90, at 689.

[31] *BGE*, 30. Bernard Reginster argues that on Nietzsche's view, it may not always be good for people to know the truth insofar as truthfulness is one of the human attributes that Nietzsche wishes to see cultivated, the ideal of truthfulness itself might provide constraints on who should pursue it and to what extent. He writes: "It may well be the case that the unqualified pursuit of truthfulness could, for certain types of people in certain circumstances, undermine the possibility of their achieving any measure of *truthfulness* at all. For example, learning the truth could, for people of a certain type in certain circumstances, wreak such psychological havoc as to damage severely their very capacity to be truthful." *The Affirmation of Life*, 265.

[32] Daniel Conway attributes to Nietzsche the universalist aim of enhancing humankind, and sees Nietzsche's commitment to "moral pluralism" as a means to this end. Cf. Daniel Conway, *Nietzsche and the Political* (London: Routledge, 1997), 6, 30.

[33] *BGE*, 239.

[34] Cf. Ibid., 221: "Women have so much cause for shame; they contain so much that is pedantic, superficial, and schoolmarmish as well as narrowmindedly arrogant, presumptuous, and lacking in restraint . . . all of which has been most successfully restrained and kept under control by their *fear* of men."

[35] *GM*, iii, 1: on the universalist context: "*That* the ascetic ideal has meant so many things to man . . . is an expression of the basic fact of the human will, its *horror vacui. It needs a goal.*"

meanings that they have to different people. And the final assessment of their value may yield the conclusion that humanity overall is best served if some people embrace them and some people do not.

Nietzsche's ranking of types clearly implies a universal scale against which human beings are measured. Even if many types are necessary, some will exhibit attributes that are rarer and more valuable than others.[36] The differentiation between higher and lower reflects this discrepancy. The question remains, though, of whether Nietzsche's universalistic value judgments are taken to be valid just for him and perhaps for people like him, or whether he believes that anyone would have to recognize them to be correct.

Nietzsche's suggestions about this are often ambiguous. They can clearly (as is evident from the diversity of the secondary literature) be made to support a variety of readings. His use of the term *we* often contributes to this ambiguity. For example, he addresses those whose value judgments involve minimizing pain (hedonists, eudaimonists, utilitarians), saying, "*Our* pity is a higher and more farsighted pity: we see how humanity is becoming smaller, how *you* are making it smaller. . . . Well-being as you understand it—that is no goal, that looks to us like an *end*, a condition that immediately renders people ridiculous and despicable—that makes their decline into something *desirable*."[37] Does he mean that his own pity is higher only relative to his own standards, or the standards of his type? Or does the "we" denote those capable of achieving a more objective view, of possessing insight into the truth about what is best for humanity? I want to argue that a case can be made for the latter, that Nietzsche's fundamental tendency in the value-criticism, if not in the meta-ethical speculation, is that of a moral realist.

THE RESIDUAL MORAL REALISM

In *Daybreak*, Nietzsche tells us that he wants to subject moral values to rational scrutiny.[38] They have previously been held, he says, to be beyond rational reproach.[39] As he begins to pursue this critical project, we can

---

[36] Cf. *BGE*, 43: "Whatever can be common always has little value."

[37] Ibid., 225.

[38] Ruth Abbey stresses the rationalism that emerges in the middle period, claiming that Nietzsche at least sometimes advocates here "a rationalized morality, requiring that values be respected and actions admired for defensible reasons rather than from habit and custom." *Nietzsche's Middle Period*, 10.

[39] He claims, in his 1886 preface, that Kant tried to make the moral realm rationally inscrutable: *D*, Preface, 3.

quickly see a tension emerge between the antirealist meta-ethics that he seems to think is entailed by it, and the inherent aim of the criticism itself. On the one hand, we find passages that indicate his attraction to moral antirealism.[40] On the other hand, he seems to be aiming for rationally justified normative beliefs, rather than rejecting the possibility of rational justification per se in the moral realm. He tells us that

> it goes without saying that I do not deny—unless I am a fool—that many actions called immoral ought to be avoided and resisted, or that many called moral ought to be done and encouraged—but I think the one should be done and encouraged *for other reasons than hitherto*.[41]

If he is aiming for rationally justified beliefs, his approach must be a cognitivist one.

I will take it to be a sufficient condition for moral realism that one take a cognitivist view of value judgments and that one think at least some of them are true (as opposed to subscribing to an error theory).[42] Recent moral realists have set out various views about how this might be the case. I do not take Nietzsche himself to have any fully developed view of whether the truth-conditions are fully mind-independent, or whether they derive from the viewpoint of an "ideal observer." He clearly does not systematically set out any realist meta-ethics. But he seems to be drawn in a realist direction in the value-criticism.

In spite of his antirealist remarks there are certainly passages where, reflecting on his own value-criticism, Nietzsche describes it in a way that presupposes both cognitivism and the possibility of insight into the truth. Take, for example, his retrospective description of the evaluative stance of *The Birth of Tragedy*, as a great insight, made possible by his daring in pursuit of the truth:

> This final, most joyful, effusive, high-spirited yes to life is not only the highest insight, it is also the most *profound*, the most rigorously confirmed and supported by truth and study. Nothing in existence should

---

[40] Cf., e.g., Ibid., 3, 108, 210.

[41] Ibid., 103. Nietzsche reaffirms this commitment to rationalism in evaluation in *D*, 107:

If the *reason* of mankind is of such extraordinarily slow growth that it has often been denied that it has grown at all during the course of mankind's existence, what is more to blame than this solemn presence, indeed omnipresence, of moral commands which absolutely prohibit the utterance of *individual* questions as to How? And to what end? Have we not been brought up to *feel pathetically*, and to flee into the dark precisely when reason ought to be taking as clear and cold a view as possible! That is to say, in the case of all our higher and weightier affairs.

[42] I have found helpful Geoffrey Sayre-McCord's account, in "Introduction: The Many Moral Realisms."

be excluded, nothing is dispensable—the aspects of existence condemned by Christians and other nihilists rank infinitely higher in the order of values than anything the instinct of decadence is able to approve, to *call good*. To understand this requires *courage* and, as its condition, a surplus of *force*: because the forcefulness with which you approach truth is proportionate to the distance courage dares to advance.[43]

In his own estimation of his value-criticism, its significance lies in the extent to which it reveals truths. And in the later works it certainly often looks as though this is his aim.

In the *Genealogy*, for example, when Nietzsche claims to be assessing the value of morality, it looks very much as though he is trying to assess its real value. And the truth about this, he claims, may be just the opposite of what it has been taken to be:

One has taken the *value* of these "values" as given, as factual, as beyond all question; one has hitherto never doubted or hesitated in the slightest degree in supposing "the good man" to be of greater value than "the evil man," of greater value in the sense of furthering the advancement and prosperity of man in general (the future of man included). But what if the reverse were true? What if a symptom of regression were inherent in the "good"?[44]

It is because he claims to have discovered such truths that he claims, in his final writings, that his work will present a tremendous challenge to humanity.[45]

The fact that Nietzsche views his moral insights as truths does not necessarily get us objectivism. As some recent interpreters have pointed out, it may be that the truth-conditions of these claims involve reference to the subjective states of individuals.[46] His view, in this case, will be that of

---

[43] *EC*, "The Birth of Tragedy," 2.

[44] *GM*, Preface, 6.

[45] Cf. *EC*, "Why I am Destiny," 1: "The truth speaks out from me. —But my truth is *terrible*, because *lies* have been called truth so far. —*Revaluation of all values*: that is my formula for an act of humanity's highest self-examination, an act that has become flesh and genius in me."

[46] This is the view that Hussain ("Honest Illusion") attributes to Harold Langsam. Langsam himself claims that truth and falsity do not apply to value judgments (cf. Harold Langsam, "How to Combat Nihilism: Reflections on Nietzsche's Critique of Morality," *History of Philosophy Quarterly* 14, no. 2 [1997]: 235–53, at 243). He does, however, attribute to Nietzsche the view that value judgments are legitimate in spite of their being subjective. Hussain fills in what the criteria for legitimacy might look like, i.e., the view that "claims of the form 'X is valuable' are true, but in virtue of the object, state of affairs, what-have-you, standing in certain relations to agents."

a subjective realist. The truth of his claims will be held to be dependent (to use Hussain's formulation) on his own pro-attitudes.[47] It is hard to see this as a genuinely realist view. It does not attribute universal validity to any judgments of the form "*X* is valuable"; and it has the consequence that if I say "*X* is valuable" and you say "*X* is not valuable," we are not in fact genuinely disagreeing.

But in any case, this view does not seem to me to be well supported by the kinds of reasons that Nietzsche actually offers us to justify his revaluations. When Nietzsche tells us, for example, that the sovereign religions so far have preserved too much in man of what ought to perish, the reason that he gives us is that they have kept the type "man" on a lower rung.[48] He does not relativize the judgment to any facts about the subjective attitudes of particular human beings. He even tells us that the "discipline of spirit needed to figure out such strange, delicate matters" requires an "affectionate and cautious neutrality."[49]

He often, in fact, seems to be presupposing intrinsic value, particularly in passages about aspects of our humanity. He writes as though human greatness would not have to be appreciated in order to be great; and the degeneration of humanity would not have to be perceived by anyone for it to be the case.[50] He also implies that values are independent of our attitudes when he asks a propos of martyrdom, "What? Does the value of something change when someone gives up their life for it?"[51]

The primary objects of value, for Nietzsche, seem to be precisely those human attributes that have been disparaged by Christianity. These seem to be held to be valuable in themselves. By positing an extrinsic ideal

---

[47] Hussain ("Honest Illusion") makes the interesting point that "one would normally [on a subjective realist view] use an agent's pro-attitudes to construct such truth-conditions; however, Nietzsche bemoans the fact that pro-attitudes themselves are constituted by evaluative judgments."

[48] *BGE*, 62.

[49] *AC*, 36.

[50] On greatness, cf. *BGE*, 285: "The greatest events and thoughts—but the greatest thoughts are the greatest events—are the last to be comprehended: the generations that are their contemporaries do not *experience* such events—they live right past them. The same thing happens here as in the realm of stars. The light of the remotest stars is the last to come to people; and until it has arrived people will deny that there are —stars out there." He seems to be implying here that greatness is not contingent on anyone's perception of it. Similarly for degeneration: *GM*, Preface, 6: "What if a symptom of regression were inherent in the 'good,' likewise a danger, a seduction, a poison, a narcotic, through which the present was possibly living *at the expense of the future*? Perhaps more comfortably, less dangerously, but at the same time in a meaner style, more basely? —So that precisely morality would be to blame if the *highest power and splendor* actually possible to the type man was never in fact attained? So that precisely morality was the danger of dangers?"

[51] *AC*, 53.

against which reality is to be measured, Christianity denies the intrinsic value of anything that exists. Nietzsche aims to correct this error:

> The parasitism of the priests (or the "moral world order") takes every natural custom, every natural institution (state, judicial order, marriage, care for the sick and the poor), everything required by the instinct of life, in short, everything *intrinsically valuable* [*was seinen Werth* in sich *hat*], and renders it fundamentally worthless, of *negative* value.[52]

Those who have been subject to this error, Nietzsche tells us, have had life spoiled for them.[53] They have failed to perceive the intrinsic value of aspects of human life.

He also uses the term *natural value* (*Natur-Werth*) in describing the immanent aspects of human life that he holds to be valuable.[54] It looks as though he is searching for a way to reconcile his naturalism with his realist orientation. It cannot be the case that he thinks that the natural and the valuable are coextensive.[55] But he does seem to hold that anything that is valuable will be natural. And his value-criticism seems to be aimed at recovering, after centuries of religious misconception, our awareness that natural phenomena can have intrinsic value.

Christianity, he claims, takes the view that anything that is valuable is nonnatural. It has postulated the existence of an imaginary realm (and hence of imaginary forms of causality in its interaction with manifest reality) in which value is ultimately located.[56] It manifests an "instinct of hatred for reality."[57] It is in this context that we must interpret the following important remark about Christian morality from *Twilight of the Idols*:

> "*There are absolutely no moral facts*. What moral and religious judgements have in common is belief in things that are not real. Morality is

[52] Ibid., 26.

[53] *BGE*, 59: "Perhaps there is an order of rank among these wounded children, the born artists who can find pleasure in life only by intending to *falsify* its image, in a sort of prolonged revenge against life. We can infer the degree to which life has been spoiled for them from the extent to which they want to see its image distorted, diluted, deified, and cast into the beyond."

[54] *AC*, 27: "Christianity grew up on this false soil, where every nature, every natural value [*jeder Natur-Werth*], every *reality* ran counter to the deepest instincts of the ruling class." Cf. also Ibid., 38: "*All* church concepts are known for what they are, the most malicious counterfeits that exist to *devalue* nature and natural values." Also *TI*, "Skirmishes," 33, on "*The natural value of egoism.*" Cf. also Ibid., 25.

[55] In *D*, 17, he criticizes views which hold that nature, as a whole, is inherently good or evil. Cf. also *GS*, 109.

[56] *AC* 57. Nietzsche outlines here the errors that he will then subject to further scrutiny in "The Four Great Errors" section of *Twilight of the Idols*.

[57] *AC*, 30.

just an interpretation of certain phenomena, or (more accurately) a *mis*interpretation.[58]

The passage has been taken as one of the strongest indications of Nietzsche's antirealism.[59] But read in this context it looks as though it is specifically Christian morality, or morality in the pejorative sense (to use Leiter's phrase) that is resolutely nonfactual.

Nietzsche despises these imaginary values precisely because they disparage what is really valuable. In *Ecce Homo* he writes: "The *lie* of the ideal so far has been the curse on reality; on account of it, mankind itself has become mendacious and false down to its most fundamental instincts—to the point of worshipping the *opposite* values of those which alone would guarantee its health, its future, the lofty *right* to its future."[60] His aim in exposing the lies of religion is to reveal what is genuinely valuable for humanity, the cultivation of which can confer this right.

As this reference to the "opposite" values indicates, Nietzsche increasingly presupposes bivalence in his later value-criticism.[61] In the preface to the *Genealogy*, referring to prevailing moral assumptions, he asks "What if the reverse were true?"[62] He claims in *Beyond Good and Evil* not just that he wants to revalue values, he wants to invert them.[63] So even where he does not explicitly use the language of truth and falsity, he seems to assume that the falseness of Christian value judgments implies the truth of their negations. This is an implicitly realist assumption, one which a consistent subjective realist (or indeed any kind of antirealist) would not make.

Nietzsche's value-criticism aims to expose errors and lies about what is right and wrong. The worst lies and the worst errors have, he insists, been propagated by Christianity and are so entrenched that it is difficult

---

[58] *TI*, "Improving Humanity," 1.

[59] Cf., e.g., Hussain, "Honest Illusion."

[60] *EH*, Preface, 2.

[61] He seems to presuppose bivalence in spite of explicitly toying with the idea that we might reject it. Cf., e.g., *BGE*, 34: "Why do we even assume that 'true' and 'false' are intrinsically opposed? Isn't it enough to assume that there are levels of appearance and, as it were, lighter and darker shades and tones of appearance?"

[62] *GM*, "Preface," 6.

[63] *BGE*, 203: "Where do *we* need to reach with our hopes? Towards *new philosophers*; there is no choice; toward spirits strong and original enough to provide the stimuli for opposite valuations and to revalue and invert 'eternal values.'" Cf. also *AC*, 46: "Every word coming from the mouth of a 'first Christian' is a lie, everything he does is an instinctive falsehood, —all of his values, all of his goals are harmful, but *who* he hates, *what* he hates, *these have value*."[63] Also, Ibid., 62: "The Christian church has not left anything untouched by its corruption, it has made an un-value out of every value, a lie out of very truth, a malice of the soul out of every piece of integrity."

for us to liberate ourselves from them.[64] But Nietzsche struggles unrelentingly to free himself from them. In his 1886 preface to *Human, All Too Human*, he explains to us how it is that the free spirit makes sense of the enigma of his own liberation. He claims that free spirits are those in whom a task becomes incarnate, and he tells us that the "secret force and necessity" of this task rules the inner life of the free spirit, even before he is aware of it. The task, of course, is the revaluation of values, or the determination of their order of rank. Those who are called to this task, he says,

> As adventurers and circumnavigators of that inner world called "man," as surveyors and gaugers of that "higher" and "one upon the other" that is likewise called "man"—penetrating everywhere, almost without fear, disdaining nothing, losing nothing, asking everything, cleansing everything of what is chance and accident in it and as it were thoroughly sifting it—until at last we had the right to say, we free spirits: "Here— a *new* problem! Here a long ladder upon whose rungs we ourselves have sat and climbed—which we ourselves have at some time *been*! Here a higher, a deeper, a beneath-us, a long ordering, an order of rank which we *see*: here—*our* problem![65]

The process of liberation, for the free spirits, is a process of discovery, at the end of which they see the correct order of rank of human values.

Freedom and Rational Necessity

In chapter 4, we saw that an antirealist reading has trouble making sense of Nietzsche's views about evaluative freedom. The views of this that it supports seem either too deterministic (the "types" view) or too open-ended (the "value-creation" views). The realist reading, on the other hand, offers us the possibility of a coherent account of what kind of independence Nietzsche's "free spirits" are aiming for. It can be construed as a form of rational autonomy. Unlike a Kantian conception of autonomy, however, it is not something that just anyone can attain.

Nietzsche's many remarks on his willing submission to necessity in his evaluations indicate that he is not recommending any purely capricious mode of valuing.[66] He says of philosophers: "Our ideas, our values, our

---

[64] *EH*, "Why I am Destiny," 7: "Christian morality—the most malicious form of the will to lie, the true Circe of humanity: the thing that has *corrupted* humanity."

[65] *HTH*, I, Preface, 7.

[66] Cf., e.g., *HTH*, I, Preface, 6, 7; *GS*, 246: "Let us introduce the refinement and rigor of mathematics into all sciences as far as this is at all possible, not in the faith that this will lead us to know things but in order to *determine* our human relation to things." As we have seen,

yeas and nays, our ifs and buts, grow out of us with the necessity with which a tree bears its fruit."[67] He does not prize untrammeled creative freedom. It would be hard to make sense of any notion of valuing that incorporated no constraints, of whatever normative standing. The question is, then, whether the constraints on evaluation that he recognizes are rational constraints.

In *Beyond Good and Evil*, Nietzsche tells us that we can attain freedom through guidance by some powerful inner necessity, that we become commanders through obedience:

> This world as it concerns *us*, in which *we* need to love and be afraid, this almost invisible, inaudible world of subtle commanding, subtle obedience, a world of the "almost" in every respect, twisted, tricky, barbed, and loving: yes, it is well defended against clumsy spectators and friendly curiosity! We have been woven into a strong net and shirt of duties, and *cannot* get out of it, —in this sense we are "men of duty," —even us![68]

The idea that freedom consists in obeying laws we give to ourselves sounds very Kantian (and Nietzsche is notoriously hostile to Kant). But the idea of freedom as submission to rational necessity does seem to make sense of his notion of independence, particularly insofar as it can be achieved through value-criticism.

Alexander Nehamas has argued that values, for Nietzsche, are created, and that the constraints governing their fashioning may be understood by analogy with the discipline involved in creating a work of art.[69] The submission to necessity can, on this model, be understood as the aspiration to a kind of inner consistency. All worldviews, on the Nehamas reading, will necessarily involve illusions and simplifications. "Free spirits" are those who can determine which set of values and illusions works best for them (though not for anyone else).[70]

---

in ibid., 335, Nietzsche appeals to those readers who, unlike "the great majority," want to "*become who we are*—human beings who are new, unique, incomparable, who give themselves laws, who create themselves." We should "become the best students and discoverers of everything lawful and necessary in the world." Cf. also, *BGE*, 32, on the apparent necessity governing revaluation: "But today, thanks to a renewed self-contemplation and deepening of humanity, shouldn't we be facing a renewed necessity to effect a reversal and fundamental displacement of values? Shouldn't we be standing on the threshold of a period that would be designated, negatively at first, as *extra-moral*?"

[67] *GM*, I, Preface, 2.
[68] *BGE*, 226.
[69] Nehamas, *Nietzsche: Life as Literature*, 26: "Socrates thinks that action must be grounded in objective value, while Nietzsche urges that values are created through action."
[70] Ibid., 61.

As John Richardson has argued, this view understates the role that truth-seeking plays in Nietzsche's project of revaluation.[71] Richardson stresses three components that are essential to the evaluative freedom to which Nietzsche aspires. The first is self-selection.[72] Freedom consists in determining one's own values, rather than accepting whatever value commitments one inherits from the processes of biological and social selection. The second is epistemic reliability. In order to detach ourselves from our inherited values, making ourselves free to create new ones, we must have a clear and full understanding of how they came about. We must overcome all forms of self-deception, particularly concerning our own actions and motivations. "Higher" values will be those which incorporate the truest picture of the world and our relation to it.[73] The third is consistency. Biological and social selection, on this view, have generated conflicting values. The aim of self-selection is to resolve these conflicts by selecting a coherent set of values for ourselves.[74]

In its emphasis on self-legislation, epistemic reliability, and consistency, Richardson's reading already seems closer to a model of rational autonomy. But on Richardson's view Nietzsche is a moral antirealist and any value judgments that are chosen will ultimately be rationally arbitrary. As we saw in chapter 4, this antirealist reading generates a problem concerning Nietzsche's generalized commitment to evaluative freedom. It is difficult to see how he could be fully committed to his own values and at the same time recommend that others should choose whichever values they like, even if it means willing ends that are incompatible with his own. He cannot coherently demand that society be organized around his chosen principles and that it should be organized around incompatible ones. And in the absence of any possibility of rational agreement, unless there is purely coincidental convergence, the assertion of his own value judgments must involve desiring that others be compelled to be subject to them, hence constraining their freedom.

This particular form of incoherence disappears if we think of evaluative freedom in terms of seeking truth, in which case the aim of everyone pursuing this freedom is to arrive at the same, correct values and principles.

---

[71] Richardson, *Nietzsche's New Darwinism*, 265: "Although [Nehamas] stresses that Nietzsche's perspectivism is not a relativism 'that holds that any view is as good as any other' (72), Nehamas seems unwilling to say that some perspectives are better by being truer."

[72] Ibid., 95–97.

[73] Cf. ibid., 266: "I think these truths function for Nietzsche not just as preconditions for self-creating but as key criteria for its success. It's not simply a minimal condition on an adequate self-creating that it be true to these deeds. It's rather a matter of the *degree to which* it is true to them: this is Nietzsche's main criterion for how 'high' a self-creating is."

[74] Ibid., 170: "Our drives and social habits (especially our habits of thought) stand in a deep conflict that has made us 'the sick animal.' Nietzsche offers freedom as solving this conflict."

It then makes sense for Nietzsche to embrace the ideal of the "sovereign individual," even if few can attain that state of being "autonomous and supramoral."[75] The few who do attain it will be those who have insight into what is best for humanity. Even where their evaluations differ, it will be parametric universalism and not relativism that permits these differences, since their ultimate standards will be the same. Nietzsche can coherently envisage a plurality of "free spirits" on this model.

THE DIFFICULTY OF VALUE-CRITICISM

Unlike the Kantian conception, however, Nietzsche's conception of autonomy does not build in any guarantee that it can be shared universally be any rational being. It is an intellectually exacting conception. It is a "privilege of the strong."[76] Very few people, he tells us in *The Gay Science*, have an intellectual conscience.[77] Many actions, he tells us, "are called evil but are only stupid." The standards used to judge them are continually changing, "because the degree of intelligence that decided them was very low."[78] In order to arrive at the right value judgments we must subject to critical scrutiny all our established moral intuitions and we must be prepared for counterintuitive results.[79]

Nietzsche rejects much of what others intuitively find to be morally right. He rejects much that many of his readers would, after serious reflection, take to be morally right. But his rejections and affirmations derive from a critical process that is sophisticated enough to point to the real cognitive problems involved in making judgments of value. Even though we might ultimately believe that he makes the wrong judgments, he shows us how intellectually demanding the process of justification can prove to be and thereby raises interesting questions about normative authority.

In his value-criticism he identifies several sources of error. First, it is very hard for us to see what is best for humanity because we tend to be mired in our own limited perspectives. Even moral philosophers, he insists, have tended to end up producing convoluted rationalizations of their parochial worldviews. In *Beyond Good and Evil*, he writes:

> Precisely because moral philosophers had only a crude understanding of moral *facta*, selected arbitrarily and abbreviated at random—for

[75] *GM*, ii, 2.
[76] *BGE*, 29.
[77] GS, 2.
[78] *HTH*, I, 107.
[79] For an interesting discussion of why Nietzsche holds that most people are unable to think for themselves, and hence of why this freedom can only be for the few, cf. Dana Villa, "Nietzsche," *Socratic Citizenship*.

instance, as the morality of their surroundings, their class, their church, their *Zeitgeist*, their climate and region, —precisely because they were poorly informed (and not particularly eager to learn more) about peoples, ages, and histories, they completely missed out on the genuine problems involved in morality, problems that only emerge from a comparison of many *different* moralities.[80]

Without a breadth of understanding of diverse moral phenomena, it is hard to distinguish rationalizations of parochial views from genuine rational justifications.

Second, it is difficult for us to see the flaws in the basic value judgments that we have unreflectively inherited. The extent to which this inherited basis of our evaluations is reflectively available to us at any given time is necessarily limited.[81] Nietzsche formulates a method for overcoming these inherited perspectives, through the discovery of tensions and inconsistencies in our value judgments and the attempt to find a position that transcends them. But these tensions and inconsistencies are nonobvious. It takes imaginative and critical effort to bring them out.

The best-known examples of this method are to be found in the *Genealogy*, where Nietzsche's rhetorical strategy is to reveal that the moral values we have inherited from Christianity can be made to look abhorrent in the light of the nonmoral values to which he appeals. As we saw in chapter 4, his aim is to discover a higher standpoint from which to judge these clashing values, a standpoint that permits us to see the overall good of the competing evaluative practices for humanity as a whole.

Another very well-known example of this kind of criticism occurs in *Thus Spoke Zarathustra*. Here Nietzsche tells us a story about the "last man":

> The earth has become small, and on it hops the last man, who makes everything small. His race is as ineradicable as the flea-beetle; the last man lives longest.
>
> "We have invented happiness," say the last men, and they blink. They have left the regions where it was hard to live, for one needs warmth. One still loves one's neighbor and rubs against him, for one needs warmth.
>
> Becoming sick and harboring suspicion are sinful to them: one proceeds carefully. A fool, whoever still stumbles over stones or human beings!

---

[80] *BGE*, 186.

[81] What we have inherited, Nietzsche claims, we take to be "natural," as in the case of priestly evaluations: "To be determined, as a matter of principle, to apply only concepts, symbols, attitudes which have been proved by the practice of the priest; instinctively to reject every other practice, every other perspective of value and usefulness —that is not merely tradition, that is *heritage*: only as heritage does it seem like nature itself. The whole of mankind, even the best heads of the best ages . . . have permitted themselves to be deceived." *AC*, 44.

A little poison now and then: that makes for agreeable dreams. And much poison in the end, for an agreeable death.

One still works, for work is a form of entertainment. But one is careful lest the entertainment be too harrowing. One no longer becomes poor or rich: both require too much exertion. Who still wants to rule? Who obey? Both require too much exertion.

No shepherd and one herd! Everybody wants the same, everybody is the same: whoever feels differently goes into a madhouse.

"Formerly all the world was mad," say the most refined, and they blink.

One is clever and knows everything that has ever happened: so there is no end of derision. One still quarrels, but one is soon reconciled—else it might spoil the digestion.

One has one's little pleasure for the day and one's little pleasure for the night: but one has a regard for health.

"We have invented happiness," say the last men, and they blink.[82]

He wants us to recognize ourselves in the last man, to identify with the aversion to suffering and desire for comfort, but to be simultaneously revolted by the spectacle of such a creature. He implies that from the standpoint of a higher value, that of human dignity, this basic attitude to suffering is flawed. The rhetorical power is clearly supposed to derive from the intractability of either position. Hence the difficulty of revaluation.

Third, the various beliefs that our value judgments incorporate are frequently false. People often make bad value judgments because they have erroneous beliefs. Nietzsche sees these bad judgments as the norm rather than the exception across human history. For the beliefs that are most deeply implicated in our value judgments are not only most often in error but are also the most difficult to revise. The emotional weight of the value judgments that they support, and the practical need to preserve the forms of life that they sustain, provide a powerful disincentive to critical reflection.

From *Human, All Too Human* on, each of his works contains long sections devoted to exposing these kinds of errors. Some are fairly mundane. For example, he corrects the error that we have the right to promise always to love someone else, when the implicit predictive claim about ourselves is unjustified.[83] Many involve broad historical judgments, which Nietzsche holds to be in error owing to a lack of appreciation of the relevant characteristics of an epoch, a culture, or a religion. The ancient Greeks, most obviously, are held to have been consistently underestimated in

---

[82] TSZ, Prologue, 5.
[83] *HTH*, I, 58.

precisely those respects that have benefited humanity most. These kinds of historical judgments are shown to have an important bearing on the way on which we view ourselves.[84]

And some factual errors, he claims, are fundamental to a whole way of thinking about value, such as the "four great errors" described in *Twilight of the Idols*: the error of confusing cause and effect (for example, seeing happiness as an effect of virtue, rather than its cause); the error of a false causality (particularly concerning our "inner world" and our motives); the error of imaginary causes (for example, "sinfulness" as a cause of the feeling of guilt); and the error of free will.[85]

The real question that his work raises, then, is not one about meta-ethics; it is about normative authority. We cannot assume, according to Nietzsche's view of valuing, that people can easily acquire normative knowledge. Most people, he suggests, are, in fact, bound to make the wrong value judgments. Inequality in our intellectual capacities leads to inequality in our moral capacities.

So there are "free spirits" and there are "fettered spirits."[86] There are those who can determine what the right values are for themselves, and those who remain subject to the illusions sustained by religious belief, by the pressure for social conformity, by the need for consolation, or the sublimated desire for revenge. Nietzsche identifies innumerable psychological and historical forces that contribute to this predicament, besides a brute, natural inequality in our critical capacities. Even if it is a contingent feature of human beings, as they have evolved so far, it is not one that Nietzsche suggests we have any foreseeable hope of overcoming. The question, then, is how we should think about normative authority in such a situation.

VALUES FOR EVERYONE AND NO ONE

Nietzsche's anti-universalism about moral knowledge consists in this set of claims about capacities. Not everyone will have access to the truth about our highest values. This antiuniversalism about moral capacities has often been mistaken for a perspectivist view that rejects universal validity. Nietzsche writes, for example, in *Beyond Good and Evil*: "Our highest insights must—and should—sound like stupidities, or possibly crimes,

---

[84] Since this theme dominates all of Nietzsche's works, there are, of course, countless examples. A particularly pithy summary of the merits and demerits of Christianity as contrasted with ancient Greek religion can be found in *HTH*, I, 114.

[85] *TI*, "The Four Great Errors."

[86] *HTH*, I, 225.

when they come without permission to people whose ears have no affinity for them and are not predestined for them."[87] Even when people are confronted with the truth, he is telling us, they will seldom have the capacity to recognize it as such. The problem of the early works, concerning intellectual authority, therefore reasserts itself in the later works. Even if Nietzsche's value-criticism can discover what is right, how can this insight be effective? It will have no popular authority.

Previous generations of German philosophers had grappled with the problem of how the moral truths discovered by philosophers might serve as a foundation for the value judgments that people actually make. Jerome Schneewind, in describing the innovativeness of Kant's practical philosophy, has helpfully brought out the contrast between two distinct enlightenment views of how this might be possible: we will refer to them as the old enlightenment and new enlightenment views.

According to the older view, moral truths are not intuitively obvious. They require a special sort of knowledge. On the Leibnizian view adopted by thinkers such as Christian Wolff, which involves the claim that God has created the best of all possible worlds, moral knowledge must be acquired through an understanding of the perfection of the universe.[88] It requires sophisticated metaphysical knowledge. Wolff felt that he himself had acquired this knowledge and he published it in the vernacular to make the basic moral principles he had learned accessible to everybody else.[89] The implication, of course, is that popular morality is only possible through deference to normative experts.

Unsurprisingly, this did not seem to everyone to settle the question of how we can come to have moral knowledge. Either we have to plough through Wolff's metaphysics (even one of his own editors describes him as "the most prolix and boring author of his century, even of modernity as a whole") or take his word for it that he is right.[90] A much more satisfactory resolution, particularly from the point of view of each of us procuring our own salvation, would be one that enabled us all to acquire this knowledge for ourselves, through the use of some faculty available to ordinary people. It would involve having what Schneewind, following

---

[87] *BGE*, 30. Brian Leiter cites this passage as evidence for the view that "Nietzsche's own evaluative perspective in undertaking the revaluation does, not, in fact, enjoy any metaphysical or epistemic privilege over its target," since Nietzsche sees the audience for his insights as narrowly circumscribed. This and other similar passages (Leiter cites *GS*, 381; *EH*, Preface, 3; *EH*, 3:1; *EH*, Preface, 4; *EH*, "Zarathustra," 6; *BGE*, 202) seem to me to reflect not a perspectivist view, but merely the idea that many people are not fit to appreciate the truth.

[88] Jerome Schneewind, *The Invention of Autonomy*, 433.

[89] Ibid., 433.

[90] Ibid., 442, citing Marcel Thomann.

Sidgwick, calls a "method of ethics," a procedure for settling normative questions that anyone can employ.[91]

This is just what Kant thought he had discovered. The newer enlightenment view is much more optimistic about our capacity for normative self-governance. Nietzsche is not impressed. He sees Kant's practical philosophy as having popular authority only because it is a rationalization of existing Protestant beliefs.[92] The justification of the categorical imperative itself is complex and controversial, as Nietzsche's own wrangles with the neo-Kantian tradition had shown him.

Given Nietzsche's insights into the complexity of value judgments, it is not difficult to see why he thinks we cannot formulate a procedure that would constitute a "method of ethics." We certainly have moral intuitions, but he thinks that these are often wrong, and even the most rigorous reflection can leave us wondering which of our intuitions are actually reliable. If there are simple rational principles that we might adopt in moral reasoning, we face the same complex problem of justification in assessing these principles. Philosophers have not arrived at uncontentious answers. If they have appeared to do this, Nietzsche claims, it is because they have "pressed into formulas" existing valuations.[93]

But the old enlightenment view does not, on Nietzsche's account, seem promising either. Reliance on expertise generates the same burden of justification as we have in relation to our own intuitions. We have to make judgments about who it would be rational for us to defer to in deciding normative issues. This is not a question that can be easily answered even by philosophers.

As we have noted, in the realm of ordinary facts we often can identify experts. Scientists have theories that can be tested according to their predictive success. We can acknowledge that there is specialist knowledge that scientists acquire, and which nonexperts do not possess. For example, the scientist might be in possession of a microscope or a telescope. But there is no moral equivalent of having a microscope, or of making a correct prediction. The criteria for what counts as expertise in the moral realm are much more opaque, and it is therefore harder to decide to whom we should defer.

Nietzsche maintains that this kind of deference has generally been misplaced. In *The Gay Science*, he writes:

In honour of the priestly type: —I think that what the people mean by wisdom (and who today is not "people"?)—that prudent, cowlike serenity and country parson meekness which lies in the meadow and

[91] Schneewind, "Natural Law, Skepticism, and Methods of Ethics," 289–308.
[92] *AC*, 10.
[93] *BGE*, 230.

earnestly ruminates and *observes* life—is also that from which precisely the philosophers have always felt the most remote, probably because they were not "people" enough, not country parsons enough.[94]

When people do defer to those who they take to be experts, Nietzsche thinks, they will be motivated to respect those whose views are least unsettling to their established beliefs and values. It is very difficult to get genuine rational justifications to override emotionally gripping normative convictions.

Those who succeed in establishing control over popular belief do so, Nietzsche claims, because they provide predictability, stability, and reassurance. He tells us that "the true invention of the religion-founders is first to establish a certain way of life and everyday customs that work as a *disciplina voluntatis* while at the same time removing boredom; and then to give just this life an *interpretation* that makes it appear illuminated by the highest worth, so that henceforth it becomes a good for which one fights and under certain circumstances even gives ones life."[95] Persuasiveness, then, has little intrinsic connection to the truth.

It sometimes looks as though Nietzsche thinks that philosophers are part of a "priestly caste," but this is not by virtue of their ability to make their normative expertise persuasive. For the "priestly caste" in Nietzsche's *Genealogy*, asceticism is a necessary means to their intellectual ends. It becomes attractive as an ideal in its own right to the impoverished and disempowered for whom asceticism is an unavoidable fact of life. But it is an unwitting by-product of their intellectual pursuits: the truths which these "priests" discover have no comparable popular authority.

Nietzsche suggests that these "priests," the intellectual classes, have deliberately exploited the ascetic ideal to control the destructive forces of *ressentiment*, but he does not claim that this opportunistic authority has any relation to genuine normative insight.[96] The evaluative phenomenon to which they give rise is not only compatible with but actually reliant on errors and lies. According to this view of the way in which popular modes of evaluation are formed, any individual who did succeed in recognizing genuine normative truths would have no special effective authority.

This is not to say that everyone's values are immune to rational reflection, only that genuine justification takes a strength of commitment of which few are capable.[97] Few of us are capable of arriving at real

[94] GS, 351.
[95] Ibid., 353.
[96] GM, iii,14.
[97] GS, 335.

moral knowledge. But many of us, it seems, will imagine that we are. As Nietzsche says in *Daybreak*, "There is today perhaps no more firmly credited prejudice than this: that one *knows* what really constitutes the moral."[98] Not only is there an absence of recognized normative expertise, but the vast majority of people do not even acknowledge the need for or existence of such expertise.

MORAL INCAPACITY AND POLITICAL IDEOLOGY

If we interpret Nietzsche to be a moral realist, then, his political skepticism will take the following form. In the modern world, political authority is concentrated in states. It is a functional requirement of states that they be accepted as legitimate (since they cannot rule through force alone). The political need for normative consensus derives from this fact. Insofar as Nietzsche wants to preserve some stable form of political authority he must accept this requirement. But at the same time, he cannot will the necessary means to this end.

Given the difficulty of achieving moral knowledge, the required consensus cannot be a genuine rational consensus. This is true in two senses. First, it cannot be produced simply by means of everybody exercising their own reason and converging on the truth. Most people will exercise their reason badly. And second, it is unlikely that consensus will be formed around rationally justified views by some other means, since those capable of perceiving genuine rational justifications have no effective authority over those who do not. Any consensus that is achieved will, then, be merely ideological.

If we see that Nietzsche's value-criticism is governed by a commitment to normative truth, we can also see why he cannot concede unconstrained ideological authority to the state. The discovery of normative truth requires rational freedom, or independence from ideology. Nietzsche cannot coherently advocate a form of political rule that is incompatible with this freedom.

But at the same time, he cannot envisage a form of political rule that is compatible with it. What would be required to reconcile normative authority and political authority is some mechanism for securing political legitimacy, some means of imposing genuine normative constraints on state power. But Nietzsche does not accept that we have discovered any such mechanism.

[98] *D*, 132.

He is particularly skeptical that democracy might fulfill this function. Like many of his contemporary Germans, both liberal and conservative, he is dismissive of the idea that democracy might have any rationalizing influence on political life, or help to impose genuine normative constraints on state power. Bismarck's strategic and cynical extension of the franchise was undoubtedly instrumental in convincing him and others that democracy meant an easily exploitable populism. Since collectivities are, on Nietzsche's view, even less epistemically reliable than individuals, the collective power of the people is unlikely to be a good guarantor of legitimacy.[99]

As Keith Ansell-Pearson points out, Nietzsche does briefly flirt with the idea that democracy might be a good protection against "physical and spiritual enslavement." Democratization is seen, in "The Wanderer and his Shadow" section of *Human, All Too Human,* as a prophylactic against certain forms of tyranny. But elsewhere Nietzsche sees it as conducive to tyranny, making the views of a manipulable public vulnerable to political exploitation.[100]

The Bismarckian struggle between "kingship and the priestly caste" provoked fears that the plastic opinion of the multitudes could be marshaled by either side. Heinrich von Treitschke, for example, described universal suffrage as "an invaluable weapon of the Jesuits, which grants such an unfair superiority to the powers of custom and stupidity."[101] Nietzsche echoes what were then conventional fears about democratization. But his fears indicate a deeper concern. No political system, on his view, can suffice for legitimacy if it does not guarantee protection for the discovery of normative truth.

So democracy, he thinks, cannot be a sufficient condition for legitimacy. It threatens to involve us in the same incoherence as political realism. It cedes to political forces (in this case via majoritarianism) the authority to render real normative insight impotent. Unless the people could be relied on to be an infallible source of truth, or were reliably guided by some genuine normative authority, they could not systematically impose valid normative constraints on state power.

On Nietzsche's view of states, the only way of making them systematically, as opposed to merely accidentally, conform to the correct norms,

[99] *BGE,* 156: "Madness is rare in the individual—but with groups, parties, peoples, and ages it is the rule."

[100] Ibid., 242. Fredrick Appel emphasizes that Nietzsche sees democracy as a powerful instrument for tyrants. He cites *WP,* 128: "The trainability of men has become very great in democratic Europe; men who learn easily and adapt themselves easily are the rule." Also, *WP,* 898, 956. In Appel, *Nietzsche Contra Democracy,* 130.

[101] Cited by Margaret Anderson, in *Practicing Democracy: Elections and Political Culture in Imperial Germany* (Princeton, N.J.: Princeton University Press, 2000), 82.

would be to subject them to real, independent normative constraints. These constraints would have to be capable of competing permanently with the state's ideological ambitions. But Nietzsche cannot envisage what form these constraints could conceivably take. And whenever we imagine that such constraints are already in place, Nietzsche warns, we are likely to be unwittingly cooperating with ideology. As we shall see in chapter 6, liberalism, like democracy, seems to him to exacerbate this predicament.

Nietzsche as a Skeptic about Liberalism

INTRODUCTION

Since Nietzsche never addressed systematically the core questions of political thought, it requires some extrapolation to see the bearing that his work has on particular normative political theories. In the case of democracy, as we have seen, his view of its limitations is drawn quite explicitly. In the case of liberalism, his engagement is more oblique and takes place largely on the terrain of debates about education. But it is interesting to draw out the nature of his arguments. We can infer from this the grounds of the hostility toward liberalism that he sporadically expresses in the later works. And so we can begin to assess whether or not his political skepticism really is resistant to the purported political solutions that were then on offer.[1]

The kind of liberalism that found support in nineteenth-century Germany might seem to address the problems that I have presented as being at the centre of Nietzsche's political concerns. Contemporary post-Kantian liberals proposed a solution to the problem of legitimacy. They were optimistic that we could have knowledge of very spare or, to adopt a more recent metaphor, "thin" principles for political legitimacy, which would be sufficient to ground political life. These would generate just enough agreement for a functioning polity, without stifling the cultural diversity which had, since Wilhelm von Humboldt, become so important to the liberal tradition.

Nietzsche is certainly not unsympathetic to the idea of minimizing state power. In *Daybreak*, he unambiguously declares that the power of the state must be limited. In a section entitled, "As Little State as Possible" (*So wenig als möglich Staat!*) , he tells us that it would be a terrible waste for the talents of society's most gifted spirits to be squandered on political and economic affairs.[2] There are "higher and rarer objectives"

---

[1] I will not attempt to spell out systematically here the implications of Nietzsche's thought for current liberal theory. For such a discussion, with particular reference to Rawlsian liberalism, cf. David Owen, *Nietzsche, Politics, and Modernity: A Critique of Liberal Reason* (Thousand Oaks, CA: Sage, 1995).

[2] *D*, 179. He is here echoing a remark made in *HTH*, I, 473, where he is countering what he sees as the socialist demand for as much state as possible.

that must be respected. In *Beyond Good and Evil*, he warns that when a people's leaders allow them to get carried away with the idea of "great politics," more important virtues than this "empty politicking" will inevitably be sacrificed.[3] Distrust of government seems to be a necessary prerequisite for intellectual integrity.

This aspect of his thought has been seen as a residually liberal element in his work, being continuous with the tradition established by Humboldt, whose own ideal of securing freedom from state action to facilitate human flourishing was still at the time an important source of liberal ideas.[4] But his concern with freedom and independence does not seem to me to be rooted in the same kind of concern for individuals.

The view that follows from Nietzsche's claims about normative authority is simply that the power of state must be limited along one specific dimension—that of its ideological authority. It is a condition of the possibility of seeking truth and normative truth that the ideological power of the state be limited. His argument therefore has a foundation which is distinct from that of liberal justifications for limiting state power.[5]

It follows from his acceptance of two important premises. First, truth in general, and normative truth in particular, are difficult to discover. In the case of normative truth, it is especially difficult for us to see how we might converge on the truth when we cannot identify appropriate experts to whom it would be rational to defer. Second, the secular state has tremendous ideological power, as well as an ideological need. It must attain legitimacy in the descriptive sense, that is, a perceived entitlement to command. It can no longer rely on the authority of tradition or religion to generate this; but it does have broad and deep powers to manipulate belief.

Simply put, his point is that normative truth is difficult to discern and we are unlikely to converge on it, but political life requires agreement. If Nietzsche were a normative skeptic all the way through, there would be no tension between these demands. He would be able to accept the realist view that the state inevitably seeks power and that we simply cannot

---

[3] *BGE*, 241.

[4] Meinecke sees the views of Burckhardt and Nietzsche, in contradistinction to those of Ranke and the German historical school, as continuous with the desire to limit state power that began with Humboldt's conception of the *Nachtwächterstaat*. Cf. "Ranke und Burckhardt," 100. Similarly, Lionel Gossman writes: "The likely source of the Basel scholars' ideal of individual freedom and independence from the state is the liberal neohumanism of the turn of the century in Germany, particularly in the writings of Wilhelm von Humboldt." Cf. *Basel in the Age of Burckhardt*, 451.

[5] Keith Ansell-Pearson points out that "like Tocqueville, Nietzsche gave a pejorative flavour to liberal individualism. Both saw modern individualism as resulting in a self-centered preoccupation with purely personal ends." *An Introduction to Nietzsche as Political Thinker*, 6.

require that this process be normatively constrained.[6] But since he has independent evaluative commitments, it would be incoherent both to have these commitments and to will their frustration by the state.

It therefore seems to be a condition of the possibility of discovering truth and normative truth, and of being capable of acting on the basis of this knowledge, that the state's ideological power be limited. Nietzsche has what we might call a transcendental argument for limiting state power. But it is an extremely minimalist one. Because it derives from a politically skeptical position, it does not entail any specification of political rights and obligations, or provide us with further criteria to distinguish between legitimate and illegitimate political actions. It does not constitute a normative political theory in the way that liberalism in its various guises obviously does.

Nietzsche's skepticism about legitimacy points to a possible tension between the demands of normative authority and political authority. Normative authority demands correctness. Political authority, or the state's ability to command, demands agreement. Nietzsche is skeptical that these demands can be made to coincide. Liberals, on the other hand, are optimistic that they might. Nietzsche identifies a particular form that this liberal optimism takes, the ideology of *Bildung*. He casts doubt on its capacity to generate uncoerced agreement and hence legitimacy.

Liberalism aims to narrow the scope of necessary political agreement as much as possible. It thereby attempts to secure agreement in spite of broader moral, religious, and cultural disagreement. But as we shall see, Nietzsche claims that it nevertheless makes substantive normative claims and ones that, in both their justification and application, are intellectually demanding and contentious. He suggests that it is, in fact, much more difficult to get this "thin" form of agreement than it is to get "thicker" kinds. So he claims that *Bildung* does not, as liberals hope that it might, guarantee convergence on the correct political norms.

Nietzsche's critique of *Bildung* implies that the basis of the liberal argument for limiting state power is insufficiently skeptical. It still holds out the naïve hope that the state's perceived entitlement to command might really be grounded in normative authority. This leads liberals to mistake state-generated political agreement for real rational convergence. They have unwittingly ceded to the state the very kind of ideological power that he sees as inimical to the quest for truth and value.

This critique of liberalism, which is grounded in his "transcendental" argument for limiting state power, may be analytically separated from his less edifying objections to liberal values such as freedom, tolerance,

---

[6] This is the route taken by Carl Schmitt and his followers. Cf., eg., "Die Tyrannie der Werte."

equality, and justice. It might nevertheless appear to be historically parochial, insofar as it is aimed at a specific form of liberal ideology. But I shall argue that it is interesting at least insofar as it helps us to rule out some of the forms that a liberal response to his skepticism about legitimacy might take.

BILDUNG AS A POLITICAL IDEAL

The German liberal tradition in the nineteenth century was diverse and complex.[7] Nietzsche has practically nothing to say about many of its central preoccupations, including issues such as economic liberalization, or the form of the legal, constitutional state. This is undoubtedly in part because he did not know very much about the empirical side of the relevant political questions. But the lack of attention that he pays to them is also determined by the fact that his starting point is the normative realm, and the kind of skepticism that he advances involves claiming that we have no clear way of linking normative authority to the world of practical politics.

His views about our capacity for normative self-governance contrast starkly with those of the post-Kantian liberals that he criticizes. The idea of *Bildung* had played a fundamental role in this tradition since its inception almost a century earlier.[8] The term has no real English equivalent, but is generally translated as either self-development, education, or culture.[9] This set of plausible translations indicates the distinctive nature of the concept and of the various aspirations that it brings together. It essentially presupposes a natural harmony between the cultivation of freedom and individuality, on the one hand, and the attainment of unity, or the basic ethical agreement necessary for political life, on the other.

It does so because the pursuit of freedom is seen necessarily to entail the kind of enlightenment that allows us to converge on rational norms. German hopes for attaining the goals of the French Revolution without violent insurrection were premised on this idea of a self-generated, reflective

[7] For comprehensive studies of this tradition, see James Sheehan, *German Liberalism in the Nineteenth Century* (New York: Humanity Books, 1978); and Dieter Langewiesche, *Liberalism in Germany* (London: Routledge, 2000).

[8] Cf. Sheehan, *German Liberalism*, ch. 1.

[9] For general studies that describe the content of this concept and its role in German political thought, see W. Bruford, *The German Tradition of Self-Cultivation: "Bildung" from Humboldt to Thomas Mann* (Cambridge: Cambridge University Press, 1975); Klaus Vondung, "Unity through *Bildung*: A German Dream of Perfection," *Independent Journal of Philosophy* 5, no 6 (1988): 47–55; Louis Dumont, *German Ideology: From France to Germany and Back* (Chicago: Chicago University Press, 1996).

form of social harmony.[10] External, institutional change was to be developed in a dialectical relation to internal, individual development. Full reflective identification with our social and political roles would then be possible. This would provide the strongest possible basis for political legitimacy.

Part of the content of *Bildung* was intended to be rationally arbitrary. The bare idea of obedience to universally binding rational norms was not a rich enough conception of freedom to accommodate the postromantic sensibilities cultivated by Goethe, Schiller, and Humboldt. The romantic stress on cultural authenticity and diversity found expression as a liberal ideal of individuality in Humboldt's conception of *Selbstättigkeit*.[11] But even this imperative that we should cultivate as many human attributes as possible was seen to be a dictate of reason.[12]

Like Schiller and Hegel, Humboldt took the view that Kant's abstract reasoning is insufficient to ground an actual historical and cultural community. *Bildung*, or self-cultivation, was therefore intended to bring reasoning into relation with the sensuous and the particular. The third *Critique*, as opposed to the second, provided the essential Kantian impetus behind the project.

This influence is clearly apparent in Schiller's *Aesthetic Letters*, which synthesize Kant's moral and aesthetic thought with more Herderian, romantic views. Schiller insists that we need to repair the fragmentation caused in modern cultures by, on the one hand, intellectual specialization, that is, specialized scientific knowledge that cannot be integrated into the everyday frameworks of meaning that form the basis of a common culture, and on the other, the mechanizing and instrumentalizing influence of the state.[13]

His paradigm for the kind of organic unity that he admires is, of course, the ancient Greek polis. This Hellenic Ideal was shared by Humboldt and

[10] See G. P. Gooch, *Germany and the French Revolution* (London: Longmans, Green, 1965); On Schiller, cf. Willoughby's introduction to Friedrich Schiller, *On the Aesthetic Education of Man*, trans. Elizabeth M. Wilkinson and L. A. Willoughby (Oxford: Oxford University Press, 1967). On Humboldt, cf. Dumont, *German Ideology*, 106. On Hegel, cf. Harold Mah, "The French Revolution and the Problem of German Modernity," *New German Critique* 50: 3–20.

[11] Raymond Geuss emphasizes the importance of Humboldt's innovation to subsequent liberal thought in his *History and Illusion in Politics* (Cambridge: Cambridge University Press, 2001), ch. 2.

[12] See Humboldt, *The Limits of State Action*, ed. J. W. Burrow (Indianapolis: Liberty Fund, 1993), 10: "The true end of Man, or that which is prescribed by the eternal and immutable dictates of reason, and not suggested by vague and transient desires, is the highest and most harmonious development of his powers to a complete and consistent whole."

[13] Friedrich Schiller, *On the Aesthetic Education of Man*: "The more intricate machinery of States made necessary a more rigorous dissociation of ranks and occupations; the essential bonds of human nature were torn apart." Op. cit., Sixth Letter, 6.

played an important role in the development and application of the idea of *Bildung* in the nineteenth century.[14] *Bildung* was intended to re-create the kind of harmony and identification with community that modern, alienated individuals lack, but it was to do so in a way that accommodated rational autonomy. Reconciliation with community was to be re-created at a reflective level.[15]

In order to facilitate this process, the state was supposed to intrude very little into citizens' lives. Its role, as Humboldt conceives it, is that of providing security, or the conditions necessary to foster diversity. It is to be the minimal, "night-watchman state." Insofar as politics does intrude into our lives, it is supposed to do so with an authority that is endorsed by our reflective, rational capacities.

This optimism about rational progress made its way from Humboldt into a broader liberal tradition by way of Mill. For both Mill and Humboldt, freedom is intrinsically linked to rational convergence, since free inquiry and public debate is seen to be the best means of discovering the truth. Mill's defense of freedom of thought and freedom of expression, like Humboldt's twin principles of *Lehrfreiheit* and *Lernfreiheit*, is not justified only on the grounds that it permits the cultivation of the authentic individual self. It is justified epistemically, since open discussion sharpens the rational faculties that lead us to truth.[16]

This kind of liberalism, then, seems promising from the point of view of political legitimacy. First of all, it is optimistic about our capacity to converge on the correct norms. And second, the kind of impartial principles that justify political actions are compatible with deeper disagreements, so we do not have to share an entire and complex worldview to converge on them. Nietzsche, however, does not think that correctness can be so easily attained or so persuasively disseminated.

---

[14] Cf. John Burrow, introduction to Humboldt's *The Limits of State Action*, xxxviii.

[15] James Sheehan points out that reconciliation between citizen and state was emphasized by German liberals at the expense of radical criticism of the existing order. Cf. *German Liberalism*, 14.

[16] Cf. John Stuart Mill, "On Liberty," *Collected Works*, ed. J. M. Robson, vol.13, *Essays on Politics and Society* (Toronto: University of Toronto Press, 1997). For post-Kantian Germans such as Humboldt, normative correctness is in the rational grasp of all autonomous individuals. Their ideal of *Bildung* does not, then, have to specify any elaborate mechanism by which convergence on normative truth might come about. Mill, however, is slightly less optimistic about this: he sees that normative truth is hard to come by and insists that once experts have managed to converge on moral and political truths, they will have to be responsible for educating the common intellect. This more "elitist" aspect of Mill's thought is emphasized by Stephen Holmes, who also criticizes Mill's conception of intellectual authority by disputing the strong analogy that Mill sees between intellectual authority in politics and in science. Cf. "The Positive Constitutionalism of John Stuart Mill," *Passions and Constraint: On the Theory of Liberal Democracy* (Chicago: University of Chicago Press, 1995).

BILDUNG AS A DISAPPOINTING REALITY

It is well known that Nietzsche identifies the most prodigious product of *Bildung* as the *Bildungsphilister*, the cultural philistine.[17] The proponents of *Bildung*, he thinks, may have intended it as a more civilized entry into modernity than the bloody-minded French had managed, but all they have really achieved is a kind of bourgeois politeness:

> Let us today take a look at Schiller, Wilhelm von Humboldt, Schleier-macher, Hegel, Schelling, read their correspondence and familiarize ourselves with their large circle of adherents: what do they have in common, what is it in them that seems to us, as we are today, now so insupportible, now so pitiable and moving? First, their thirst for appearing morally *excited* at all cost; then, their desire for brilliant, boneless generalities, together with the intention of seeing everything (characters, passions, ages, customs) in as beautiful a light as possible—"beautiful," unfortunately, in the sense of a vague and bad taste which nonetheless boasted of a Greek ancestry. It is a soft, good-natured, silver-glistening idealism which wants above all to affect noble gestures and a noble voice.[18]

The problem is not just that their ideal of *Bildung* has failed to be realized in practice, on Nietzsche's view. The ideal itself is flawed.

The very superficial appreciation of the Greeks that motivates the *Bildungsphilister* is taken to be evidence of this. The Hellenic ideal that had gripped the German imagination since Winckelmann's *History of Art*, in 1764, was certainly a more polite vision of the Greeks than Nietzsche's own evocation of orgiastic excess.[19] But Nietzsche does not just object to the classicist aesthetic that these figures espouse; he insists that they have completely misunderstood the deep forces that shape human cultures.[20]

---

[17] *UM*, i, 2.

[18] *D*, 190.

[19] On the history of this ideal, see E. M. Butler, *The Tyranny of Greece Over Germany* (Boston: Beacon Press, 1958); and Suzanne Marchand, *Down from Olympus: Archaeology and Philhellenism in Germany, 1750–1970* (Princeton, N.J.: Princeton University Press, 2003).

[20] It is interesting, though, to compare Schiller's and Nietzsche's responses to Greek sculpture. Nietzsche is clearly aiming for psychological realism, rather than an imitable ideal. In his *Aesthetic Letters*, Schiller writes:

> They transferred to Olympus what was meant to be realized on earth . . . they banished from the brow of the blessed gods all the earnestness and effort which furrow the cheeks of mortals, no less than the empty pleasures which preserve the smoothness of a vacuous face; freed those ever-contented beings from the bonds inseparable from every purpose, every duty, every care, and made *idleness* and *indifferency* the enviable portion

Nietzsche's own portrayal of the Greeks aimed for a certain kind of psychological realism and was influential in that regard.[21] He wanted to do justice to the irrational forces that produce cultures. His cultural criticism, here as elsewhere, often involves large and unsupported assertions about empirical psychological matters that he is ill-equipped to judge. But there is one aspect to his approach that seems both to have some historical plausibility and to be relevant to our current concerns.

Nietzsche believes that the kinds of certainty and agreement necessary to forge political unity or establish de facto political authority are not likely to be achieved through rational reflection. In *The Birth of Tragedy*, Nietzsche contrasts the cohesiveness of a culture grounded in myth with "abstract man, without guidance from myth, abstract education, abstract morality, abstract law, the abstract state."[22] This seemingly romantic, organicist view would be less interesting were it not for the fact that it is linked to his general thesis concerning normative authority.

Even if our reason can discover the right abstract principles, Nietzsche is still skeptical that these can exercise sufficient authority over the human psyche to ground a form of political association. Since such principles do not seem to be self-evident, in order for them to be recognized, those who discover them would have to be capable of wielding effective authority over those who have not.

The liberal hope for a "thin" form of political agreement might seem like a realistic one, since it rests on the specification of impartial principles to

---

of divinity—merely a more human name for the freest, most sublime state of being. . . . the Greeks effaced from the features of their ideal physiognomy, together with *inclination*, every trace of *volition* too; or rather they made both indiscernible, for they knew how to fuse them in the most intimate union. (15th Letter, 9)

Nietzsche, on the other hand, asks, "Why did the Greek sculptor repeatedly have to represent war and battles with endless repetition, human bodies stretched out, their veins taut with hatred or the arrogance of triumph, the wounded doubled up, the dying in agony? Why did the whole Greek world rejoice over the pictures of the battle in the Iliad?" "Homer on Competition," trans Carol Diethe, appendix to *On the Genealogy of Morality*, ed. Keith Ansell-Pearson, 188; *KGW* III-2, 278. For a general study of Nietzsche's relation to Schiller, see Nicholas Martin, *Nietzsche and Schiller: Untimely Aesthetics* (Oxford: Calrendon Press, 1996).

[21] See E. R. Dodds, *The Greeks and the Irrational* (Berkeley: University of California Press, 1951). Dodds says in his introduction that his own work is "a study of the successive interpretations which Greek minds placed on one particular type of human experience—a sort of experience in which nineteenth-century rationalism took little interest, but whose cultural significance is now widely recognized." Nietzsche is clearly taken to be the pivotal figure underlying this development.

[22] *BT*, 23. Tracy Strong has emphasized this ongoing romantic element in Nietzsche's view of the state, which involves seeing the state as a sponsor of fragmentation, eroding organic cultural unity: *Nietzsche and the Politics of Transfiguration*, 200–201.

which any rational person can supposedly assent. But according to Nietzsche (as we shall see in the next section), it is in fact much easier for us to establish the "thicker" forms of agreement that do not demand rational transparency.[23]

It is difficult for political philosophers, Nietzsche perceives, let alone just any bourgeois recipient of a classical education, to arrive at uncontroversial, rational (and therefore impartial) principles for political action. Little agreement has been established amongst experts. Many of the philosophers who promulgate versions of Kantian and Hegelian claims do not understand clearly the philosophical justifications underlying these positions.[24] The abstractions propounded by Kantian and Hegelian philosophers, according to Nietzsche, have appeared to have broad cultural authority in Germany, but only where they have happened to coincide with the existing political status quo.[25] Unanimity is not, on this view, likely to be the product of our individual, autonomous deliberations.

Impartial principles for political action are indeed very difficult to articulate and defend. It is hard to draw a clear and uncontroversial line between permissible and impermissible forms of state interference. The twentieth-century history of liberal theory seems to have borne out this insight. Such principles and procedures as philosophers have come up with would require us to take very sophisticated attitudes toward ourselves and our beliefs and values.[26] Normative correctness of this kind, then, does not seem to be a very promising foundation for basic political agreement.

Bildung was supposed to bridge just this gap between justification, on the one hand, and social and political practice on the other. It was intended, Nietzsche points out, to reshape all public institutions in such

---

[23] In adopting this vocabulary, I do not mean to assimilate Nietzsche's view to that of recent "communitarian" critics of liberalism. The ferocious galvanizing force of nonrational, collective forms of identity is something that Nietzsche deplores, but it is bound to triumph, he thinks, over more abstract and reflective allegiances.

[24] Cf. *UM*, i, 6, where Nietzsche claims that in spite of David Strauss's laying claim to Kant's authority, in fact "he has no notion how to derive from Kant's critique of reason support for his testament of modern ideas."

[25] Ibid., iii, 8.

[26] One example of just how sophisticated these attitudes might have to be may be found in Thomas Nagel's defense of impartiality as a means of resolving moral disagreement in liberal societies. He tells us that "the parties to such a disagreement can think of themselves as appealing to a common, objective method of reasoning which each of them interprets and applies imperfectly. They can therefore legitimately claim to be appealing not merely to their personal, subjective beliefs but to a common reason which is available to everyone and which can be invoked on behalf of everyone even though not everyone interprets its results in the same way." "Moral Conflict and Political Legitimacy," *Philosophy and Public Affairs* 16, no. 3 (Summer 1987): 215–40.

a way that people could reflectively identify with them.[27] It did not require that just institutions be constructed from scratch, starting with first principles, but rather that we gradually modify society from within in accordance with the dictates of reason. However, Nietzsche's concerns about normative authority apply equally to this model of gradual rational convergence.

Reflection seems, on the contrary, to break down agreement. The view that we should be reliant on our own reason has the effect of eroding established, unreflective sources of agreement, such as those of tradition, religion, or deference to established social hierarchies.[28]

Nietzsche claims that this brings about a disjunction between the internal convictions of individuals and the demands of the collective, social institutions in which they participate. This is the predicament that he describes as the consequence of *Bildung*. He claims to have perceived in his contemporaries

> the remarkable antithesis between an interior which fails to correspond to any exterior and an exterior which fails to correspond to any interior—an antithesis unknown to the peoples of earlier times. Knowledge, consumed for the greater part without hunger for it and even counter to one's needs, now no longer acts as an agent for transforming the outside world but remains concealed within a chaotic inner world which modern man describes with curious pride as his uniquely characteristic "subjectivity."[29]

The aspiration to normative self-governance, on his view, makes us more vulnerable to the hegemonic power of the state because it erodes the intermediary forms of authority that might have served as a bulwark against state power. It deprives us of the very ability to shape social institutions that it is intended to confer on us.

Unwitting Illiberalism

Nietzsche identifies two ways in which the faith in *Bildung* might have unwittingly illiberal consequences, inadvertently consolidating the ideological power of the state. First of all, it encourages people to perceive as autonomy what is in fact an occluded form of authority. The hegemony of the state is then rendered invisible. Second, people are liable to mistake

---

[27] Cf. *UM*, i, 2.

[28] Nietzsche is particularly worried about the atomism that ensues from this breakdown during the period of the *Untimely Meditations*. Tracy Strong has emphasized this feature of his concerns: *Nietzsche and the Politics of Transfiguration*, 201.

[29] *UM*, iii, 4.

forms of unanimity that are generated through nonrational means for rational convergence. Ideological subordination is then taken for free assent.

It should again be emphasized that Nietzsche is not concerned on behalf of the deluded multitudes, whose illusory "feeling of self-determination," whose "pride in the five or six ideas their head contains and brings forth," only in fact makes life more pleasant for them.[30] His commitment to limiting state power is derived solely from his commitments to the pursuit of truth and value per se, not as goods to which human beings are entitled, but as ends in themselves. But this minimal basis is sufficient to ground his concern about the potentially illiberal effects of liberalism.

In his "Lectures on the Future of our Educational Institutions," Nietzsche's first contribution to a significant public debate, he warns of the development that permits the exercise of state authority to be mistaken for autonomy. He contends that the form of contemporary educational institutions is determined by two tendencies:

> on the one hand, a drive towards the greatest possible widening of education [*Bildung*], on the other hand the drive to diminish and lessen it in itself.[31]

The desire to educate as broad a public as possible results in an impoverishment of the educational process. One tendency demands that education be carried into the widest circles, while the other asks *Bildung*

> to give up its highest, noblest and most exalted claims and to content itself with the service of some other life form, for instance, the state.[32]

The perceived success of *Bildung*, or assent to shared political norms, is presented as the result of the stifling, not the fostering, of criticism.

As we saw in chapter 1, he is particularly critical, in this period, of the liberal intellectuals who were cooperating with Bismarck and Falk's repressive *Kulturkampf* legislation of 1873–74. This problem concerning their relation to state power has deeper roots, though, in the German liberal tradition. When Wilhelm von Humboldt, in 1791, articulated his account of the necessary limits to state power in relation to *Bildung*, he intended the state to concern itself only with the security of its citizens. But as Prussian minister for education in the 1800s, whose duty was to provide a complete reform of German educational institutions, he inevitably found it necessary to expand his conception of the role of the state. State action was the only available means of effecting the social changes necessary to institute general education. Its authority also permitted the

---

[30] *HTH*, I, 438.
[31] *KGW* III-2, 139.
[32] Ibid., 159.

reshaping of educational institutions themselves, albeit in accordance with the demands of *Bildung*.[33]

German liberalism therefore continued to be characterized by an ambivalence in relation to the state, whose power was used to institute an educational program to which state authority was notionally subordinate.[34] It was also used, with the endorsement of many liberals, to resolve doctrinal disputes that arose from religious differences. *Bildung* was effectively dependent on state intervention. This history would seem to account for Nietzsche's remark, in *Twilight of the Idols*, that "liberal institutions cease to be liberal as soon as they are attained: later on, there are no worse and no more thorough injurers of freedom than liberal institutions."[35] His experience in the early 1870s had taught him that in covertly ceding power to the secular state, we can have our freedom silently stolen from us.

In this early period Nietzsche makes clear that he thinks the supporters of this supposedly liberal *Bildung* are in fact permitting the state, through its supervision of culture and education, to manufacture a bogus form of individuality that implicitly serves political ends and to which the state then appeals as a source of legitimation.[36] The concept of the *Bildungstaat*, on such a view, permits a circular self-legitimation of political power.

This is the situation described in the first of the *Untimely Meditations*, where Nietzsche sees the state consolidating its power through an appeal to manufactured public opinion. It is in the same essay that Nietzsche introduces the second of his concerns, as outlined above, about unintended consequences. The defenders of *Bildung*, he claims, are mistaking nonrational forms of agreement for the consensus toward which *Bildung* has been striving.

In the aftermath of the Franco-Prussian War, nationalist sentiment swept across the new *Reich*. After 1871, liberals increasingly turned to nationalism as a source of cohesion.[37] Nietzsche also identifies jubilance at the military victory, antipathy toward the French, and Bismarck's personal authority as a leader as powerful unifying forces.

What Nietzsche deplores is the preposterous situation in which the self-deceived proponents of *Bildung* actually claim this form of unity as their own cultural success.[38] This self-deception, though, is seen as a natural temptation given the inevitable failure of liberal *Bildung* to establish any genuine source of cohesion or unanimity. He especially sees this tendency

[33] Cf. Sheehan, *German Liberalism*, 43.
[34] Ibid., 43.
[35] *TI*, "Skirmishes of an Untimely Man," 38.
[36] This view recurs in his unpublished essay of this period on classical education, "Wir Philologen."
[37] Cf. Sheehan, *German Liberalism*, 273–78.
[38] *UM*, i, 1.

in those whom secularism has deprived of a meaningful existence, that is, the kind of integrated subjective and objective existence which *Bildung* promised but failed to restore. He tells us that "since their sundering from religion, hearts in these circles have felt a sense of emptiness which they are seeking provisionally to fill with a kind of substitute in the form of devotion to the state."[39]

Nonrational, emotional allegiances seem to Nietzsche to have a stronger galvanizing force than any reflective commitments. He concedes that individuals have critical faculties that cannot be finally extirpated by any imposition of an ideology. But he also sees that these critical faculties are liable to be suspended if people feel reconciled to social institutions that they mistakenly perceive as the product of collective reasoning and to which they might therefore rationally assent.

He perceives a powerful tendency in his compatriots to absolve themselves in this way of any further rational responsibility. He takes popular forms of Hegelianism to be evidence of this. Their purported identification of the rational with the real is a "deification of success."[40] And later he claims the unconditional homage paid to Schopenhauer, Wagner, and Bismarck as manifestations of the same retreat from the burdens of rational justification.[41] Given this tendency, we can see why Nietzsche should claim in his later work that liberal institutions only promote freedom so long as they are being fought for, but not when liberals have power and people feel that freedom has already been attained.

Where the authority of the state appears to be rooted in normative authority, Nietzsche warns us, we should be wary. The alliance of state power with an unjustified belief that we have attained moral knowledge constitutes the most insidious kind of ideological threat. And the state is good at striking up such an alliance with moral opinion. Zarathustra tells us that every people "has invented its own language of customs and rights," but the state "tells lies in all the tongues of good and evil."[42]

CONCLUSION

Nietzsche is more skeptical than his contemporary liberals about our capacity for normative self-governance. The Kantian basis of German liberal thought had permitted the romantic valuation of authentic, individual

[39] *HTH*, I, 172.
[40] *UM*, i, 7.
[41] *D*, 167. He suggests here that it might still be possible "to make of a nation of credulous emulation and blind and bitter animosity a nation of conditional consent and benevolent opposition."
[42] *TSZ*, "On the New Idol."

self-expression and the enlightenment valuation of rational justification to be reconciled. For Nietzsche, the Kantian synthesis that was articulated through the concept of autonomy has broken down. The beliefs and value judgments that result from free, individual thought are not likely to be rationally justified.

It is tempting to assume that Nietzsche then chooses the romantic value of creative self-expression over rational justification. This certainly remains a powerful theme throughout his work. Alexander Nehamas, in particular, has demonstrated what a rich philosophy of self-creation might be derived from his remarks in this vein.[43]

Some interpreters have taken this theme to be the basis of an illiberal, aristocratic, Nietzschean politics.[44] But Nietzsche's romantic, aesthetic commitments remain in tension with his powerful epistemic and ethical commitments. Even if the unappealing political vision that seems to be entailed by the former surfaces from time to time in Nietzsche's work, I hope to have shown that the political skepticism that he derives from the latter constitutes a more interesting critique of liberalism.

As we have seen, Nietzsche does not (and cannot coherently) advocate a normatively unconstrained politics. He shares the view that reason should be authoritative, but does not believe that we can rely on the rational capacities of even an enlightened public to secure this. Moral knowledge is hard to come by. Experts seldom agree. And if large swathes of agreement are to be found elsewhere, this is likely to be the result of pragmatic consensus, not a convergence on genuinely justified beliefs.

Nietzsche is therefore more skeptical than liberals about the possibility of political legitimacy. If we could rely on a class of normative experts, analogous to a priestly caste, we might be able to integrate the demands of normative and political authority. Our acceptance of the state's authority could be grounded in recognition of the relevant norms. Recognized expertise would solve Nietzsche's problem, and in a brief but intriguing moment in *Human, All Too Human*, he indeed reaches out for such a tantalizingly simple solution:

> It is easy, ridiculously easy, to erect a model for the election of a law-giving body. First of all the honest and trustworthy men of a country who are at the same time masters and experts in one or another subject have to select one another through a process of mutual scenting out

---

[43] Alexander Nehamas, *Nietzsche: Life as Literature.*

[44] Cf. esp. Bruce Detwiler, *Nietzsche and the Politics of Aristocratic Radicalism.* Detwiler claims that "in every case Nietzsche assesses the political sphere from a theoretical framework that adjudges the issue of cultural vitality and cultural decline to be paramount. In every case he favors the kind of politics he associates with cultural vitality and the enhancement of man" (8).

and recognition: in a narrower election those experts and men of knowledge of the first rank in each department of life must again choose one another, likewise through mutual recognition and guaranteeing. If these constituted the lawgiving body, then finally in each individual case only the voices and judgments of those expert in the specific matter would be decisive and all the rest would, as a matter of honour and simple decency, leave the vote to them alone: so that in the strictest sense the law would proceed out of the understanding of those who understand best.[45]

But, of course, this confidence is short-lived. Even within the same volume, he acknowledges that it is hard to know what political expertise would look like, let alone normative expertise.[46]

Nietzsche did not envisage any political solution to the skeptical predicament that he confronted. He was not interested in imagining constitutional arrangements that would permit a pragmatic, politically feasible compromise. Neither liberalism nor democracy seemed to him to offer viable solutions.

In *Beyond Good and Evil*, Nietzsche predicts that the democratization of Europe will lead "to the production of a type that is prepared for *slavery* in the subtlest sense," that it is "an involuntary arrangement for the cultivation of *tyrants*—taking that word in every sense, including the most spiritual."[47] The resort to plebiscitary democracy and charismatic leadership, which subsequent generations of German were to advocate, is predicted here but not endorsed. That is the resort of normative skeptics, who do not mind giving up on normative authority altogether. Nietzsche remained committed to the quest for truth, including normative truth. Given the ends that motivate him, he could never, therefore, endorse relinquishing to the state the ideological power that it inevitably seeks. The constraints of his historical situation prevented him from seeing either liberalism or democracy as possible means to this end of preserving the conditions of possibility of truth and value.

Unlike liberals, he detached his hopes for truth and for the authority of reason from any agenda for popular enlightenment. He could not

---

[45] *HTH*, II, "Assorted Opinions and Maxims," 318.

[46] *HTH*, II, "Wanderer", 277: "How badly we reason in domains where we are not at home, however well we may be accustomed to reasoning as men of science! It is disgraceful! But it is also clear that in the great world, in affairs of politics, it is precisely this *bad reasoning* that arrives at decisions on all those sudden and pressing questions such as arise almost every day: for no one is completely at home in that which has newly developed overnight; all political thinking, even in the case of the greatest statesmen, is random improvisation."

[47] *BGE*, 242.

acknowledge that the development of reason, and therefore the greatest hope for truth, might require publicity. He scorned Kantian hopes for the *Öffentlichkeit* that might advance our understanding through debate, seeing only the tyranny of an impoverished *öffentliche Meinung*, or public opinion.

But given the lack of recognized normative expertise to which he draws our attention, we might justifiably wonder whether this public demand for reasons, even if it does not fully live up to its most optimistic enlightenment promise, is not simply the best that we can do in our search for normative truth. Although we might still, for the most part, fall short of acquiring real moral knowledge, let alone making it effective, the constant demand for reasons might at least keep alive the possibility.

And if this quest is not feasible without constraining the ideological power of the state, it certainly seems possible for us now to think more creatively than Nietzsche did about institutional and constitutional solutions to this problem. He did not imagine that democracy could play a role in the kinds of constitutional arrangements that might secure this end. And he was clearly unaware of any potential for constitutional self-binding.

So it is tempting to utter the usual "if only" of those who find something compelling in Nietzsche's work. If only he had envisaged the possibility of a liberal democracy. And if only his boundless contempt had not prejudiced him against everything liberal and democratic. But even if he had had the political foresight and the appropriate attitudes, this would not have vanquished his deep political skepticism. So long as there is still a gap between the demands of normative authority and the demands of political authority, legitimacy remains a mere aspiration. Nietzsche's insights do not entail the view that we should give up on this aspiration, rather that we should preserve the conditions of its possibility, without ever assuming that it has been fulfilled.

Acknowledgments

Although this book was written in Princeton, I began working on Nietzsche as a graduate student in Cambridge. I am grateful to my PhD supervisor there, Raymond Geuss, and also to John Dunn and Istvan Hont, who taught me a great deal. I must also thank David Owen and Michael Tanner for their comments on my thesis. During this period, and subsequently, Bernard Williams was a close reader and brilliant critic of my work, for which I will always be grateful. Jonathan Lear also gave me helpful comments at this stage.

I continued my work on Nietzsche as a Research Fellow at King's College and would like to thank the fellowship of King's for their support. I benefited particularly from conversations about my work with Ross Harrison, Stefan Hoesel-Uhlig, Halvard Lillehammer, and Michael Sonenscher. I am very grateful for Richard Bourke's criticism and advice throughout this period. I also owe a great debt of gratitude to Michael Tanner, who I must thank for continually deepening my appreciation of Nietzsche's work through many fascinating conversations not only about the writings themselves, but about the cultural and ethical issues that motivated them.

In the year 2004–5, I was a member of the Institute for Advanced Study in Princeton. I would like to thank the institute for providing me with an especially congenial intellectual environment. My colleagues at Princeton University have also provided me with much-appreciated support. I have benefited from close reading of my work by Charles Beitz, Stephen Macedo, Alexander Nehamas, Philip Pettit, and Jennifer Pitts. I have received much helpful advice from Paul Benacerraf, Patrick Deneen, Daniel Garber, Christopher Eisgruber, Robert George, Gilbert Harman, Mark Johnston, George Kateb, Victoria McGeer, Jan-Werner Müller, Sankar Muthu, Paul Sigmund, Jeffrey Stout, Alan Patten, Maurizio Viroli, and Keith Whittington.

I am also grateful for comments on my work from the following: the audience at the Institute for Historical Research in London; the audience at "Nietzsche and Morality," a conference organized by Mathias Risse at the Center for Human Values in Princeton, especially Nadeem Hussain and Bernard Reginster, who emailed helpful suggestions afterwards; and Kinch Hoekstra, Sharon Street, and David Velleman.

I would like to thank my readers at Princeton University Press, as well as my editor, Ian Malcolm, for his support and encouragement.

I owe an enormous debt of gratitude to Lanier Anderson, who read the manuscript for the press and gave me extremely detailed critical comments and suggestions. He has helped to make this a much better book than it would otherwise have been. The remaining faults are of course my own. Thanks also to Aaron Voloj Dessauer for vetting the proofs.

I would like to thank my friends Andrea Ashworth, Lucy Harman, Erika Kiss, Victoria McGeer, and Sharon Street for all their help; my sister, Kerry Shaw, for her endless help and advice; and my parents, to whom this book is dedicated. Finally, I owe an incalculable debt of gratitude to Paul Boghossian, who has been an indispensable source of criticism, advice, encouragement, and support.

Index